# The Adaptive Enterprise

## IT Best Practices Series

This book is published as a part of the IT Best Practices Series—a collaboration between Intel Press and Addison-Wesley Professional, a division of Pearson Education. Books in this series focus on the information technology challenges companies face in today's dynamic, Internet-based, business environment, as well as on the opportunities to improve IT performance and thereby gain a competitive edge. Some of the books explain proven strategies to help business executives and managers develop needed capabilities. Other books show technical professionals exactly how to implement specific solutions. The series overall reflects Intel's Best Practices Program, developed with leading researchers, vendors, and end-users to meet the challenges and opportunities described. These Best Practices recognize that companies must be agile and adaptable in the face of diverse and rapidly changing technologies, and, in particular, must be prepared and able to integrate multivendor, e-Business tools. Thus, the theme of this series is: *Making it all work together.*

Books in this series include:

*The Adaptive Enterprise:*
*IT Infrastructure Strategies to Manage Change and Enable Growth*
—Bruce Robertson and Valentin Sribar

*Securing Business Information:*
*Strategies to Protect the Enterprise and Its Network*
—F. Christian Byrnes and Dale Kutnick

*Enriching the Value Chain:*
*Infrastructure Strategies Beyond the Enterprise*
—Bruce Robertson and Valentin Sribar

For detailed information about these and other books, as well as announcements of forthcoming books in the Series, visit the Intel Press and Addison-Wesley Professional Web sites:

www.intel.com/intelpress
www.aw.com/cseng

# The Adaptive Enterprise

IT Infrastructure Strategies to Manage Change
and Enable Growth

## Bruce Robertson
## Valentin Sribar

INTEL
PRESS

Addison-Wesley
Pearson Education

Boston • San Francisco • New York • Toronto • Montreal
London • Munich • Paris • Madrid
Capetown • Sydney • Tokyo • Singapore • Mexico City

# Contents

## Chapter 4   Developing Adaptive Services   131

## Chapter 5   Services Starter Kit   153

## Chapter 6   Processes and Methods   177

## Chapter 7   Packaging and People   207

# Appendix A   Component Catalog   231

# Glossary   277

# Index   293

# Preface

*The Adaptive Enterprise* has one clear objective: to provide you with IT strategies to manage change and enable growth.

Starting in 1999, META Group developed information on IT infrastructure and operations to serve a group of clients who were adapting to the new demands of online commerce. Working with these clients, we coined the term "adaptive infrastructure" to describe their results.

The IT Best Practices Series published by Intel Press explains the strategies for developing Internet-based capabilities and solutions to meet key challenges in your business. It reflects Intel's Best Practices program, which was developed with leading researchers, vendors, and end-users to show business and IT decision makers how to *make it all work together* for increased business performance. Unlike the mainframe era, distributed e-Business is a loosely coupled and event-driven phenomenon in which Internet-based solutions run on a diverse set of multivendor configurations. That has changed the rules for business, and *The Adaptive Enterprise* is designed to help IT decision makers manage change and enable growth in their new, customer-centric e-Businesses.

*The Adaptive Enterprise* is for executives and IT professionals at companies large and small. In this book, we explain how to achieve success in infrastructure planning by changing the way things are done, by making applications become easier, more cost-effective, and quicker to integrate. We explain how to run these services for the long term with high quality.

## Acknowledgments

Books written for the IT Best Practices Series draw on the talents of many contributors, reviewers, and advisors.

In particular, the authors would like to acknowledge the following key contributors to the book. Thanks to Peter Burris for his seminal thoughts and for his active support of both the IT Best Practices program and the book series. Brian Hellauer and Donna Maciver tirelessly translated raw analyst research into structured and readable manuscript content.

We thank the following individuals who were important advisors: Dan Fineberg, who conceived the IT Best Practices program of which the book series is a key part; Rich Bowles for defining the IT Best Practices Series within the overall program and driving it from concept to reality; Jerry Braun for supporting the program, even when economic conditions made scarce resources even more precious. Finally, we give special recognition to Deb Catello for her conscientious and high-quality content reviews and to Chris Thomas for his leadership in identifying key tenets and themes.

Other individuals contributed to our project by keeping us in touch with our audience through their feedback on various parts of the books. We recognize and thank these special reviewers: Pierre-Andre La Chance, Chief Information Officer at Kaiser Permanente's Northwest Region Center for Health Research, for his reflections on the significance of processes within his organization; Steve Borte, Director of Services at ObjectFrontier, for his suggestions and his candid perspective as a seasoned IT professional; Cloy Swartzendruber, senior consultant and independent contractor, for his in-depth review of the content and his detailed feedback on the book's approach to the subject.

Finally, thanks to Ryan Bernard of Wordmark and Associates for his diligent efforts while turning our manuscript into a book.

—Bruce Robertson
Vice President for Adaptive Infrastructure Strategies
META Group

—Valentin Sribar
Senior Vice President and Co-Research Director
META Group

# Chapter 1

# The Case for Adaptive Infrastructure

Everywhere you look today, change is occurring at warp speed. And nowhere is it happening faster than in the business world. Those of us who have ridden out the business cycles of the last two decades understand that change is a given. But, with the rise of the Internet and e-Business, change isn't something that you decide to do anymore: It's something that can be forced on you daily.

You hear a lot of talk about business agility, but what does this really mean? It certainly isn't the ability of the CEO to leap tall buildings in a single bound. Agility means being prepared for change at a moment's notice. It also means you must have the infrastructure in place to support change without throwing away everything and starting over after each change because a completely new start takes too much time and is almost always too expensive.

The reason organizations need an adaptive infrastructure is very simple: More change happens in business than IT or the business can anticipate. To cope with the many unforeseen circumstances and competitive demands, businesses must create and possess a certain flexible, adaptive range.

Developing this flexibility requires an infrastructure planning process that makes it much easier to introduce new business initiatives and to grow initiatives that are already under way.

This chapter explains the fundamental approaches to adaptive infrastructure, so that you can start creating a more focused, organized way of dealing with changes in your organization. An adaptive infrastructure approach requires you to create deliverables in three areas—platforms, patterns, and services—and follow a five-step process for infrastructure planning. Concentrating on the delivery of solutions or "infrastructure products" and reusable components will provide you with the keys to success.

## What is IT Infrastructure?

Before getting started, it helps to agree what the term "IT infrastructure" actually means. Generally, infrastructure is a relative term meaning "the structure beneath a structure." This definition implies different layers of structure, which metaphorically provide support or services, as shown in Figure 1.1.

In the physical world, the term infrastructure often refers to public utilities, such as water, electricity, gas, sewage, and telephone services. These utilities are just more layers of a total structure that includes IT infrastructure. Each layer of infrastructure has certain characteristics, including:

■ Shared by a larger audience than the structures it supports

■ More static and permanent than the structures it supports

■ Considered a *service*, including the people and processes involved in support, rather than just a physical structure or device

■ Often physically connected to the structure it supports

■ Distinct from the structures it supports in terms of its lifecycle (plan, build, run, change, exit)

■ Distinct from the structures it supports in terms of its ownership and the people who execute the lifecycle

The notion of a separate ownership and lifecycle (especially the design and run phases) is fundamental to the concept of infrastructure set forth in this book. This concept contradicts an assumption implicit in many object-oriented application development projects—that all reusable components should come from one set of designers, or that all designers should use a common framework such as Java 2 Enterprise Edition (J2EE). Discarding that assumption means you must design with a much looser coupling in mind.

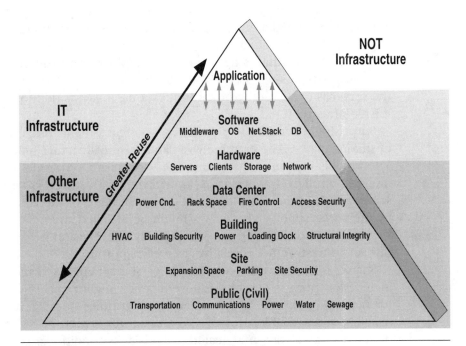

**Figure 1.1** Types of Infrastructures

In contrast, those things understood as IT infrastructure (networks, servers, etc.) are already separate in ownership and lifecycle from application development. Expanding the notion of infrastructure is one key goal of an adaptive infrastructure strategy.

## The Idea of Shared Infrastructure

When you think collectively of the people, process, and service aspects of a structure, you can more easily refer to it as a *system*. Not all infrastructure is physically connected to the structure it serves. For example, many people consider mail delivery, fire fighting, police patrolling, and garbage collection to be infrastructure services, yet none of these services must be performed while in physical connection with a building.

Infrastructure is easily described when it is clearly shared by many applications. Strictly speaking, however, many physical infrastructures aren't shared by multiple applications. The notion of infrastructure must also include the idea of an *unshared* infrastructure, which means every application has its own infrastructure.

Certainly, in some cases, it's best to consider a separate component still part of an application—even if it is not shared much. Consider an appliance, which is a bundle of hardware and software that is planned, built, and run as a single unit. Now consider a common off-the-shelf software package that is designed to be deployed and run on any common server type such as UNIX or Windows 2000/.NET Server. Even if the server isn't shared by other applications, it seems odd to think that it isn't infrastructure.

Surprisingly, even if the physical component isn't shared, other types of sharing may still be extremely valuable to infrastructure practitioners. The key distinction is that while the server isn't physically shared by multiple applications, it shares its lifecycle with other servers of the same model, in the sense that it is designed, built, changed, and exited by the server vendor. That server might be installed and managed using shared operational processes. Accordingly, the division between structure and infrastructure is relative, as well as porous.

Shared infrastructures certainly offer some benefits, which usually include lower costs due to greater efficiency, higher quality due to better management, and faster implementation times because it's already installed and available. However, a shared infrastructure is not always better, nor is it always practical in real business conditions. The value of shared versus unshared infrastructure is discussed in detail later in this book, but keep in mind that both kinds exist, and both are still infrastructure.

## Creating Your Own Definitions

The previous section discusses one way to define infrastructure, but other definitions abound. For instance, some people define infrastructure as "anything that is shared across multiple business units," which includes large corporate applications, such as enterprise resource planning (ERP), customer relationship management (CRM), supply chain management (SCM), or even e-mail applications. Given that much new development treats these packages as infrastructure to be leveraged, this definition also shows that the job of maintaining applications has passed to a different group of people from the designers and developers of the application. Clearly, ownership of the solution is a key condition when defining layers of infrastructure.

Another common definition of infrastructure might be "anything that isn't fun anymore!" Many application developers and business units that enjoy the planning and execution phases of a project have no interest in actually supporting in-place infrastructure once the operational phase begins. You see this happen also with marketing departments that hastily and gladly give up ownership of the Web site after the first significant infrastructure meltdown. In fact, this kind of thinking is a clear indicator of the need for some separation of ownership and lifecycle.

You can create your own definition of infrastructure, but remember the general rules and cases already discussed here. The next few chapters provide more specifics on the technology side of particular infrastructure components.

## Why Infrastructure (Suddenly) Matters

As time goes by, more businesses are buying, commissioning, and even renting applications in one form or another. Meanwhile, fewer companies are building their applications internally from scratch. As a result, an adaptive infrastructure strategy becomes crucial to providing a versatile, flexible, and agile foundation for application deployment.

As business units increasingly make the application selections for their companies, infrastructure becomes a key focus for IT personnel. Therefore, an adaptive infrastructure should exhibit several key traits:

- ■ Efficiency. The ability to provide reusable components that are reasonably priced and can be turned around quickly for application development projects.

- ■ Effectiveness. The easy integration of all components in a way that supports their robust operation.

- ■ Agility. Effective planning and design processes that allow companies to develop new applications quickly and to re-purpose or upgrade their existing infrastructure to support new requirements for existing or new applications.

Infrastructure matters because as your organization turns to third parties for more of its applications work, getting the infrastructure right is what's left for you to do. From a practical standpoint, if you are implementing a major new application package, what differentiates your effort isn't the application itself, but how successfully or quickly you get it running and how well it works. In many cases, these problems aren't application issues; they're infrastructure issues.

Most important, the Internet has made applications and infrastructure increasingly visible to customers and to the general public. Today, much of your organization's reputation and brand identity depends on the quality of your IT infrastructure and operations, not just on your applications.

With the Internet as a common currency in the business world, any lack of integration, robustness, or agility on your part becomes immediately and embarrassingly obvious to key customers, no matter where they are in the world. When you made mistakes in the past, only your employees knew and it wasn't a big deal. Now, if you have problems, the whole world knows. CNN may broadcast a report on how your Web site hasn't been up for five hours! That's definitely poor advertising for the company's brand.

An infrastructure that frequently fails, or doesn't support the traffic load, or can't provide a single integrated view of your complex organization can cost your company immediately in lost sales and lost goodwill. When you realize what's at stake, you begin to see why savvy organizations are investing more to make sure that their infrastructure doesn't lag far behind their business vision and applications. Unfortunately, once your lack of robustness and agility is exposed, you cannot change things very quickly. Having an adaptive infrastructure will ensure that you don't get caught flat-footed when your time comes to shine on the world's stage.

## The Clash of Cultures

So you'd like a better infrastructure but you're a little short on cash? IT people realize all too well how difficult it can be to sell infrastructure improvements to the organization. In companies with less enlightened management, any IT department trying to reach the goal of an adaptive infrastructure will encounter two common yet fundamental reactions.

- Stability is good. People often feel it's good to have an infrastructure that is stable, unchanging, and predictable. Certainly, predictable, systematic behavior must be achieved at some level. However, infrastructure must also be flexible, even breakable, to be fully leveraged by business.

- Infrastructure costs are bad. Second, businesses usually regard IT infrastructure as a cost to be minimized or a necessary evil. However, as business increasingly becomes "informational" in nature, the systems for information capture, management, and delivery become even more central to business success.

A clear misalignment between business and IT organizations dominates infrastructure decision-making. Business is chronically disconnected from what is happening on the infrastructure side. Here's the way it typically works:

1. High-level executives work with high-level consultants to determine strategic direction. This direction might take the form of some broad initiative, such as becoming more customer-focused, creating unique new offerings, integrating with suppliers, or becoming a low-cost provider.

2. Usually, this initiative drives some major application development. However, information about these decisions often reaches infrastructure planners in the form of rumors or hearsay and, usually, after the decision has already been made. Infrastructure planners should be involved in the decision-making process. All too often, they aren't.

3. Meanwhile, the systems and applications are developed and customized behind a wall of consultants and systems integrators. The resulting application code, servers, and other components often show up in the operations center when the application is about to be promoted into production, expecting that IT can support it without any extra costs.

4. Not surprisingly, this disjointed solution often results in applications that do not perform nearly as well as intended. Such applications can even degrade the performance of other applications, because developers don't understand the complexities of a shared network infrastructure within the organization.

5. This approach further increases the complexity of managing the whole infrastructure. Fresh applications often arrive with new or different components, which require an already over-stretched IT organization stretch itself further to support these variations.

6. Unfortunately, the need to support everything often leads to mediocre support at best, or expensive and ineffective outsourcing at worst. For excellence in business as well as infrastructure, you must be able to focus on what's critical to the business. Of course, outsourcing isn't all bad; it's a legitimate business requirement and you must assign skills and effort to this indispensable approach. However, outsourcing infrastructure must be well thought out and not executed only as a reactive or simple coping strategy. Other-

wise, the infrastructure becomes expensive, slows things down, and usually ends up generating quality problems.

7. Finally, this situation places IT in the unenviable situation of developing an ongoing investment strategy with little or no idea of what new applications will look like—or even what type of business they must support. Not surprisingly, this way of doing business can get quite expensive. While technology vendors deliver constant improvements in price and performance, major infrastructure investments are still multimillion-dollar decisions.

The gap between business and IT, as well as between application development and infrastructure within IT, often causes havoc. Some of the issues can be addressed through better communication. Fundamentally, however, infrastructure planners within IT must be prepared to take their own initiatives. To solve the problem, infrastructure planners must introduce standard practices and procedures into the planning, design, and implementation phases. These standards should create and accommodate adaptability.

## What's the Problem with Most Infrastructure?

Simply stated, the problems outlined above manifest themselves in many different ways. Do any of these comments sound familiar to you?

- Costs too much. You can't get funding, can't figure out costs, or can't articulate value.

- Too slow. You can't get applications out the door fast enough to be effective. The time to market must be faster.

- Nothing works together. Your systems are incomplete, overly complex, or unpredictable. Data and processes from one application may not be available to another.

- Handoffs don't work. Ownership isn't clearly defined. Handoffs don't work between IT groups such as application developers, infrastructure planners, and operations. People are always dropping the ball. Key assignments aren't being made to get work done.

- Too much theory, not enough practice. People don't know enough about technology, or they are waiting for technology that will take too long to arrive, so they are paralyzed by uncertainty.

- Lack of focus. Planners spend all their time responding to a pager and never have time for key planning activities.

What else causes problems in your infrastructure today? Is it technology, processes, or people? What problems would your IT infrastructure customers identify? You should have a good idea of the exact nature of the problems in your organization before you start suggesting solutions. Then, as you move toward solving problems, you can tie your solutions back to the problems they are meant to solve.

## What's the Solution?

Even though your problems may seem unsolvable, in fact you have some very clear and workable solutions to your dilemma. You can stop the vicious cycle of problems described above in various ways:

- **Plan your infrastructure end-to-end.** When you plan infrastructure, you can't just plan a piece at a time and hope it comes together. To be adaptive, your infrastructure planning efforts must become more extensive. They must consider all layers of the IT model and fit new components into a complete infrastructure solution that can service an entire application. This book provides a number of successful techniques, such as categorizing infrastructure into *patterns* that can help you do a more thorough job of planning.

- **Design an adaptive infrastructure.** Your infrastructure shouldn't just meet today's requirements; it should be ready to scale, adapt, change, or grow to deal with challenges already looming on the horizon. Once you identify these challenges, you must face them squarely and start designing for them immediately. This book explains the fundamental concepts of adaptive infrastructure and explains how to identify your major challenges. The answer to being more adaptive usually involves focusing more on people and processes, instead of focusing only on the infrastructure components.

- **Execute a reuse-centric strategy.** A key reason for building an adaptive infrastructure is that many design standards and actual physical components of the infrastructure can be reused. Reinventing the wheel for every application only makes your infrastructure increasingly unmanageable and slows down its delivery. This book explains how to identify key infrastructure patterns within your organization and how to structure them to leverage a set of reusable adaptive infrastructure services.

- **Overcome the tech-only focus.** Many IT people seem to focus on making product choices or architecture choices, while ignoring the people and processes needed for successful operation. You can make great technology choices, but if you don't have the right people and processes, your choices will be useless and you won't get the success you need from them.

■ Choose the right technology and products. Of course, striking a balance doesn't reduce the need to always select the best technologies and products for your infrastructure and application delivery needs. The latest, best-of-breed solution might not always be the right one for your organization. Quite often, it turns out that the best engines are not made of the best individual parts as much as they are made from parts that work best together. The same holds true for IT infrastructure.

■ Balance immediate needs with long-term goals. Few people have the proverbial luxury of stopping the train to redesign the railroad tracks. There simply isn't time to do that in today's fast-paced world, and the costs would be horrendous. To be successful, you must be able to change what you are doing *while you are still doing it*. This theme is repeated throughout this book. You must strike a balance that helps you transform while you are performing. This book shows you how to create this balance, and it gives you a few specific approaches that can work for you.

## The Philosophy of Adaptive Infrastructure

Obviously, developing an adaptive infrastructure isn't something that happens overnight. To create major change within your organization, you must start by changing yourself—by adopting a new way of thinking and a philosophy that will guide you toward your goals.

### Striking a Balance

Adaptive infrastructure strategy must include the people, processes, and technologies that provide ongoing support for an organization's applications.

To achieve success, you must strike a balance that doesn't neglect or place undue emphasis on any of these three areas:

■ Technology. This category includes the hardware, software, and leveraged third-party services that constitute the infrastructure. Too much focus on technology is known as the "silver bullet syndrome," the idea that a particular technology will solve all your problems. In the real world, silver bullets rarely exist.

- People. In this category, you can include the roles, skills, and organizational structures involved in the infrastructure lifecycle processes. Over-reliance on people creates a "hero mentality," which assumes that by working harder and being smarter, you can do everything by working around the clock to get it done. This is one of the most pervasive problems in IT departments today. Now that the euphoria has subsided over "get rich quick" stock options in the Internet Age, employees won't work around the clock, and even if they do, it is at a serious cost to their health and well being. Make sure your behavior doesn't reinforce hero mentality. While heroes should be rewarded, the key is emphasizing how things will be done differently in the future, so that people don't have to be heroes and don't have to drive themselves to the point of burning out.

- Process. This category includes standards and information that define the lifecycle of infrastructure (design, procure/build, customize, configure, deploy/install, manage, change, exit). Actually, too much focus on process is quite rare. Some companies are a little too process-centered, but many more IT organizations lack a systematic approach.

To strike a balance, you must know enough about technologies to pick the right technology. You must understand the people skills required to get the job done, without expecting superheroes to come in and save the day. Process is an increasingly important focus because it's not enough to have a visceral understanding of adaptive infrastructure strategies; you must focus on process as well. As explained in Chapter 6, you need a set of effective processes and methods that will help you bring about change. Don't try to accomplish important things by chance, and don't make people figure it out as they go. Doing so rarely leads to consistent, replicable success. After all, the goal of a great infrastructure program is not that things go well once, but that everything goes well consistently, from project to project.

## Key Organizing Principles

One way to look at adaptive infrastructure is to see it as a set of components, patterns, and services, along with the people and processes necessary to tie them together. These key organizing principles drive much of the content in this book:

- Platform is an organizing concept that groups individual component technologies into technical domains (or layers).

- Patterns are organizing concepts that facilitate rapid mapping from business requirements to end-to-end infrastructure designs. Patterns structure component selections from many platform layers.

- Services are "infrastructure applications" that shift responsibility for certain services out of the application domain into the infrastructure domain. Services provide a set of physically shared components, such as a network or a credit card processing service, which multiple applications can leverage.

Figure 1.2 shows that all the elements of adaptive infrastructure work together to support applications in an organized way.

If applications are the physical manifestation of real business processes, then all the elements of infrastructure must work together successfully to ensure their flawless performance.

The art of adaptive infrastructure, however, is not to cater to every application on its own terms. Doing so only creates more "stovepipes" (or applications resistant to adaptive infrastructure) within your organi-

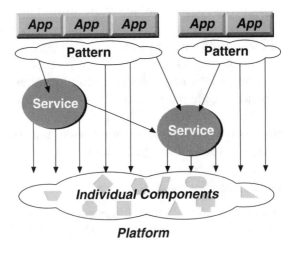

**Figure 1.2** Key Organizing Principles for Adaptive Infrastructure

zation. Instead, you can make both the application and infrastructure development processes more manageable by defining infrastructure "patterns" that you can manage more effectively. These patterns are built on a foundation of key services that you have clearly identified as crucial to your business operation. These services, in turn, are based on individual components working together as part of your adaptive infrastructure platform.

On one level, the first step in building an adaptive infrastructure is to identify and catalog all these elements—the patterns, platforms, and services, along with the people, processes, and packaging that will make your IT organization successful. Once you organize your world this way, you can avoid the dilemma of having to start from scratch each time a new application rolls out, asking questions such as, "What exactly do I need for service levels?" or "Which component do I select?" Instead, you will have pre-built solutions that you can apply or adapt at a moment's notice, which will provide your organization with ultimate agility.

Everything you need to create an adaptive infrastructure strategy boils down to the six fundamental concepts discussed on the following pages. These concepts set the tone for your infrastructure planning efforts. They form the core strategies of this book and map directly to the remaining chapters.

## 1. Identify and Catalogue Technologies

If your decision-making attitude is, "I bought from Vendor X, so now everything is solved," you're probably thinking the wrong way about the problem. The notion of platforms emphasizes organizing hardware, software, and networking components (technologies) into common application runtime targets that maximize component reuse and systems integration while providing a base level of shared services.

To manage your infrastructure well, you must first identify and catalog all the components by their functional categories.

By organizing components into categories, you can assess the complexity of managing hundreds of components. As you begin the organization process, you will start to see the components used to deploy applications fitting into different layers of stacked infrastructure, as shown in Figure 1.3.

The component items in the layers below the line (e.g., a particular server) are all purchased, not physically built. In contrast, those above the line may be internally developed, particularly if they represent areas of potential competitive advantage. And where the application and the infra-

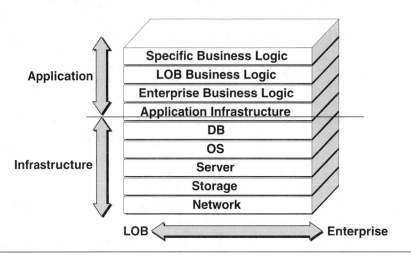

**Figure 1.3** The Infrastructure Stack

structure worlds intersect, systems integration becomes a crucial element. This integration typically focuses on various uses of middleware to combine applications, processes, data types, and underlying infrastructure as necessary.

Chapter 2 provides more detail about these layers and the organizing principles behind categorizing and managing component technologies.

## 2. Develop Reusable Infrastructure Patterns

One important way to resolve some problems is to simplify wherever possible. The best way to simplify is to identify patterns within your infrastructure that can be supported, augmented, nurtured, and reused across applications to ensure success during an endless succession of business initiatives and application rollouts. Using these end-to-end sets of infrastructure components (from many platform layers), you can clarify and unify technology, planning, and operational processes, as well as personnel experiences.

It's a losing proposition when you react to the wide variety of application development requests by trying to maintain expertise in every type of infrastructure. To make things more manageable, select a few key patterns to build your expertise around, and then use these patterns to support business projects in a repeatable way. By starting with a core set of patterns and tweaking them as necessary, this makes things easier and less expensive for everyone. In other words, simplify and prioritize.

The old barriers that prevented you from simplifying are starting to fall away. Standardization of network protocols, for instance, not only simplifies your job, but also helps you deliver a better, more focused, and ultimately more credible result to your business managers. Thinking in terms of patterns can help you handle ongoing plan-build-run work quickly and efficiently, even in places where you cannot set standards easily—and particularly at the product level, where technology innovation is fastest and maturity is a distant goal.

If you create standardized infrastructure patterns that are robust, flexible, and reusable, this will help you streamline the process of providing infrastructure for application developers and business units. The infrastructure pattern matching (IPM) methodology, outlined in Chapter 6, will help you work with your internal customers to set infrastructure investment priorities that reflect real business requirements. Figure 1.4 shows how a pattern-based method unites as it simplifies.

Using pattern-based methods, you can avoid the old problem of creating internal "stovepipes" that are isolated from the rest of the infrastructure and don't integrate well with the rest of the business. Instead, you will have an infrastructure that integrates much more easily, serves multiple applications more efficiently, and actually outlives the applications it supports. Pattern-based infrastructures reduce the incredible variety of

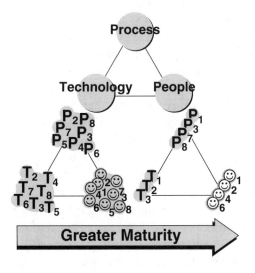

**Figure 1.4** Goals of a Pattern-based Infrastructure

technologies, processes, and people (skills, roles, etc.) that are required for accurate application delivery, which will result in more focused and repeatable excellence.

Chapter 3 explains how to define, categorize, and catalog patterns, and it provides a starter kit of nine patterns that you can use to begin building an adaptive infrastructure.

## 3. Develop Adaptive Infrastructure Services

The next step in organizing your infrastructure thinking is to structure components from platform layers into various classes of services to be used by patterns. A service exists when someone delegates the responsibility for performing a process to a service provider. A service provider can be any person or system that can perform a task repetitively. In the outside world, service providers include people such as bank tellers and plumbers. In the IT world, a service provider might be a storage area network, a database, or an IT help-desk person. Unlike a component, which is focused solely on technology, an adaptive infrastructure service is a shared set of technologies that is implemented once, with a common set of processes and people skills, to be reused by multiple applications. While these services are not the entire end-to-end set of infrastructure services for an application, they can be reused by such infrastructure patterns.

To be truly efficient and reusable, services must be decoupled and become separate processes from the person or system that interacts with them. By defining services in this way, you can start removing the stovepipes from your IT infrastructure.

The network itself is an ideal example of the concept of adaptive services. The network has been removed from the application for so long that people tend to forget the days when each application required its own special type of network. Today, no one thinks of the network as part of an application; it's a service on which the application runs. No one builds a unique network just to host a single application. Not too long ago, however, such an arrangement was painfully common.

In recent years, IT infrastructure has evolved to the point where most people use a single network service, namely TCP/IP, to support all applications. While networks are still dedicated for specialized applications, such as the wireless networks used in the power industry to dispatch repair trucks, this practice is relatively rare.

Integration is another important area where services are being decoupled from applications. Enterprise application integration (EAI) uses message brokers to move data transfer functions out of the applications themselves and into a reusable service that can be shared by all applications. The trend, obviously, is to turn reusable shared components over to the infrastructure where they can be more easily maintained and shared across applications as services. This is the kind of building block approach that an adaptive infrastructure strategy can help you achieve.

Chapter 4 explains the organizing principles behind adaptive services. Chapter 5 provides a starter kit of services you can use for your own infrastructure, with special emphasis on Transactional Integration and Identity Infrastructure services.

## 4. Use Good Tools

Once you have identified patterns, platforms, services, organizational issues, and old problems that must be fixed, you should sit down with a robust set of tools and processes and begin the journey toward organization and clarity. Chapter 6 introduces the following processes and methods that you can use to simplify your job.

**Infrastructure Pattern Matching (IPM).** If you're an infrastructure planner, what the business really wants from you—in addition to credibility and leadership in the IT arena—is the ability to quickly estimate the cost, schedules, and risks associated with new projects. Infrastructure Pattern Matching (IPM) helps by providing systematic answers to three fundamental questions: Who are the users, where are they, and what work is being performed? Answering these questions helps you define service-level commitments, analyze costs, and identify the core technology issues that affect the infrastructure's ability to support business initiatives.

**Periodic and Annual Processes.** Having structured, repeatable processes with concrete outputs or deliverables will make a difference in terms of the speed, quality, and cost of everything you do. Chapter 6 shows you how to organize two planning processes that you will execute repeatedly. One of them is periodic (or *strategic*) infrastructure planning to review your standard infrastructure patterns and services on a regular annual cycle. The other is per-project (or *tactical*) infrastructure planning, which is done for each application or new technology being introduced into the organization. Figure 1.5 shows the relationship between tactical and strategic processes.

With a robust set of tools and a well-defined set of processes, your team is able to respond to application support requests in a repeatable, structured way in a matter of hours, rather than in weeks or months. In

**Figure 1.5** Tactical Versus Strategic Processes

the process, you will generate enormous credibility for the adaptive infrastructure concept and for your whole IT organization.

**Portfolios.** Anyone who uses Quicken or Microsoft Money knows that half the battle in financial management involves keeping your planning portfolios up-to-date. Waiting until tax time to update your portfolios can be extremely painful. The key is to apply discipline and a set of easy-to-use tools to continuously update your portfolios. The portfolio concept is also an important tool of infrastructure planning, as shown in Figure 1.6. Infrastructure portfolios keep you organized as you identify, catalog, and manage your patterns, platforms, and services on an ongoing basis.

Once you develop a set of infrastructure portfolios, people will know where to find the details when they need them. A portfolio can be something as basic as a physical filing cabinet with folders in it or a directory structure with word processing documents, spreadsheets, and diagrams. The best way to make a portfolio sharable is to put it on an intranet site using a database or content management system to deliver the information to the widest audience.

The contents of a portfolio are fairly predictable. For instance, in the Pattern portfolio (see Figure 1.6) you might have a Web Publish folder with use cases, architectural diagrams, and service level metrics showing the service levels that the Web Publish pattern will meet. A reference manifest might show the product names and version numbers to be used for the database component of this reference architecture.

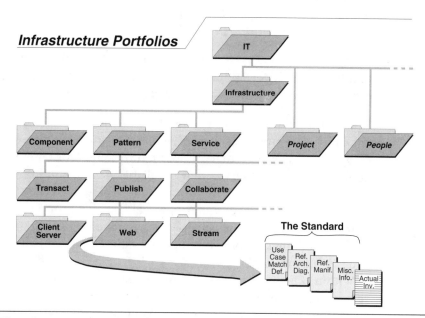

**Figure 1.6** The Concept of Portfolios

Techniques for building and using portfolios are discussed later in this book. Chapter 6 provides more detail on proven infrastructure planning methods such as infrastructure pattern matching, predictive cost management, and impact assessment labs.

## 5. Get Organized

For infrastructure planning to work, it has to be more than just a "good idea." It has to become an essential part of your business.

The only realistic way to incorporate infrastructure planning into your business is to create new roles and responsibilities, job titles, and even new groups or departments where necessary. Someone must own the processes of infrastructure planning and development to ensure that it is completed. Staffing with a full-time equivalent person (FTE) will ensure that at least one person is no longer being distracted by day-to-day operational responsibilities. What's more, infrastructure planning roles must be clearly separated from traditional application development roles. Separating the roles allows each group to focus on its particular strengths, particularly if they offer a shared service with separate lifecycles.

**Infrastructure developers** can be responsible for designing, implementing, and managing the interfaces between enterprisewide resources and the infrastructure shared by multiple applications.

**Application developers** provide project-related interface requirements to infrastructure developers who ensure that interfaces are implemented efficiently, securely, and with management controls.

At the group level, having a team of infrastructure planners and developers can create priorities across an array of infrastructure projects. The team can make sure that infrastructure standards, including components, patterns, and services, are available. Perhaps more important, the team can guarantee that the infrastructure standards are reused for particular application development projects. Such a group can also identify potential areas for reuse, not only of technologies, but also of project management methodologies, documentation, and some of the processes and people involved.

Within this more refined focus, infrastructure planning professionals can recognize when unique components are required and determine what they will cost. Planners can maintain a longer-term view of infrastructure requirements, and they understand the cost/return dynamics of infrastructure building. They can also shift the focus from an emphasis on particular technologies to continuous improvement of the delivery process.

By focusing on reuse, product or solution delivery, and the other concepts presented here, infrastructure planning becomes a more organized and tangible process. Presenting a range of potential infrastructure choices to internal customers, including application developers and business users, places the ultimate decision with those who are responsible for creating value within the enterprise. Business users can actually start comparing the benefits of one project to the other, ultimately making the determination from a business standpoint. Infrastructure planners indicate the cost options, but business users must determine the benefits.

Obviously, creating this type of organizational structure requires a clear definition of the relationship between infrastructure planners and application developers, as described in Chapter 6. In addition, planners must establish credibility and maintain constructive relationships with the people who manage project teams within the different business units. Chapter 7 gives further detail on how to organize people and processes into distinct roles and responsibilities, as well as how to encourage compliance with adaptive infrastructure standards and policies.

Chapter 7 also provides more detail on the organizational issues that you will encounter and explores alternatives for staffing and organizing your infrastructure team.

## 6. Describe Value Through Packaging

You can learn all the engineering principles, design methodologies, and pattern approaches that you want. You can create your own infrastructure development group and achieve perfection in all your processes. But if you can't sell your approach to the business and continually show the value of what you're doing, then all is for naught.

*Selling* is the main idea here. Business unit managers who hold the purse strings must understand the *value* of what you are proposing. Only when they see value will they be willing to loosen the purse strings and give you the investment dollars and management support that you need.

One of the most important techniques you can use to sell the value of adaptive infrastructure to upper management is the concept of an "infrastructure product." This product is an ongoing, reproducible, and repeatable set of services that your IT organization can deliver to the business.

For example, in a retail store environment, line executives will sign on much quicker for a world-class system that sustains a particular retail function, such as point-of-sale transaction processes, than they would for a world-class systems administration function. Retail executives will always be more interested in the in-store process, which they see as more valuable. When dealing with these types of concerns, your emphasis should be on packaging and pricing infrastructure products that support those efforts. Don't just solve your own infrastructure problems; solve your customer's problems too. At the very least, make a connection that shows how the work you must do to address your own issues will also end up solving their problems.

In addition, business leaders often have specific applications that they will pay extra to see delivered well, such as e-Business systems, enterprise resource planning applications, customer relationship management solutions, collaborative engineering capabilities, or accounting applications. Once you master the quality-of-service issues, you can create premium subscription services for applications, while ensuring that these services are handled in a premium fashion. Such applications can then justify additional expenses such as online backup and around-the-clock support, because of the higher value perceived by the business.

Once your organization accepts the concept of infrastructure as a set of packaged products and services, infrastructure planning becomes an ongoing process of refinement. It focuses more on increasing the service levels offered to the business. As you add more infrastructure and applications, the entire conglomeration starts behaving in an almost organic fashion. The objective is to optimize ongoing investments, while maintaining a balance between what the infrastructure delivers and what applications require.

As with any other business, deliverable products should be packaged in a coherent manner and supplied in a consistent, repeatable fashion. They should be organized to match what the business values. If infrastructure costs go up, you must tie these increases to real business needs and value. With a product-delivery mindset, the idea of *reusability* becomes more important in your approach.

Chapter 7 explains how to develop packaged infrastructure products and communicate their benefits to managers in a way that will earn levels of funding for future infrastructure development projects commensurate with their business value.

## Benefits of Adaptive Infrastructure

So far, most of the benefits of adaptive infrastructure have been fairly obvious. Other benefits may not be so apparent. Some of the less understood benefits are detailed below.

### Developing an Adaptive Range

Understanding exactly what is "adaptive" about adaptive infrastructure can be a complex task. A number of dimensions are involved in quantifying the flexibility or adaptive range of infrastructure, as shown in Figure 1.7.

One obvious measurement is cost. Everyone wants a fixed, low cost, but how you deliver it is the real problem. Speed is the next measurement that attracts the most attention. Speed refers to the timeliness with which IT can respond to users and implement the business processes they want. However, speed is a derivative measurement. Certainly, buying more powerful hardware can increase the transaction rate, but infrastructure isn't equipped with a speed knob that can be turned up or down as needs dictate. To increase speed, other dimensions must be addressed.

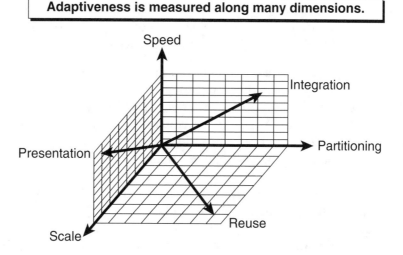

**Figure 1.7** Measuring Adaptive Range

**Scalability.**   You can build in some headroom (adaptive range), so that boxes and boards don't have to be swapped when increasing the number of users for an application. That is a relatively easy (though expensive) way to be adaptive, but it isn't sufficient to accommodate the rapid changes in business processes that users are creating.

**Presentation.**   Another dimension that affects virtually every IT organization is presentation: the way information is presented to users or business partners. Historically, the presentation layer has shown little adaptiveness. Organizations now spend a great amount of time and effort converting more traditional 2-tier, client/server applications into Web-based applications. Unfortunately, designing Web-only presentation solutions is equally limiting. Other presentation methods, such as personal digital assistants (PDAs) and interactive voice response (IVR), can't support a full-page Web display and will require completely new development efforts, which are expensive and time-consuming.

Presentation independence alone doesn't guarantee sufficient adaptability, however. Infrastructure planners should be very focused on the front end, but if the application-to-application integration issues aren't addressed simultaneously, the result is taller "stovepipes."

**Partitioned complexity.**   The ability to partition functionality and complexity within the infrastructure is another measure of adaptability. If the infrastructure cannot be effectively partitioned, the resulting complexity will spread throughout the organization and eventually become unmanageable. You must effectively manage the interfaces between applications and between infrastructure components, both for the enterprise and for applications used by external partners.

**Integration/reuse.** Infrastructure integration and reuse are also measures of adaptability. The typical organization requires a dramatic increase in the reuse of infrastructure code, other technology components, and skills to increase adaptability and speed of deployment. Reusable code is the opposite of legacy code. Whereas legacy code can be difficult to maintain, enhance, and integrate, the most adaptive code can be adjusted as the business evolves.

These factors and more contribute to the adaptability of an organization's infrastructure. This book discusses many of these issues in greater depth.

Increasingly, you must describe the value proposition for infrastructure directly to the business users in terms of the discrete service levels that they want delivered. By turning to a discussion of service levels, you can influence business users to consider more than just the immediate impact of a single application. You must convince the business to consider the value of adaptability, because it will take more money, effort, and time to deliver than single implementations.

## The Importance of Reusability

Of all the concepts discussed so far, reusability is the most crucial. The patterns, platforms, and models used to create an adaptive infrastructure all depend on reusability. Without an effective approach to this issue, it will be difficult to apply the additional rigors of specifying pattern components and creating predictive cost models.

Reuse isn't simply a matter of being thrifty or making do with whatever hardware happens to be lying around the shop. In fact, reuse often involves just the opposite—weaning business units away from archaic legacy systems that are no longer cost-effective and replacing flawed applications or integrating them with other applications within the enterprise.

When implementing a reuse policy, the biggest challenge is getting people used to the new policy and getting them to fund it appropriately. It's difficult to tell business executives that their infrastructure requirements are physically impossible, or that they can't have an application because it's too difficult to support.

Many business units have the financial and human resources to subsidize non-standard implementations, but they don't. Instead, the IT department ends up absorbing the extra expense to support the deviation, or devoting extra resources and effort to making sure it works properly. This will continue until you present errant business units with a reasonable alternative or a bill for the extra time and effort. If the business units only encounter half-hearted resistance from IT, you will probably spend most of your time doing ad-hoc support, and you can forget about creating an adaptive infrastructure.

Reuse policies are both a logical precursor to and an integral part of implementing adaptive infrastructure techniques. Designing reusability well requires that you leverage all the concepts introduced here, particularly patterns and services. Once your organization is ready for reusability, or actively practicing it, you are ready to implement an adaptive infrastructure.

## Reusable Components

The following table is a list of the infrastructure components that should be included in any reuse efforts.

## Reuse and Adaptive Infrastructure

The concept of reuse has been around since the arrival of object-oriented programming (OOP) languages in the 1980s. OOP promised that developers could write applications, then reuse large blocks of code, called "objects," in other new applications.

OOP failed for a number of reasons. The concept was too complex and fine-grained for the average programmer to grasp. In many cases, software developers created objects that were so specific to a particular application that it was difficult to reuse them without a major rewrite.

As a result, developers were forced to start from scratch each time. Still, the OOP concept was compelling enough that others have since attempted to introduce reuse at higher levels of abstraction, such as security, middleware, and networking.

Scalability was another problem. An organization with a 100-percent object-oriented approach had to support millions of objects. This proliferation resulted in a separate object for every customer in a particular database. The history of some of object-oriented database wars shows this simply doesn't work, as shown in Figure 1.8.

**Table 1.1** Reusable Components

| Basic Components | Metacomponents (Define standards for architecture, interoperability, etc.) |
|---|---|
| Network<br>- Circuits<br>- Routers, hubs, etc.<br>- Management software | Business rules |
| Hardware<br>- Servers<br>- Storage<br>- Workstations | Process models |
| Software<br>- Applications<br>- Subsystems<br>- User interface designs<br>- Utilities (backup/recovery, security, audit, error handling, etc.)<br>- Code fragments, macros, object classes, etc. | Documentation templates<br>- Technical architectures<br>- User manual outlines<br>- Operations methods |
| | Action diagrams<br><br>Data models<br>- Types<br>- Definitions<br>- Structures<br><br>Algorithms<br><br>Plans<br>- Project<br>- Deployment<br>- Testing |

Note: A more extensive infrastructure component list can be found in the component catalog listing detailed in Chapter 2.

In fact, reuse is best achieved at the infrastructure level, not *within* applications but *between* applications. For this reason, you should focus reuse efforts on broader external components.

A banking and financial services firm, for example, might have multiple credit authorization processes to support various business units. To promote reuse, you could consolidate these various applications into a single credit authorization module. It doesn't matter whether this common module is object-oriented or not. Reusability stems from the fact that different applications share it.

Third-party software vendors are leading the way in this area. SAP, for example, includes integration components in its architecture in the form of Business APIs (BAPIs). PeopleSoft leverages middleware from BEA Systems to integrate various modules, processes, and data types within its application suite. These types of components and middleware are crucial for organizations that are integrating existing applications into e-Commerce and supply chain solutions.

Applications that present IT services to external business partners depend heavily on component-oriented solutions. Each part of the supply chain becomes a component with interfaces exposed to its neighboring component, permitting the development of some fairly complex supply chain configurations.

The key to success in infrastructure planning is to change the way things are done so that applications become easier, cheaper, and quicker to integrate. Success also means being able to run these services long-term with high quality.

Another form of reuse that emerged in the 1990s involves placing a "wrapper" around legacy applications using interface definition language (IDL) models such as CORBA or DCOM. This practice is a perfect example of internal applications not needing to be object oriented. Typical mainframe applications can be migrated into a component framework by wrapping them inside an IDL.

Today, approaches such as Java 2 Enterprise Edition (J2EE) and Microsoft .NET are moving further down that path. These approaches provide not only "wrapper" capabilities, but also the beginnings of a set of Web services that can be leveraged across applications, processes, data types, and businesses. Web services represent the latest opportunities for leveraging and reuse at the intersection of the application and infrastructure worlds. These approaches take advantage of standards such as Extensible Markup Language (XML); Universal Description, Discovery, and Integration (UDDI); Simple Object Access Protocol (SOAP); and Web Services Description Language (WSDL).

▲ **Internal Components (Fine-Grained), NOT!**

- Object-oriented programming constructs
- Programming patterns
- 1 million customers = 1 million customer objects

▲ **External Components (Coarse-Grained)**

- Merging 12-credit authorization process into one
- Accessing SAP business process via BAPIs
- Integrating existing applications into e-Commerce and supply chain solutions
- Wrapping legacy applications with IDL

**Figure 1.8** What Kind of Reuse Is Achievable?

In summary, successful reuse efforts don't get deeply involved with fine-grained componentization. Rather, these broad efforts emphasize integration components and focus on the infrastructure level.

## Is Your Organization Ready?

Now that you understand the concept of adaptive infrastructure, it's time to determine whether you are ready to use the techniques and concepts described in this book.

The following questions can be revealing:

- Has your organization ever not purchased an IT product because it did not comply with some specified level of interoperability or failed to fit current or planned infrastructure practice?

- Does your organization have a technical architecture group? What is it responsible for?

- Has your organization ever funded a reusability study? Who paid for it?

- Exactly what are your infrastructure successes and failures? What would your customers, including application developers, business managers, and partners, say are your strengths and weaknesses?

The answers to these questions will provide a fairly clear picture of whether your organization is pursuing an infrastructure reuse strategy, or if it is ready to do so. If your organization actually has managed to veto a product purchase, you might want to analyze exactly how that was accomplished.

## Summary

To summarize what's been discussed in this introductory chapter:

**Success depends on the appropriate IT focus.** Your focus should be on solution or IT product delivery, not technological prowess. Any IT organization will find it difficult to differentiate itself positively based on how effectively it handles its systems administration. Delivering basic technology services is like having the lights come on when you flip a switch. The real value proposition for IT is not making the lights work, because this is expected of you anyway. Instead, the real value proposition is delivering sharable support services for applications in a way that promotes reuse, cost savings, and agility.

**An "infrastructure product" mentality helps simplify options and drive competencies.** Thinking in terms of infrastructure products leads to a delivery mentality. Creating tangible infrastructure products reduces the amount of uncertainty for your IT department and, ultimately, your organization. You should focus on core infrastructure patterns and services, looking for ways to reuse pattern and service assets and expertise while emphasizing consistent delivery with people and process improvements.

**Developing adaptive infrastructure requires a change in culture and relationships.** Successful implementation of adaptive infrastructure will change the relationship between business users and the IT group, but it should also change a key piece of the IT culture: the application developer community. Your efforts will create a new class of workers—infrastructure planners and developers, who will have application developers as their customers.

**The ultimate goal is for IT and business to develop strategic investment priorities together.** The typical IT department can develop a suitable infrastructure plan at a given point in time. Developing a plan that reflects and accommodates developments within the business, then updating and managing that plan, will require close coordination with business managers.

**Reuse is the linchpin of adaptive infrastructure.** Substantive reuse is impossible at the application level. Instead, reuse must be fostered at the interface level, among application components. A number of adaptive infrastructure concepts are designed to facilitate reuse, including adaptive infrastructure services, infrastructure pattern matching, predictive infrastructure cost models, and the role of the infrastructure planner.

# Chapter 2

# Laying the Foundation

**N**ow that you understand the basic features and benefits of adaptive infrastructure, the question naturally arises: "How do I get started?" As mentioned in Chapter 1, developing an adaptive infrastructure involves breaking down the raw infrastructure found in any organization into three distinct domains, or layers:

- Platforms represent the aggregation of common technologies.
- Patterns provide a way to organize infrastructure end-to-end and relate it to applications.
- Services involve infrastructure that isn't application-specific, but that is shared physically at the implementation level across more than one application.

These three domains arise out of "raw infrastructure," but they are inter-connected and work together as a group, as shown in Figure 2.1.

The goal is to identify universal structures and processes that are truly reusable and that can adapt to future business and technical needs. To do this, you must understand the role of each element and how it fits into your adaptive infrastructure strategy.

This chapter begins the process of building an adaptive infrastructure by looking at the *platform level* and identifying the layers and specific component technologies within it. Later chapters help you map these

**How should IT infrastructure deliverables be formulated?**

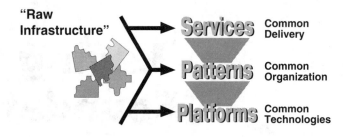

**Figure 2.1** The Three Basic Levels of Adaptive Infrastructure

components into infrastructure patterns and services for use in the infrastructure planning process.

## How To Catalog Technologies

To catalog technology, you start with a raw list of infrastructure components, one that changes as often as technology changes, and organize it into a platform model. Simply listing the technologies without organizing them isn't enough. A lack of organization would leave you with the prospect of planning your infrastructure piecemeal, with too much emphasis on individual technologies and not enough on integration. It will leave you with optimized parts but not an optimized whole.

Your platform model will have layers based on technology groupings that will allow your expertise to be focused effectively, rather than being distracted by the sheer complexity of it all. As new technologies arrive, your platform model will help you determine how they can be harnessed, since you can compare the function of the new technology to the layers and components in your current platform.

You can see what a component catalog looks like in Appendix A. You can use that example as part of your initial portfolio of components.

Notice the sheer size of this list. With scores of components and hundreds of example products, this sample should remind you of the sheer complexity of the problem you are trying to solve. Cataloging all of these components will not be a simple task, but it is the unavoidable first step that you must take toward making your infrastructure more adaptive and manageable.

The reason is simple—you can't take 100 components and understand them all without organizing them into categories. Having categories in place will help you map your technologies to the patterns and services, which are so important in developing and delivering adaptive infrastructure.

## Getting Organized

How should you organize the components in your catalog? There is no set answer; in fact, you could map them to a number of different common structures:

- By technology similarities
- By architecture domain
- By program
- By process
- By support group

Take technological similarity, for example. Many components are involved in making networks happen, so they can be categorized as networking technologies. Just as you can categorize by an architecture domain, such as security, you can also group anything related to security under a single umbrella.

You can organize by program, grouping together components that support e-Business or customer relationship management, for instance. You can organize by process, recognizing that a certain number of components will be involved when the process is executed. You can even categorize by support group, using the logic: "If I have people who support this group of products, this is how the products will map to the people." Naturally, some of these options may overlap.

Categorizing components will help you start simplifying some of the complexity, but categorizing alone will not solve the infrastructure puzzle. Building your efforts around a technology catalog will lead to fiefdoms of infrastructure expertise, not a complete vision of how all the infrastructure works together. For a complete vision, you need the patterns and services identified in later chapters. These elements will improve your ability to focus implementation of shared infrastructure from one or more layers of this model.

## Building the Platform

As you start organizing your technologies into a coherent model, you are creating a platform on which your adaptive infrastructure will rest.

In much the same way that a collection of utilities and services form the basic infrastructure of a city, platforms provide the common infrastructure on which hardware, software, and networking function. Platforms, like utility conduits, should help maximize component reuse and systems integration, simultaneously providing a basic set of shared services that can accommodate considerable variability among applications (such as type of work, user class, location). Obtaining platform services should be as simple as accessing electricity or other utilities, and it should be totally transparent to end-users. This task is not easy or even completely achievable. You will always find newer areas with problems. However, the techniques covered in this book will help reduce them.

Based on the model in Appendix A, you will find most adaptive infrastructure platforms contain three basic sets, or *strata*, of components:

- Physical. All components dealing with the tasks of physical connectivity, storage, and processing, including routers, disks, and servers, plus user devices such as desktops, laptops, mobile phones, and personal digital assistants.

- Functional. All components involved in data manipulation, logical storage, data exchange, transformation, and workflow. This category includes operating systems, relational databases, message brokers, application servers, and integration servers.

- Interface. The components providing system-to-person interaction, such as interactive voice response or graphical user interfaces, or system-to-system interaction such as application programming interfaces (APIs).

Each stratum is further broken down into composite component layers. Each layer is a collection of infrastructure components that are logically associated with delivering a fundamental infrastructure capability.

Collectively, these component layers form the high-level tiers of the infrastructure platform, as shown in Figure 2.2. In this stack, each successive component layer within each tier builds on the functions of the component layers beneath it. The final result of your efforts is a set of infrastructure components that can be used by application developers in a standardized way.

The rest of this chapter focuses on defining each layer in the platform. These component layers will become specifically organized into

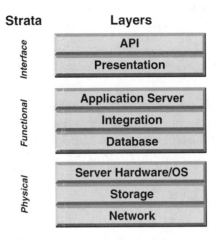

**Figure 2.2** The Adaptive Infrastructure Platform

usable systems by patterns and services. Then the layers will be defined and standardized as part of a toolkit that is used by infrastructure planners and application developers to select, organize, and integrate various services. As explained in Chapter 1, such toolkits will help you promote reuse and integration strategies that will ultimately simplify delivery of infrastructure.

The goal is not to explain the details about each component (another book in this series addresses critical e-Business components). Instead, the goal is to make sure you have at least this traditional model as a foundation for future planning efforts. After defining these layers, which probably map closely to the way you already think about infrastructure planning, this book introduces new ideas—an approach to defining patterns and services that make planning infrastructure better than this simple platform model.

The following pages note the basic function of each layer, describe key strategies for each layer, and list the components in each layer. It will also define where more layers might be useful and identify the common need to add more components over time. You should standardize on a model for use within your organization, including common icons used to diagram infrastructure components.

This use of common models, and even icons, addresses one of the first steps you must take to have an adaptive infrastructure. Your organization must have a common set of semantics, as well as commonly accepted ways of communicating. Then, if you need to choose between opposing viewpoints, at least everyone understands the debate, even if they don't agree with the conclusions.

## Physical Components

The physical part of your platform includes server hardware devices and operating systems, any storage infrastructure that you support, and the network infrastructure itself. The following is a complete discussion of each, starting from the bottom up.

### The Network Layer

The network layer is primarily concerned with locating and communicating among entities in a secure and manageable way. This layer provides a universal protocol (TCP/IP) that is essential to an adaptive infrastructure platform. Components in the network layer include firewalls, routers, switches, proxy and caching services, and load balancers. At a lower level, which usually doesn't need to be detailed, network components also include physical wires and fibers, as well as transmission services typically provided by telecommunications service providers such as AT&T, British Telecom, and NTT.

Integration of components in the network layer is much easier, thanks to the rise of TCP/IP as a standard networking protocol and lower-level standards, such as Ethernet and its higher-speed derivatives. A few years ago, this commonality wasn't something you could take for granted. Today, most businesses have network and desktop operating systems that support TCP/IP-based networking and applications over standards such as switched, high-speed Ethernet.

Why IP? Because it provides a reliable and ubiquitous infrastructure for delivering data and applications across all types of network boundaries, including the Internet. Over the last decade, IP has become the *de facto* standard for business-to-business communication and data sharing.

What's more, the vast majority of current business applications require IP support. By definition, any application that uses one of the major databases, such as Oracle, Microsoft SQL Server, or IBM DB2, assumes that your network supports IP.

IP support is also included within the major desktop operating systems. Internet, virtual private network (VPN), intranet, and extranet applications cannot work without it.

IP prevalence is important for another reason: the convergence of voice and data traffic. Merging voice and data networks will become an increasingly critical issue within larger organizations, particularly those with significant call center operations. While this book does not cover the particulars of such convergence, organizations that might be heading in this direction must sort out transport issues within the network layer to prepare for that possibility.

Just because you have IP, of course, doesn't negate any of the other protocol layers on your network such as Novell IPX, IBM mainframe SNA, and Digital's LAT. However, the dominance of TCP/IP will help your organization offer service levels more simply and with a greater degree of quality at a lower cost. It's easier to support a more homogenous network.

Of course, IP is just one component of the network layer, but it is a key one. This change to a single standard for the protocol component of the network layer is profound; unfortunately, a single common infrastructure is not that common for many other components in other layers—or even in this layer.

Below TCP/IP, many networking components must be planned, including hardware, services, and technologies such as VPNs, frame relay, leased lines, and so forth. However, TCP/IP provides a simple yet critical transparency layer between this lower-level complexity and upper-layer usage. You can see this approach more clearly in the discussion of services in Chapter 4. The network is usually offered up as a service to applications, which makes it more than just the sum of its components.

Many organizations further structure their networking layer with sets of grouped components. By adding staffing and processes to these bundles and using them more in planning, you will be defining services. Simply bundling common technologies further in the network is a start to planning them better.

### Trends in Networking

Current and long-term trends in networking focus on a number of different models:

**Local/campus networks (LANs).**  These days, businesses without local area networks are few and far between, and the days of rationing network connections are over. The price/performance of network hardware continues to improve at a dramatic rate, while available bandwidth continues to grow. Falling hardware prices make it easy for network designers to build in considerable power at a reasonable cost, including 10/100 Mbps network interfaces, Gigabit Ethernet backbones, and LAN switching. In fact, local networks can be safely "overdesigned" from a bandwidth standpoint, trading the expense of overprovisioning for lower management and maintenance costs and higher quality.

The remaining issues in campus networks have to do with the timing and uniformity of technology upgrades. First, the organization should be riding, not fighting, the improving price/performance curves. Ethernet, in its many forms, has won. Token-ring networks should be a relic of the past, and user requirements should be organized so that upgrades take place systematically, in concert with equipment leases or desktop upgrades. The ultimate goal should be the creation of a generic campus infrastructure that supports all applications in use within the campus.

**Wide area networks (WANs).** The WAN is indispensable for businesses with far-flung locations. Due to its nature, however, it's trickier to provide a generic infrastructure for a WAN than for a LAN. The level of service is dictated by the size and location of the remote sites, the applications they support, and the costs of network equipment and services required.

A three-layer WAN architecture, shown in Figure 2.3, helps account for these various possibilities. The top level covers high-speed, aggregated campus traffic within a major metropolitan area. This service is typically delivered via synchronous optical network (SONET), synchronous digital hierarchy (SDH), or fiber-optic networks, and is usually available and cost-effective for large sites in limited geographical regions. The middle tier is a hybrid of leased line, frame relay, and IP interconnects, which connects the majority of sites at access rates of T1 or below. The final tier, for small, remote locations, is a hodgepodge of network technology. These sites use whatever happens to be available, including Integrated Services Digital Network (ISDN), Very Small Aperture Terminals (VSAT), analog dial-up, and xDSL/cable modems.

**Remote access.** VPNs are often seen as a cost-effective alternative to conventional remote access solutions and WANs. VPNs can offer major benefits, particularly flexibility, cost-effectiveness for selected configurations, and the ability to connect dynamically with outside organizations. Pitfalls do exist, however, including security risks, efficiency, and manageability issues. Therefore, users should not use VPNs indiscriminately, or in place of more stable and supported WANs. Instead, they should differentiate among the various types of VPN services (dial, branch office, and electronic commerce/extranet) and devise separate adoption strate-

Users will deploy three-tier WAN architectures: metro-area SONET/SDH transitioning to ATM (1998–99); enterprise frame relay transitioning to IP (1999–2001); and low-speed alternatives (e.g., X.25, VSAT) serving outlying locations (through 2002+). Packet over SONET will coexist with ATM within carrier networks through 2002.

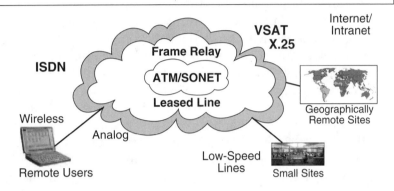

**Figure 2.3** Three-layer WAN Architecture

gies for each, based on specific connectivity requirements, service costs, and technology maturity.

## Differentiating IP Service

As IP becomes the single platform for all applications, the focus must shift from building the IP foundation to enabling differentiated services on top of that foundation. These services will differentiate quality-of-service (QoS) guarantees and better security, along with more robust directory services, not just domain naming services (DNS). Technology issues will be resolved slowly, but the real challenges will be the determination and end-to-end implementation of QoS policy, particularly across organizational boundaries, such as business unit to business unit, or enterprise to service provider, as well as between networking layers.

Creating these enhanced services is one of the many ways you can competitively differentiate aspects of your infrastructure and present them as packaged products that can be delivered more effectively to the business units. In fact, determining the level of enhancements initially will be more of a business decision than a technology decision.

Network architects would like to have *carte blanche* to install a network that can handle every possible application and contingency. The other extreme would be a bare-bones configuration with minimal QoS guarantees. The reality, of course, falls somewhere in the middle.

You should plan now to involve business units in decisions to determine which applications get enhanced network services at the expense of others. With increasing QoS requirements, networking personnel should not make prioritization decisions, but force the business to address these issues head on. Options should be presented based on cost and on outcomes of prioritization decisions.

Not surprisingly, the technology component of this equation remains muddled. You could deploy numerous QoS options, including filtering, prioritization, traffic shaping, multicast, and caching, along with network monitoring. The complexity of QoS decision-making could drastically curtail its effective use in enterprisewide deployments, making QoS something that applies only to WAN links and firewalls.

Initially, for most organizations, QoS solutions should focus on ensuring the reasonable performance of mission-critical interactive applications, at the expense of more unpredictable traffic that adversely impacts critical data flows, such as e-mail and file transfer. Network and application upgrades eventually will enable QoS solutions to support specific applications and user profiles.

## The Storage Layer

The storage layer is primarily concerned with handling the need for short-term and long-term data storage within the organization, including the backup and redundancies that are vital to data security and disaster recovery. Figure 2.4 shows hardware components of the storage layer.

Decisions in the storage layer will only become more critical over time. What is more pressing: the need for processing power or the need for storage? Where are systems typically underutilized? And where do capacity problems occur more frequently? In many organizations, storage is the place where you will see the most performance problems.

Storage, then, is a major hardware component of the shared services infrastructure you are trying to develop. It will be fairly simple to get users to understand that the server is just a tool and that the goal is to select the right tool for the task at hand. It will be more difficult to establish distributed, consolidated storage as part of the shared infrastructure. While many organizations are adept at handling servers, relatively few are good at handling distributed storage.

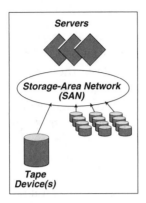

**Storage Layer Components (Hardware)**

Examples:

- Business continuance hardware (disk and tape)

- Business continuance software (tape backup, mirroring, etc.)

- Host interconnect

- Storage area network (SAN) interconnect

- Storage server

**Figure 2.4** Storage Layer Components

## Trends in Storage

As storage interconnects continue to provide additional bandwidth for storage input/output performance, and as Fibre Channel (FC) interoperability issues dissolve, storage will be deployed more and more as a service, rather than a technology tied to particular server choices. Performance enhancements will come with clusters, then increasingly from products that develop the notion of the storage area network (SAN).

The SAN concept involves offloading storage and backup/recovery traffic from the user/application network using various interconnect technologies. SANs can also use traditional network protocols, such as Ethernet, to offload storage traffic onto a dedicated network. You can also use traditional storage interconnects such as FC and Ultra small computer systems interface (SCSI) to satisfy the same requirements. Clearly, portions of the SAN concept have been in place for years, and many IT organizations enjoyed great performance benefits by implementing a dedicated Ethernet or Fiber Distributed Data Interface (FDDI) network for backup and recovery in the early 1990s.

Before long, the concept of an enterprise storage standard will be commonplace. IT shops will have multiple storage pools aggregated by application type connected to a robust SAN. Servers will not attach directly to storage subsystems but to a logical storage subsystem.

The issue here is data movement. For instance, many users with large data warehousing applications are extracting the data from a production system, physically transferring it to another system, then reloading it. With a SAN, the transfer can be logical, not physical. This transfer requires additional data translation facilities, but it works better than shipping something over a conventional network, where all kinds of problems may be caused or encountered.

The main concern is avoiding the logical controls that a database manager provides. Application A should not be writing to Application B's data independent of the database manager, unless the architecture also includes a storage controller that maintains the logical business rules.

Increasingly, storage vendors will add more functionality to storage controllers, including switches for the SAN. Basically, these products will be controllers that can support multiple hosts. Data requests come into the controller from multiple sources, and the controller routes them around.

Backup and recovery services, meanwhile, must maintain some consistency in the configuration of the storage. In a multihost environment, a backup/recovery solution should be able to execute independent of any individual host. A master/slave relationship is not desirable here, because if the master is lost, then backup/recovery capabilities are lost.

### An Appropriate Storage Strategy

To save money, consolidation strategies will be established—first by co-locating servers, then by using SANs for storage consolidation. (See the section on consolidation below.) This type of consolidation is easier to do than full server consolidation with like or mixed workloads. Mainframes can do this, but distributed systems will have trouble consolidating application instances. Everyone should have a storage strategy that promotes consolidation, often across multiple platforms.

Increasingly, the most strategic aspect of storage strategies will be software focused. The ability to manage data and information across many business processes and applications, as well as across physical servers and storage devices, represents the next level of value in storage services. If you have an overall strategy for information storage and its accessibility across geographies and mediums (e.g., memory, disk, tape), it will enable both improved disaster recovery and business continuity and the use of information as an asset across the enterprise.

## The Server Layer

The server layer includes both the server hardware and the operating system software, such as Microsoft Windows 2000/.NET Server, Sun Solaris, HP-UX, IBM AIX, and Linux, as well as traditional mainframes and minicomputer host systems running OS/390, OS/400, and others.

These basic server components are bundled with more sophisticated capabilities to create file servers, Web servers, application servers, database servers, and integration servers. Figure 2.5 shows the hardware and software components of a server layer.

When organizing this layer, you should realize that the days of organizing infrastructure around the capabilities of a particular vendor's hardware platform are essentially over, since hardware is becoming the least expensive component of application infrastructure.

For this reason, you should place less emphasis on server selection as a criterion for planning infrastructure. Beware of picking only the most capable solution for all problems, because less powerful servers may work better for many applications than more powerful ones. More important, you should limit the degree to which the choice of server hardware influences the selection of applications, middleware, and network infrastructure components. Surprisingly, infrastructure planners tend to place the most emphasis on server selection.

However, minimizing the influence of servers within the organization does not completely eliminate the issues surrounding their selection. The most prevalent issue remains the choice of server hardware and operating system, which has coalesced around three favorites:

- Microsoft Windows 2000/.NET Server
- UNIX
- IBM System S/390

Gaps in performance, scalability, and price among these three platforms have narrowed significantly in recent years. Nonetheless, even though the differences are disappearing, each type of server possesses strengths or weaknesses that make it suitable for supporting certain environments.

### Trends in Server Hardware and Deployment

Server components will continue to have aggressive price and performance gains, with microprocessor value continuing to follow Moore's Law. More than likely, next-generation bus technologies will address the common bottlenecks associated with input/output and moving information around the microprocessor. These technologies will bridge the server and storage worlds, fulfilling the server's role in speeding up the movement of information between storage and server devices.

Microsoft Windows 2000/.NET Server will be the long-term dominant player and will provide the widest number of options for application soft-

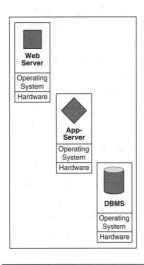

**Server Layer Components (Hardware/Software)**

Examples:

• Operating system software

• Hardware

• Web server

• Application server

• Database server

• Integration server

• File server/network-attached storage (NAS)
  ...and other hardware servers

**Figure 2.5** Server Layer Components

ware. The UNIX platforms will consolidate around three product vendor choices:

■ Sun Solaris

■ IBM AIX

■ HP-UX

Many of the basic techniques used for distributed systems management, database management, and communications are technologies that grew out of the UNIX realm. So, even if UNIX loses market share, skills that were built in the UNIX realm will persist and continue to be valuable.

System S/390 will remain the most expensive choice and will also have the smallest installed base by units, but it will not disappear completely. Some applications require System S/390 or MVS OS/390, due to the inherent advantages in scalability and availability. For instance, if an application includes a non-distributed job that needs to be scheduled with tight interdependencies among other applications with similar characteristics, then S/390 may provide an advantage over other platforms. Even though organizations might need to continue supporting one or more of these platforms for the foreseeable future, new applications no longer target the mainframe platform.

*Basic Issues in Server Selection*

From an adaptive infrastructure standpoint, the primary concerns related to server selection revolve around the following issues:

**Total Cost of Ownership.** Each server architecture will offer consistent levels of quality from a pure hardware or OS standpoint, and each will have its own strengths. Therefore, total cost of ownership (TCO) concerns will focus on supportability, availability of skilled development and implementation staff, and recurring support costs for hardware, software, and operations. In TCO-optimized shops, component costs will decline to less than 25 percent of TCO, making vendor support considerations more important in server procurement strategies. Since one now finds less variance among the three platforms than in the past, they also will share much more commonality in microprocessor designs and in the basic operating system services being presented.

The differences lie in the fact that certain server platforms benefit from years of server-oriented use. Some vendors understand the requirements for a shared piece of hardware and have built an entire infrastructure to support them. Others have demonstrated the ability to support complex applications. A demonstrated expertise in support is the critical component of reduced TCO.

**Playing to the Windows 2000/.NET Server's Strengths.** In the world of Microsoft, the vendor market might not be as mature as elsewhere, but the potential advantage is simple: application choice. What Microsoft promised with Windows 2000/.NET Server is a consistent, coherent infrastructure out of the box. The promise is not less expensive systems, which Microsoft calls a by-product of consistency. Nor is there a promise of better quality or better support. The Windows 2000/.NET Server value proposition is that software vendors will write their applications to run on Windows. As a result, organizations will get the widest possible range of potential applications for enterprisewide deployment. Additionally, these applications will become more consistent over time, reducing support problems.

More important, the richness of applications written for Windows 2000/.NET Server, from a business function standpoint, is often superior to applications written for other platforms, because software vendors can take the money saved by eliminating different platform-dependent versions and use it to improve application functionality—unless they decide to improve their bottom lines.

In that sense, the software market is no different from any other market. Suppliers will direct their efforts toward the largest potential payoff. What is unclear is how each server platform will ultimately be supported. On platforms that have weaker support from software vendors, new application features may arrive several years later than more supported platforms.

**Technology Consolidation.** Many of the more obscure UNIX variants will continue to fade away, while Solaris, AIX, and HP-UX retain market share. Linux will be used more as an operating system for Web and appliance servers than for application and database servers. In the Windows 2000/.NET Server world, system vendors will attempt to differentiate their Windows 2000 implementations by adding various utilities and services on top, such as clustering and systems management, particularly in Windows 2000 Data Center Server. The basic point about Windows 2000/.NET Server is this: Keeping the Windows 2000/.NET Server choice simple keeps Windows 2000/.NET Server deployment simple.

**Server Consolidation.** In addition to technology consolidation, server consolidation will occur during the next few years. This issue is critical to developing an adaptive infrastructure platform, because users currently have many ways of configuring and using servers. Server consolidation will generate some savings, but in very targeted and specific ways. Organizations will find themselves somewhere on the server consolidation curve (see Figure 2.6), and they must decide how far along the curve they need to move.

At the bottom of the curve is random server proliferation. Someone will say, "I have applications to stage, and I am buying a server. Can I drop it in?" This syndrome results in the kind of usage patterns found at one organization, where 850 servers were deployed, none with a utilization rate greater than 18 percent. This approach is not the best way to solve the problem.

The first move up the curve should involve physical co-location of servers and storage. Co-location tends to foster common management approaches, while leveraging staff and promoting storage consolidation. Co-location can generate some noteworthy savings, but it still represents a fairly rudimentary consolidation strategy.

Likewise, you might find it fairly simple to consolidate storage systems to leverage file and print services, despite any networking complexities. Still, these first two levels of consolidation are the ones that provide the easiest (most risk-free) cost of ownership improvements.

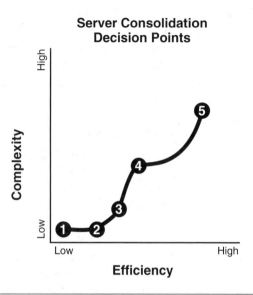

**Figure 2.6** The Server Consolidation Curve

Real efficiencies can be found in the next step of the curve, which consolidates similar, or "like-workload," applications. The best example of this server consolidation currently involves file/print and groupware systems, including e-mail and calendaring. These consolidations centralize common applications and storage systems from disparate distributed servers. Groupware applications are well suited for consolidation, since concern for complications such as transaction collisions is minimal. In metropolitan and campus environments, networking complications also can be mitigated using appropriate bandwidth. However, many times it makes sense not to centralize even these types of servers, especially where long distances and slow wide area network services separate large user populations. For example, a 500-person facility in Malaysia is much better off using a local groupware server than having to connect back to North America for e-mail and calendar access.

Other applications might not do as well when highly centralized or consolidated. A given application may not scale well on a single server platform. A single server might have a realistic maximum number of simultaneous users, no matter how powerful it is.

The most advanced server consolidation involves mixed-workload consolidation. This approach can provide the most efficient use of storage, servers, and personnel such as database administrators. However, variability becomes much more of a factor. Slight differences in applications will lead to huge differences in performance and behavior. You should probably not mix workloads unless you place them on a platform that is designed specifically to be partitioned, or you have done a thorough analysis of commonality and variability on the workloads. The latter method helps ensure that workload differences are at a minimum and that dependencies are well understood.

Having many different applications running on a single server means that you will spend much time and effort optimizing the last 10 percent of the server's performance, resulting in higher cost for support, expertise, and training. Many organizations avoid overburdening servers and keep loads below 80 percent to avoid management costs or the costs of upgrading to high-end hardware platforms from cheaper commodity platforms.

Over time, this approach will become more common as applications can scale incrementally with multiserver designs. (See the 3/N-Tier pattern in Chapter 3 for detail on the stateless server farm architecture.) The least expensive configuration may not be one with fewer servers, particularly when you take cost-of-ownership issues into account. Putting all servers into a centralized data center, even if you have many of them, will lower the total cost of ownership significantly—so real server consolidation may not be necessary.

With this focus on server selection, remember that as infrastructures get more complex, including e-Business and 3/N-Tier designs, a given application will need multiple servers and they *do not* all need to be the same server OS/hardware platform.

## Functional Components

The functional part of your platform includes the software that provides database systems, integration servers, and application servers. The following sections discuss each of these in turn, focusing on key trends to consider when planning each.

### The Database Layer

This layer includes all the software components used to deliver database services, including mainstream database products such as Oracle, DB2, and Microsoft SQL Server, as well as other components that are less visible to the business, such as gateways, middleware, and voice messaging repositories.

Except for data warehousing, the database market has been relatively stable in recent years with the ascendance of the dominant market players: Oracle, IBM, and Microsoft. Still, the proliferation of cross-enterprise applications, like data warehousing, knowledge management, and customer care, is increasing the demand for integrated access to previously independent data stores, such as RDBMS, Web site content management systems, e-mail, and spreadsheets. Specialized data stores, which enhance performance and support a variety of data types, will continue to support specialized applications.

## Trends in Database Technology

As demands on the "corporate information asset" continue to expand, the federated database architecture (FDA) will supersede universal database engines as the preferred DBMS infrastructure within the next few years. FDA provides autonomous, local processing for individual data stores, but also provides a way to integrate them globally for applications that require it.

In an adaptive infrastructure context, your goal is to give the people who manage applications a transparent way to improve the performance and reliability of the applications they support. For example, a single data warehousing application might have several data stores associated with it that must be joined in a single query, including a database for the data mining portion, a star schema configuration supporting online analytical processing (OLAP), any number of relational database managers, and other data types. Access to each data type should be simplified, or encapsulated in an infrastructure service to the greatest extent possible, in order to minimize the learning curve for application developers.

The FDA approach initially will affect data warehousing installations, followed by knowledge management and lightweight transaction processing applications. To support FDA, database vendors will provide new features such as improved tool transparency, distributed query management, and most important, better, faster, and cheaper platforms and engines.

Still, these activities will require considerable effort from database administrators to promote reuse throughout the organization. Many of these functions, including schema integration and index coordination, are far from easy. Creating consistent, enterprisewide rules and practices for data administration and design is the most important step—and it remains a major challenge within distributed environments.

Initially, reuse will require a gateway layer that can span a few types of data stores without requiring you to write new and uniquely supported access methods. Many vendors are heading in this direction, including IBM (Data Propagator, Data Joiner), Sybase, Microsoft (OADB), and any number of smaller vendors.

### Database Selection

From a component standpoint, most organizations approach the database layer by choosing a particular DBMS server platform and sticking with it. Most users *cannot* do this well, because their applications demand particular products, or because merged organizations made different choices in the past, or because new technology enhancements (or pricing changes) introduce new options.

Even so, most users have narrowed their choices to just a few platforms: Oracle, Microsoft SQL Server, or IBM DB2 universal database server (UDB). With the discussion of patterns in Chapter 3, you will discover a better way to describe the various database choices—a technique that allows some variety while keeping a strong structure so that the variety does not get out of control.

## The Integration Layer

As shown in Figure 2.7, this layer contains all components that provide integration services between back-end applications and other Web servers, application servers, or database servers. Components may include adapter toolkits, application adapters, integration servers, electronic data interchange (EDI) gateways, file exchange servers, and more. The integration function could be internally focused, such as enterprise application integration (EAI), or externally focused, such as inter-enterprise integration (IEI).

Integration servers provide a way to integrate e-Business applications with enterprise and legacy systems at the application layer. Application servers are used to build applications, and integration servers are used to integrate applications once they are built. These two types of products are the main drivers in a rapidly converging middleware market.

As the market continues to converge, even these two types of products will overlap, supporting features necessary for both application building and integration. Ironically, as these product classes overlap, the evolution to Web services will result in these capabilities being called on from a wider variety of places, including external service providers.

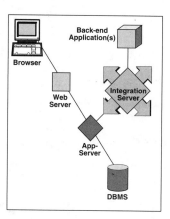

**Integration Layer Components**
Examples:
- Enterprise application integration (EAI) server
- Inter-enterprise integration (IEI) server
- Application adapter/adapter toolkit
- Integration transport software
- Process modeler/execution engine
- Computer telephony integration (CTI) server
- EDI gateway
- File exchange server
- Integration transport server
- Middleware encryption software
- Process modeler/execution engine

**Figure 2.7** Integration Layer Components

Architecturally, integration servers include the following components, as shown in Figure 2.8:

- Adapter provides interfaces for applications to send or receive business events to or from other applications, such as placing, changing, or canceling orders

- Transport moves the business events around the network, often using messaging middleware such as MQ Series or using publish and subscribe services, all of which will likely become a subset of Web services over time

- Formatting transforms business events from one application-specific format to another using standards such as XML

- Routing defines which applications receive which events

- Business Process Automation (BPA) is a state-handling run-time environment, generally used to control the execution of long-lived transactions

When well implemented, such hub-and-spoke transactional integration services will make these aspects of integration transparent to application developers. Furthermore, these services will be easier to support as a key organizational asset, because applications won't need to know what format or protocol other applications are using, or where they are located.

Stateless integration servers provide a loosely coupled integration, which is a better technical foundation for implementing enterprise application integration (EAI) than component-based application servers

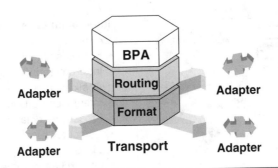

**Figure 2.8** Integration Server Components

such as Java 2 Enterprise Edition (J2EE) and COM+. It's a good idea to use application server infrastructure for building application functionality, but separate integration server infrastructure to integrate these applications.

While generally appropriate for most integration problems, this approach doesn't work for everything. The need for state-handling capability and transaction-handling features on application servers will cause the application server and integration server platforms to eventually converge. Thus, Web services derived from Microsoft 2000/.NET Server or J2EE will become the long-term solutions. These services will leverage numerous lower-level standards, including:

- Extensible Markup Language (XML)
- Universal Description, Discovery, and Integration (UDDI)
- Simple Object Access Protocol (SOAP)
- Web Services Description Language (WSDL)

Ideally, Web services will enable application developers to leverage existing capabilities wherever they may be found, whether within core infrastructure offerings, enterprise applications, partner/supplier applications, or even on the Internet.

### Best Fit for Integration Servers

The complexity involved in integrating any given business process is determined by many factors, including:

- Throughput (events per second)
- Number of applications involved

- State-handling requirements
- Number of interfaces involved
- The quality of those interfaces

State handling is a good example of issues that will require you to reduce complexity. As integration becomes increasingly crucial to successful business strategy, you must transform subjective concepts such as "complexity," "collaboration," and "automated business processes" into objective technical requirements to be supported by the infrastructure. State handling is the only feature that will force you to implement additional infrastructure to support first-generation stateless EAI infrastructure.

An example of an integration process—one that is handled best and most straightforwardly by using a stateless integration server—is the process of routing a customer's Web-based orders to the distribution center nearest the customer, then sending e-mail to the customer indicating that the order has shipped. To support this process, the integration server hosts an order routing service that uses an EAI rules/routing engine to determine which distribution center should fulfill the order. The server then uses an EAI formatting engine to create the order in the appropriate format required by the pick/pack/ship application at the chosen distribution center.

Since state doesn't need to be maintained as an order moves from the Web storefront or call center to the distribution center, the state-handling capabilities of an application server are unnecessary. While developers could use Visual Basic, C++, or Java to execute this logic within an application server container, the rules/formatting feature of an integration server offers faster time-to-market and greater flexibility. The common hub-and-spoke topology of such integration services also enables simpler management and easier leverage than using code in or between applications.

To enable "real-time" inventory checks, however, the integration server must be able to maintain the state of a given order as it queries the inventory status of the various distribution centers. Initial routing is still based on proximity to the customer shipping address. However, the inventory level of that distribution center is checked, and if the item is out of stock, the order is rerouted to an alternative distribution center. If the item is completely unavailable, the customer is presented with the option of back-ordering the item or canceling the order. This state-handling capability is beyond the functionality provided by an integration server's rules and formatting engines.

## A Best Practices Approach

When faced with state-handling issues, examine how long the state must be maintained and how dynamic the changes in business logic will be. Generally, application servers must maintain sessions to maintain state, which is fine for quick transactions but not feasible for lengthy ones. An integration server, with its process automation engine, would be a better fit for more long-lived processes such as coordinating the provisioning and billing of a retail bundle of land-line, wireless, and Internet networking services among various back-end provisioning and billing systems.

In either case, an application developer should not have to know whether the order routing logic is handled by an application server, by an integration server, or both. This functional partitioning is the key to business process agility. Defining such application services—using a combination of application server and integration server technologies—will be a premium skill set that helps maintain an optimum separation between application and infrastructure development.

## The Application Server Layer

The application server layer contains the software that supports business logic. Obvious examples are 3-tier applications involving products such as IBM WebSphere and BEA WebLogic, or tools associated with Microsoft 2000/.NET Server and its framework. As opposed to the server operating system software discussed earlier, the application server layer contains software that makes it easier to leverage application service functionality.

Keep in mind that this layer does not contain the applications themselves. Instead, it provides front-line components upon which the applications are directly built.

## Application Server Trends

Application servers are being rapidly adopted, but they are still in their infancy, accounting for roughly 10 percent of new application development and packaged software acquisitions. This situation will change dramatically as organizations begin to adopt component-based development standards and as application software vendors respond to the demand for componentized products.

Within a few years, the norm for best-practice IT organizations will be to use applications that are assembled from built or purchased components and combine them with Web-based services built on compatible component models.

The rapid ascendance of e-Business, along with the realization that business logic must reside on the server instead of the client, has propelled the application server to center stage. When this market was in its early growth stage and crowded with products, business units often selected incompatible products for different projects. Today, organizations must choose between J2EE and .NET as their primary enterprise application integration architecture.

You will find architectural similarity in both camps, but take special care when picking vendors of appropriate components within the J2EE camp.

This crucial choice should be based on explicit, well-defined business requirements and constraints. Enterprises that fail to make a clear choice between J2EE and .NET as their primary application server platform will lack infrastructure agility and will be at a disadvantage relative to more-nimble competitors.

Given current trends, most large organizations will have both J2EE and .NET, and they will need strategies for maintaining the least variety possible. This topic is the core of the discussion of the 3/N-Tier Transact pattern in Chapter 3.

### Selection Criteria

When considering which framework to use, J2EE and .NET are both viable alternatives. In fact, most large organizations will need to deal with both to some degree. Using the Extensible Markup Language (XML) and more sophisticated Web services in the future will help bridge the two when necessary. However, all organizations need to choose one or the other as their primary application integration framework.

Deciding between J2EE and .NET doesn't necessarily limit your product choices in other infrastructure layers. For instance, both work with any Web server or database management system. In practice, however, your choice of a primary application server platform will typically lead to related infrastructure choices. For example, choosing J2EE will require UNIX platforms such as Sun Solaris, HP-UX, IBM AIX, and possibly Linux. Choosing .NET implies a more substantial enterprise role for the Microsoft Windows server environment.

In the early stages of deployment, you may find that less code is needed to make your application server run than to integrate your newly created application server layer with existing, monolithic applications and databases. However, as you develop, acquire, and deploy more new componentized applications on your chosen application server, the application server layer will steadily expand to encompass ever more enterprise and line-of-business applications. Eventually, most applications will be component assemblies running on the application server with only vestiges of legacy applications and data sources. Naturally, the more you design for 3/N-Tier architecture, the easier integration becomes.

## Interface Components

The interface components include API and presentation layers. The following is a discussion of key trends in each.

### The Presentation Layer

The presentation layer probably offers the widest assortment of hardware and software tools you will have to deal with in your technology catalog. The choice of user interface devices for desktop or mobile environments ranges from PCs to cell phones, personal digital assistants (PDAs), browsers, and telephones. Presentation server components are also in this layer, including traditional terminal servers, streaming media servers, interactive TV, e-mail servers, and Web servers such as Microsoft Internet Information Server (IIS). This layer may support presentation methods such as interactive voice response (IVR), wireless application protocol (WAP), and computer telephony integration (CTI)—each with its own hardware and software options, as shown in Figure 2.9.

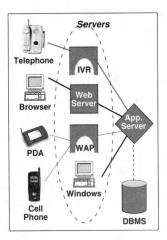

**Presentation Layer Components (Software/Hardware)**

Examples:

- Web server
- Wireless Application Protocol (WAP) server
- Integrated voice response (IVR)
- Voice/telephone
- Terminal server
- Streaming server
- Interactive TV
- E-mail MTA
- Telephone
- Desktop/notebook hardware
- Personal digital assistant (PDA)
- Embedded services (e.g., in vehicle systems, intelligent appliances)

**Figure 2.9** Presentation Layer Components

## Multiple Points of Interaction

Obviously, much of the component choice involves picking the right presentation model for the right application and user environment. To provide agility, your infrastructure might need to support, or integrate with, a number of different presentation models. Today's applications will need to be displayed on tomorrow's presentation devices.

Increasingly, the rise of e-Business is creating a demand for multiple points of interaction (POI) for customers, partners, employees, and suppliers. Web content could be displayed through a desktop browser, a PDA, a cell phone, or one of the many Internet devices rapidly making their way to market. Today's applications need more than one user interface for essentially the same information and processes.

For this reason, one of your key goals should be to tie together all systems and present a consistent user experience across increasingly varied points of interaction. Tying application logic only to a Web interface defeats this goal. You may have encountered this problem before with Windows-centric 2-Tier client/server designs, which made it very expensive to move to a Web interface. A new infrastructure approach is necessary, one that must change application developer behavior so that multiple points of interaction are included in the design. Organizations must cleanly separate presentation logic from application logic to promote proper 3/N-Tier design principles, as discussed in Chapter 3.

To provide this consistent user experience and to make business logic reusable, your company should develop applications in a disciplined manner that decouples the presentation logic so the same application logic can be reused across all points of interaction. Unfortunately, most companies have not focused enough attention on separating out the presentation layer, either because it is easier and faster to design for the Web only or because they chose solutions that do not offer presentation flexibility.

Multiple access devices such as cell phones require particular ways of interacting with the end user. You should re-examine front-end presentation logic to accommodate the entire range of anticipated presentation requirements, such as the smaller screens on mobile devices, or the voice output of telephones. You should also take a look at the assumptions built around user data input. Instead of building all your assumptions around a keyboard-input model, future applications may require you to cope with more limited input methods such as mobile device keypads, or voice recognition software.

## Cost and Complexity

If you don't develop a proactive approach to these issues, your company could find itself devoting considerable effort over time to re-engineering application presentation and user data entry logic. You might end up having to re-architect the entire application and infrastructure to support multiple end-to-end interaction chains for each access device, with significant implications in terms of cost and complexity. Supporting new access devices implies a thorough reassessment of infrastructure requirements to ensure that the new devices will be supported efficiently. For example, you may have to re-examine your network design to cope with dissimilar bandwidth, latency, and reliability characteristics of individual communication channels. You may also have to re-examine application server configurations and back-end application connectivity modes.

Many organizations are tempted by quick fixes that simply give a "face lift" to the presentation layer. They also tend to give lower priority to access devices other than Web browser-powered desktop workstations and laptop computers, mainly because most U.S.-based Internet initiatives are focused on markets where home and office PC penetration rates are high, including the U.S., northern Europe, and Japan. Alternative Internet points of interaction are considered "exotic" and significant only in niche geographies such as mobile/WAP in Europe and the Asia Pacific region, or interactive TV in the U.K. and other parts of Europe.

Even among companies that *do* recognize the need for multiple points of interaction, many have fallen prey to an additional misconception that threatens their success: the idea that other points of interaction will be simply an extension of their current Web browser interface. The popularity of simplistic tools designed to add mobile access to existing e-Business front-ends was an early indicator that many companies were relegating multiple points of interaction infrastructure investments to an accessory role.

One example of these Band-Aid solutions was the development of HTML-to-WML converters, part of the WAP Forum's Wireless Access Protocol (WAP) standard for mobile Internet services. Early solutions also include page converters for mobile environments, as well as HTML-to-MHEG-5 translators in interactive TV systems.

In the final analysis, particularly for e-Business applications, individual points of interaction will require significant end-to-end planning for the underlying infrastructure to succeed in attaining expected service levels and reliability. In addition, these infrastructures will require you to acquire and master a broad range of divergent technologies.

## The API Layer

One of the key principles of adaptive infrastructure is the idea of breaking out APIs as a distinctly separate layer in the infrastructure stack, as shown in Figure 2.10. Creating a separate layer for APIs makes it easier to separate applications from the infrastructure, which is essential to avoid stovepipes and create a shared, reusable infrastructure.

In the past, programmers wrote applications from the business logic all the way down to the operating system. Currently, however, most application developers are insulated from the operating system by at least one layer of "packaged" infrastructure tools such as Enterprise Java Beans (EJB), IBM's CICS, and Tuxedo. This is rapidly moving to a more sophisticated layer of application/Web services in the form of application servers such as Microsoft .NET Server, IBM WebSphere, and BEA WebLogic.

However, the application developer must still fill in the large gap between the packaged infrastructure and the business logic at the core of the application. In addition, the application developer must become adept at tuning and debugging the infrastructure itself.

Just as organizations separated the database administration function from application development in the past, adaptive organizations are beginning to create a role that separates infrastructure development from application development and its corresponding APIs.

The new role of infrastructure developer relieves application developers from most infrastructure-related responsibility. Once this is done, the application developer can concentrate on the business analyst role and avoid having to spend a lot of time working as a systems programmer.

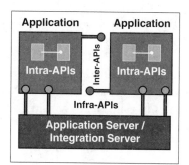

**API Layer Components (Software)**

**Intra-API**—exposes business logic used within an application

    Examples: COM IDL, EJB IDL

**Inter-API**—exposes business logic used between applications

    Examples: Rational Rose

**Infra-API**—exposes infrastructure services to application and infrastructure planners

    Examples: J2EE, .NET, LDAP

**Figure 2.10** API Layer Components

In this new role, the infrastructure developer can take responsibility for selecting and configuring the packaged infrastructure (.NET, EJB, etc.) and may even start building reusable extensions for it, including macros, custom wizards, code templates, and run-time libraries. This shared set of tools can help save application developers time and alleviate much of the tedium of infrastructure performance tuning and debugging.

Much of the separation between the infrastructure developer and application developer function occurs at the API level. To promote this idea, this book divides APIs into three types, each of which will require distinct standards and methodologies. Over time, API developers should be segmented along these lines so that they can become adept at creating reusable components.

### Infra-APIs

Infra-APIs include low-level technology services, such as security, naming, or object invocation, which application developers and infrastructure developers use to create business logic. Increasingly, Infra-APIs and the services they encapsulate are provided off-the-shelf as a built-in part of application servers, such as EJB or .NET.

However, infrastructure developers will still need to create certain Infra-APIs, and provide them to application developers to use in the development process. Use of Infra-APIs is how application components will actually tap into lower-level application services, such as initialization, housekeeping, memory management, and fail-over. The low-level code has nothing to do with business logic; it just makes business logic execute more effectively.

Examples include container servers and integrated development environments (IDEs) that invoke off-the-shelf services and create new infrastructure services. For example, IBM WebSphere would be a container server using IBM VisualAge as its IDE. Open Database Connectivity (ODBC) and Lightweight Directory Access Protocol (LDAP) are other examples of standard APIs. In contrast, organizations occasionally will build their own interfaces for services, such as authentication when using the specific development environments employed within the organization or the application package they have chosen.

### Intra-APIs

Intra-APIs help business logic communicate *within* individual applications and typically are not exposed to other applications. Since they are not reused outside a given application, they are created and managed only by the application's developers.

Examples of infrastructure solutions that support this kind of API include visual modeling tools, such as UML tools that are being offered as a built-in part of IDEs and container servers to promote productivity and single-source shopping. For example, IBM's WebSphere includes a built-in modeling tool called Rational Rose.

### Inter-APIs

Inter-APIs help business logic communicate *between* applications. They expose the application business logic that will be used by other applications. Because this logic affects other applications, Inter-APIs should be defined and managed by infrastructure developers. This category of API includes very large but simple Web services, such as credit card verification, offered by centralized IT to any business unit application needing it.

Solutions supporting the development of such interfaces include container server IDEs, visual modeling tools, and adapter software development kits (SDKs). For example, Java 2 Enterprise Edition (J2EE) version 1.3 includes the Java Connector specification, which provides a standard API to provide connections from a Java application to applications written in other technologies. This feature is emblematic of the shift away from stand-alone EAI/IEI solutions toward having integration components embedded in application servers.

### How to Handle APIs

Application and infrastructure developers must create a formal policy and framework for creating, cataloging, and storing APIs. Infrastructure developers must combine the application requirements and the principles generated by the architectural group to design efficient, secure, and manageable interfaces.

Organizations must use division of labor to increase componentized development with suitable architectural oversight to ensure reuse and compatibility. As the application infrastructure center of gravity converges on component-based infrastructure platforms, users must further evolve and formalize the infrastructure developer and architect roles.

Who will design APIs that support multiple applications? Not the application developer, but the infrastructure developer. Application developers are responsible for designing APIs that work only inside of their applications (Intra-APIs). But APIs that are built for multiple applications must be managed by people who aren't focused on individual applications.

The problem of managing APIs across multiple applications raises some interesting issues, such as:

■ How do you set up an integration server to leverage both Infra-APIs and Inter-APIs and create a service approach?

■ What is the process used to develop APIs that will be used across multiple applications?

■ Should any infrastructure people be involved?

The answer to the last question is an emphatic "Yes." You will be much more successful if infrastructure developers are involved. If you let the application teams figure it out for themselves, they will end up with an endless variety of APIs, many of them redundant, with no central way of managing them all.

In any case, good application design will increasingly involve designing programming—not user—interfaces for simpler, faster, and cheaper integration. This technique will vastly improve infrastructure, even if implemented with moderate success. It should become the best reason to take a lot of care when creating standards or planning infrastructure. It is key to the value of the 3/N-Tier Transact pattern discussed in the next chapter, but it is worth discussion in any pattern.

## Is Anything Missing?

Now that you have considered the entire range of components, take some time to look at your own infrastructure and see how it maps to the Component Catalog in Appendix A. Is anything missing?

### Other Components?

If other infrastructure components become a part of your infrastructure pattern or service portfolios, they should be mapped as a separate component layer if they are:

■ Reused often

■ Politically correct, i.e., adding them will not cause problems in IT

You might need to incorporate more components and create more layers over time as innovation continues. For example, in Figure 2.11, management tools exist for each layer's components, but overall management may be a separate service.

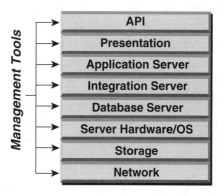

**Figure 2.11** Adding New Components

As application tools continue moving into the infrastructure, you should anticipate changes, such as more application server types in the application server layer. The current application server layer is mainly for transactional applications. As more collaboration servers and analytic servers are executing business logic in a way that is reused across multiple applications, you will want to add more components to this layer than you see now.

Also, as the definition of specific management components increases, you should anticipate changes such as the following:

■ Individual component manager tools, also called element managers, will be included in the same layer as their managed components. Each component could have its matching management component. Clearly, you should do this only when the component is commonly addressed separately. Otherwise, lump such tools into a single "element/component manager" component as a catchall.

■ Multicomponent managers that manage a group of components in one layer should also go into that layer. One example is HP Open-View managing all Simple Network Management Protocol (SNMP) devices at the network layer. You could add a "layer manager" component generically for each layer.

■ Multicomponent managers that manage a group of components across multiple layers could be handled by either placing them in one existing layer, by adding a whole layer for management, or by creating a service for management that draws components from multiple layers.

One final example: An online analytical processing (OLAP) tool with both a database layer component and a reusable application service component should be put in the application server layer *if it is reused heavily.* Other components will be added to the layers over time.

## Other Layers?

If other common sets of components generally are lumped in as part of your complete infrastructure model, you should make a layer out of them and include them in your component portfolio if any of the following applies:

■ They are often referred to as a group (such as security, management).

■ Including them will not overly complicate politics in IT.

■ Including them helps simplify infrastructure complexity. (Keeping the layers to 10 or less is a good rule of thumb.)

■ The components will not form a service themselves.

For example, security can be used as a shared layer by isolation, identity, and permissions infrastructure, as discussed in Chapter 4. Figure 2.12 shows how a security layer might be added.

Instead of simply creating layers, however, focus more on creating services that are physically reusable instantiations of product combinations

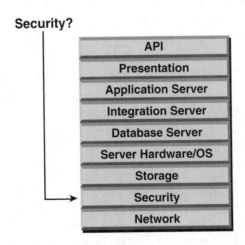

**Figure 2.12** Adding a Security Layer

to be used by multiple applications. Then components from multiple layers can be used even if they do normally fit nicely in a layer. For example, avoid putting security databases or directories in the new security layer, particularly if they might be used for more than security purposes.

## Summary

This chapter has taken infrastructure components and helped you start thinking about ways to organize them. Once you organize components into layers, you will have a portfolio that you can immediately start showing to the business or to application developers.

As new technologies arise, this new component structure will help you organize your thinking about it to the point where you can easily identify the proper roles of the new components and where they fit in the infrastructure. As part of the categorization process, you might identify which expert is responsible for the new technology or who would be assigned additional research and analysis tasks.

This approach is only logical, and it matches the way the real world actually works. Most people, when building any kind of architecture, do technology analysis quite well; they often realize, however, that this is not enough.

### Designing for Operations

For many organizations, management presents a unique challenge —usually to the operations staff. To better operate and manage infrastructure, however, it would be best to design-in management.

How do you design-in management? By insisting on reusable management APIs, such as Application Response Management (ARM), SNMP, XML, and HTML consoles. Since most management needs only hooks, your applications and the infrastructure they are built on must have management interfaces.

Some of these interfaces are SNMP based, but any design paradigm should include designing in the hooks. The earlier discussion of Infra-APIs should guide your thinking, as should the discussion of services in Chapter 4. Monitoring of user response time could be a centralized management service, just like an SNMP console.

Here are some examples where management components have been designed into platform layers and services, or where they become a whole service unto themselves:

- Element management. Put each component into a layer, as discussed earlier.

- User management. This is a key aspect of components in the identity infrastructure service, which specifically may be offered by the directory service or Web Single Sign-On (SSO) components, or built on top of them as another application, tied into a portal, for example.

- Network operations. This could be a service in the form of a network operations center (NOC). While somewhat automated using tools, such as HP OpenView, much of a network operations center is the people and manual process issues that you also need for a service.

Designing for better operations will require coordinating with operations personnel and process. In any case, structured thinking about management could involve new components and new platform layers. Most critically, it should involve pattern thinking, and especially service thinking, to be best achieved in actual practice. At the very least, management must be built into the infrastructure planning methodology itself. Consider it an attribute of any design, plan, or standard that you create.

# Chapter 3

# Identifying and Using Patterns

The fundamental concepts presented so far are quite useful from an organizational standpoint. But they don't help much when someone wants a new application deployed and suddenly asks you to provide a complete infrastructure design, along with a full range of cost estimates.

Instead of cobbling together a hasty response, an adaptive infrastructure strategy gives you the ability to reply quickly and accurately with a set of proven options. Using a blueprint that you have already tested, you can reply in a matter of hours with detailed plans, architecture diagrams, costs, and schedules.

The key to this tour de force is the idea of "patterns," which are complete, predesigned end-to-end solutions that can be simply and quickly molded to fit the latest business requirements. By identifying and creating a series of reusable infrastructure patterns, you can be prepared to propose solutions that are faster, cheaper, and better for most of the application requests that come your way.

An adaptive infrastructure strategy starts paying off when you begin visualizing basic infrastructure patterns and seeing how easily they can be adapted to describe the existing applications within an organization. You can use the common patterns and pattern-oriented thinking described in this chapter to simplify your own infrastructure planning and make application development easier.

## What Are Patterns?

Technology and business evolution can wreak havoc on your infrastructure in many ways. Difficulties occur when you try to consolidate incompatible hardware and software infrastructures after a merger or acquisition, or when you try to create an enterprisewide intranet to enhance workplace collaboration. Globalization efforts can easily descend into chaos. And each new application that you deploy can bring with it new infrastructure challenges or just further add to the chaos. Yet it doesn't have to be this way. If your infrastructure is planned and maintained properly, new applications can be incorporated rapidly and efficiently.

Figure 3.1 shows the goals of a pattern-based architecture.

The infrastructure necessary for a given application is determined by who uses it and how they use it. Since users interact with applications in a small number of ways, and applications interact with other applications in a small number of ways, it is easy to describe an application by the types of interactions it employs, thus defining its infrastructure requirements. The adaptive infrastructure patterns outlined here have evolved to a point where they reduce many possible infrastructure options to a small num-

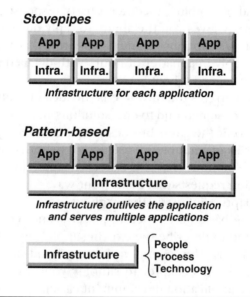

**Figure 3.1** Goals of a Pattern-based Architecture

ber of descriptive archetypes, so you can use them to plan for simplified and reusable infrastructure configurations.

## Designing for the Future

If left unmanaged, a growing business's IT infrastructure would evolve very much like a one-bedroom house evolves with a growing family. Anytime a need arises, a new room gets tacked onto the structure, or a new doorway is cut in an existing wall.

The same thing can happen in IT. While no organization should expect to run all their enterprise applications on a single IT infrastructure, it is impractical and inefficient to allow networks, hardware, software, and business processes to grow unchecked with separate decisions and implementations each time an application is deployed.

In a way, good infrastructure design works the same way a real estate developer plans a subdivision or a master-planned community. Though thousands of homes are to be built, all are based on a set of perhaps 10 basic designs. And while each design can be customized, the builders already know these 10 designs and have worked with them often. By improving on these 10 designs, a wide range of homes can be delivered without massive amounts of customization.

Meanwhile, having 10 predefined home styles keeps homebuyers from spending the extra time or money to have an architect design each of their homes from scratch. The ideal is to get the whole subdivision built by a primary contractor, doing quality work quickly and cheaply.

Will there be compromises on each house? Yes, of course. But more houses will be built faster, ideally with higher quality.

The same rationale applies to adaptive infrastructure. In the place of builders, substitute application and infrastructure developers who will be reusing the same patterns repeatedly. When you want to add a new business application, such as a new Web site, CRM program, or data warehouse, your developers should recognize that it shares patterns of interaction and use with other applications in the infrastructure. This approach means that less time and money is wasted establishing a new, and likely redundant, infrastructure implementation.

As explained earlier, reusability is the absolute hallmark of an adaptive infrastructure. Recognizing patterns in your infrastructure allows you to reuse existing technology, business processes, and the skills of existing personnel. It also lowers the risks associated with integrating an increasingly complex number of individual components into actual systems that support real applications.

In general, patterns should be considered a reuse of designs, rather than a reuse of built systems. The latter is what services do, as explained in Chapter 4.

## Relating Patterns to Platforms

Patterns and platforms are both fundamental parts of the overall adaptive infrastructure methodology. Patterns are the information, insight, and experience—the "what is" and "how to"—that are common to an existing class of applications. This information is captured in a form that makes it easier to reuse with future applications of the same class.

Patterns also capture experience and best practices for projects that result from real application requests by the business, and they emphasize end-to-end reuse in a logical rather than physical way. The services discussed in Chapters 4 and 5 emphasize shared physical infrastructure in more detail.

Reusability is the key to making patterns effective. Once you've designed a successful application using a full spectrum of infrastructure components, you can use most (if not all) of that experience to design, build, deploy, and run the next application that needs similar resources. For example, after you figure out how a mainframe application runs on mainframe infrastructure, you can deploy other mainframe applications on the same infrastructure much more quickly and efficiently.

Of course, mainframe infrastructure is very mature, stable, and well understood by the organizations that use it today. But other technology innovations in multi-tier and e-Business computing are so new that most people don't have the same experience and comfort level.

Figure 3.2 shows the relationship of patterns, platforms, and services.

Patterns can help structure, capture, and limit the complexity of these more distributed and complicated infrastructure solutions. With so much that can go wrong in an N-tier application and its related infrastructure components, a complete system design is required. This design should go beyond just the best-of-breed decisions within one particular component or platform layer. It should focus instead on the best decision for all the components and platform layers together, weaving these into the best solution for a given application, or better yet for an entire class of similar applications.

As seen in Chapter 2, the adaptive infrastructure platform includes layers of component technologies such as network, storage, server, and database. Whereas patterns deal with applications, platforms deal with technologies. And, while platform requirements are IT-driven, pattern

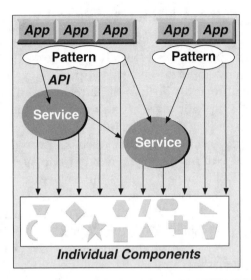

**Figure 3.2** Patterns, Platforms, and Services

requirements are more directly driven by business needs. They are designed to address application requirements by providing a proven and tested solution.

## Why So Few Patterns?

Eighty to ninety percent of all infrastructure needs can be consistently accommodated by a set of less than ten patterns. While the specifics of these patterns may change to accommodate new technologies, and they certainly will differ in detail from company to company, the number of patterns needed is almost always relatively small.

And it *should* be small. When you have too many options to choose from, complexity becomes a problem. Since it's difficult to maintain expertise in too many areas, designing a limited set of patterns will help you keep your focus.

Another benefit of patterns is response time: You want to get the designs *done* so you can use them. If you have too many patterns, you'll have a lot of blueprints but never use them in any concrete way on real projects. And that would be wasted effort.

## Are Patterns Just for New Infrastructure?

The pattern matching approach does more than help describe future best practices, such as using the N-Tier Transact pattern for new applications. This approach enables you to view infrastructure as a portfolio of patterns and underlying components, shedding light on what you already have installed by providing an inventory of existing infrastructure.

Once such an inventory is made, you can manage this portfolio of patterns just like any other portfolio, determining when to buy, hold, or sell various infrastructure investments. Ironically, one of the biggest shortcomings of most infrastructure organizations is not the "buy/hold" aspect of portfolio management, but the "sell" aspect. Now that Year 2000 has come and gone, infrastructure organizations no longer have a compelling reason to eliminate anything again, which could be disastrous. In addition to bringing new infrastructure on board, patterns should be used to help design exit strategies.

Patterns help you manage the complexity of the entire existing infrastructure, rather than only describing blueprints for the future. By learning what patterns you already use—but perhaps didn't recognize that you had—you can learn what experiences may prove useful in continuing your existing patterns or in adopting new or different ones.

To some extent, the future should be based on the past. Innovation doesn't necessarily mean completely changing everything you do, every time you do it.

Details on how these basic functions will be accomplished can help differentiate patterns. For instance, how much growth can a pattern design accommodate?

Specific "how" questions differentiate the Transact patterns in the Starter Kit. The answer to "what" is the same for all three. For example, do you want to be able to add multiple points of interaction, such as the Web, interactive voice response (IVR), and mobile devices? Or will consistency across multiple points of interaction be fairly unimportant to your business?

## Are Patterns Just for New Infrastructure? (continued)

One type of pattern might allow this access easily, and another might not. The main challenge is meeting the needs of your business. If your organization's brand promises consistency across points of interaction, you should implement the appropriate pattern infrastructure.

So before you start planning for future development, you should first take inventory of your existing infrastructure, particularly the infrastructure that is likely to change. Determine what patterns you already have and whether they are viable, require modification, or need a complete overhaul. If a pattern needs changing, determine whether existing applications should be upgraded or whether you will focus on adopting new applications that do things in a different, more advanced manner.

The practical goal when identifying patterns is to accommodate basic differences between applications. So keep in mind the 80/20 rule and leave the last 20 percent of the differences outside of the standards. In other words, pick patterns that apply to most of the work, get them designed, and start using them—that's the real benefit.

## Asking Who, Where, and What?

How are patterns determined? The details of Infrastructure Pattern Matching (IPM) are covered in more detail in Chapter 5. But basically, you can start by asking the key questions:

- Who are the users?
- Where are they located?
- What kind of work do they need to accomplish?

In many cases, patterns may be differentiated simply by asking "what?" For example, two-way real-time collaboration is completely different from taking orders that a user keys into a system. On the other hand, many transactional applications can run on all three of the Transact patterns we define. The deciding factor for choosing a Transact pattern might be service level requirements, quality of service requirements, or cost restraints.

In some cases, "Where?" and "Who?" could be more appropriate questions to ask. One of the Transact patterns doesn't work very well when users are not located in main offices over LAN-speed connections. So when you ask why there are three Transact patterns, it's really a matter of history and installed base that requires having three different versions.

## The Starter Kit

META Group research over the last 10 years has yielded much information about how organizations use infrastructure. During that period, the actual list of patterns has evolved considerably. Today, META Group recognizes a set of nine starter patterns, shown in Figure 3.3, that cover three basic interaction types:

- Transact patterns. Applications in which business data is written and stored for a long period of time, such as online customer orders and other transactions.

- Publish patterns. Applications with read-only data, such as online marketing information.

- Collaborate patterns. Applications where information contained in files and documents is shared between two or more users, such as a product design document shared by a development team.

Figure 3.3 provides a set of thumbnail diagrams showing how each of the patterns work. Each pattern is covered in more detail later in this chapter, along with a more detailed view of each conceptual diagram.

The nine patterns detailed in this chapter provide a model for patterns that you might have or that you might need in the near future. These model patterns can be modified or augmented as current and future applications demand, and as current infrastructure allows. At minimum, this high-level starter kit must be refined or fleshed out to match your current practices, experience, and goals.

In fact, most enterprise applications loosely match one (or more) of these nine patterns. While patterns can be merged or modified to suit a particular need, the starter kit fulfills most application requirements.

Developing these patterns within the typical organization is usually a familiar exercise. Most organizations already have existing infrastructure and an architecture that may encompass a number of the patterns. However, seeing a whole set of infrastructure decisions and experiences standardized at such a high level—not just one layer or component at a time, and in an application-centric way with an end-to-end view—should

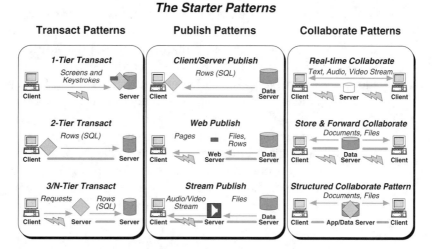

Patterns capture experience and best practices for
business/application projects as designed for a
particular end-to-end set of components or services.

**Figure 3.3** The Nine Starter Patterns

prove useful in unlocking decision making about future investments and approaches.

In fact, few organizations need to develop all of the patterns outlined. Once you've designed a good set of patterns, adding or aggregating the infrastructure to support a new pattern requires a strong business case. You should not end up with new patterns each time an application is added or each time a minor component change is required for a particular application. Your standards must have some stability, or the whole infrastructure becomes unmanageable.

## How Detailed Should It Get?

While most of the previous discussion highlights how valuable the broad scope of a pattern is and how much of a blueprint it is, the patterns that you develop must also have concrete depth and immediately usable detail. In fact, the detail level is often what differentiates one organization's 3/N-Tier Transact pattern from another's. Both are named the same, but the details can be quite different.

A complete and more mature pattern blueprint specifies the details of architecture, technology, product, and configuration. Remember that it's not just the architecture being captured, but also specific decisions on technology and products.

For one pattern, you might use a particular database product or a certain vendor's network load balancer. Configuration details can be standardized even for other more mature patterns that are commonly and widely implemented. In Store-and-Forward Collaborate, for example, all file servers may be set up with a common file system, login script, drive mapping, and security configuration. Less mature (newer) patterns may lack detailed configuration standards at first, but as they mature, these standards should be added. The relationship between pattern maturity and level of detail is shown more clearly in Figure 3.4.

Now that you understand what patterns are all about, let's examine each of the major patterns in the Starter Kit. A later book in this series will describe in more detail a few completely refined pattern designs.

## Transact Patterns

Transact patterns include any application that "writes" structured information to a system or data set. Many applications fall under this umbrella, including those that involve simple updates to a centralized database, remote modifications to a portal profile, or business process execution for large-scale enterprise resource planning (ERP), customer relationship management (CRM), and supply chain management (SCM) systems.

Typically, transactions let you Create, Read, Update, and Delete (CRUD). Request/reply interactions are also common. The changes invoked by a

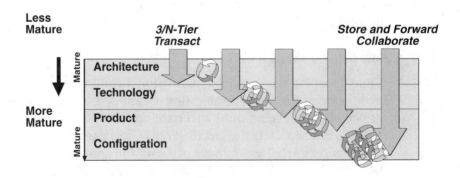

**Figure 3.4** Pattern Maturity Differences

transactional business event are small as measured in bytes of data, on the order of a field or record, or at most, a business contract. This pattern usually requires centralizing the business state, by implementing a database management system (DBMS) to make coordination of state changes easier. Thus, a DBMS is usually a standard component of Transact patterns.

Transactions that fall into this pattern all exhibit or require ACID properties:

■ Atomic. The function in question is a logical unit of work.

■ Consistent. The transaction represents repeatable, verifiable behavior.

■ Isolated. The transaction does no work or has no impact outside of its "atomic" scope.

■ Durable. The function retains its integrity; if some pieces are interrupted, the entire transaction is rolled back.

Once part of a business initiative or application is identified as transactional, it can be subclassified using the following logical tiered structure:

■ 1-Tier Transact, or Host Transact, where all data processing is done on the host system in a monolithic application

■ 2-Tier Transact, which typically brings the presentation and business logic to the client side, leaving the database management on the server

■ 3/N-Tier Transact, which, in addition to separating data management like 2-Tier, separates the presentation logic from the business logic and allows for the most flexible infrastructure, but with the most developmental complexity and often the highest costs

The following sections cover each of these patterns in greater detail.

## The 1-Tier Transact Pattern

This pattern includes batch processing applications or online transaction processing (OLTP) applications without logical abstraction between the presentation, application, and data logic. Although the application itself is fully centralized, users may be widely distributed over wide area networks (WANs).

Most mainframe systems support 1-Tier transactional applications, with resource (data), business, and presentation logic all designed into a single application. These applications are then displayed on separate desktop devices, such as terminals and PCs, via simple terminal emulation running over networks. This environment allows massive servers to be constructed. Many organizations have mature systems with this setup.

Unfortunately, most new applications are smart PC applications that are not designed to run on mainframes at all. While much data and business logic is already on mainframes, many organizations no longer design applications to run exclusively there. Instead, they use newer paradigms, such as client/server and the Web, and just hope to access as much of the data and business logic from these existing systems as they can. In turn, this practice has created a need for the transactional integration service discussed in the next chapter.

The 1-Tier Transact pattern is also called the "host pattern," and it includes systems like CICS and IMS, as well as batch applications and applications based on flat-file databases. All are part of this pattern.

Typically, host applications run under IBM's OS/390 operating system, but some companies use AS/400, UNIX, and even Microsoft Windows 2000/.NET Server platforms to support this pattern as well. The 1-Tier Transact pattern typically targets internal employees, primarily in the campus and branch environments and has, in fact, been optimized for this behavior for more than 20 years.

### Benefits

Due to its maturity, the benefits of host pattern uses are well known.

■ Availability. With its long history, the host pattern's availability is a common strength familiar to infrastructure developers. Uptimes of 99.99 percent are frequently achieved.

■ Scalability. The host pattern excels in the number of concurrent users it can support. In fact, it is the ideal pattern in situations where more than 5,000 single-scope concurrent users must be supported. Likewise, it is the best pattern for situations where large volumes of operational data—more than one terabyte—must be written.

■ Reliability. This pattern is also the most reliable. System recovery problems are often handled automatically, usually in less than a minute. Support for transactions and operational process depths are also unmatched. Queries can be compiled, and subsystems deeply tuned, to achieve throughput of more than 15,000 transactions per minute with less than one second response time.

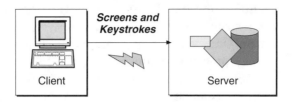

**▲ Description**

 ▶ **Presentation and data access logic is inseparable from business logic**

**▲ Service Level Matches**

 + **Scalability**

 + **Availability**

 − **Everything else**

**▲ Commom Examples**

 ▶ **CICS**

 ▶ **IMS**

 ▶ **Flat-file-based applications**

 ▶ **Batch applications**

**▲ Popularity**

 ▶ **The majority of mainframe applications are based on this pattern**

**▲ Practices**

 + **Wrapper (maybe migrate)**

 − **This pattern is not a best practice**

**▲ Futures**

 ▶ **Although applications based on this pattern will exist for the foreseeable future, no new applications should be based on this pattern**

**Figure 3.5** The 1-Tier Transact Pattern

*Weaknesses*

The weaknesses of the host pattern are equally well known.

■ Expensive. Users can expect to pay a 40 to 50 percent premium for CMOS-based mainframe hardware versus other platforms. Similarly, traditional mainframe-based software licensing approaches are often significantly more expensive than distributed systems.

■ Inflexible. While the host is adept at providing large numbers of users with large amounts of data, providing data to external applications usually requires a significant engineering effort. Likewise, supporting modern graphical user interfaces has been a challenge.

■ Lacking agility. The shared nature of applications can generate significant interrelated workload dependencies that can slow down deployment efforts, making the pattern sluggish from a business management standpoint. Development is difficult, with development cycles often lasting several years.

■ Lack of applications. Packaged application support is declining precipitously. Most applications are no longer designed for a traditional host environment, with everything in COBOL, for instance. Rather, they are client/server or Web oriented, using new tools and infrastructure that, in many cases, cannot be run on traditional mainframe systems or cannot exhibit single-tier design. (See the other patterns for detail.) So, the buy-not-build culture of most organizations means that new applications are never deployed in terminal-emulation-centric systems anymore.

■ Resource intensive. Limited access to market applications and tools generally minimizes opportunities to buy applications. Thus, organizations must carry a large staff of developers to support this pattern. Such a staff typically takes at least 18 months to build an application, meaning that application portability will always be several years behind the market norm.

This statement of weaknesses does not imply that the mainframe type of server layer component is to be used only in this pattern. It is common to see mainframes used to support 1-Tier Transact applications, but the mainframe can support applications of different patterns. For example, the mainframe running IBM's DB2 could be a DBMS server in a 3/N-Tier Transact application. However, this situation is not a traditional host computing or 1-Tier Transact infrastructure pattern. In this new case, the mainframe is being used in a different pattern.

*Best Practices*

So, what should you do?

■ Put wrappers around legacy host code to encapsulate them and make them reusable. If hosting applications survived the Year 2000, they are unlikely to go away. Getting to the data as well as business logic in these existing applications is a key problem for most organizations. A great deal of mainframe-based data must still be leveraged by new applications using different infrastructure patterns. To make the applications of this pattern reusable, organizations must employ transactional integration services (covered in Chapter 5).

■ Don't use this pattern for new applications due to ongoing improvements in other patterns. Also, don't expect to see lots of new applications appearing on the mainframe, at least not as part of a 1-Tier Transact pattern.

■ Don't use components optimized only for this pattern in other patterns. One always hopes that existing investments can be leveraged for new applications, but at some point you must simply move on. No component heavily optimized for one pattern is likely to fit well in others. For example, 1-Tier Transact infrastructure, and mainframes in particular, has not been suitable for e-mail ever since those systems were modernized to support graphical user interfaces and offline PC-based processing. As the technology market moves on to other solutions, the left-behind infrastructure becomes more costly to upgrade and maintain. Over time, by focusing on keeping new applications off this infrastructure, you can carefully balkanize the older infrastructure and limit its impact on technology change in other areas or patterns.

■ Stop investing to upgrade components in this pattern. Most organizations have already made this pattern fit the new standards for networking and desktop infrastructure in the distributed world. They've updated terminal emulation to run on PCs, and taken the emulators off the IBM systems network architecture (SNA) and Token Ring networks. So, the effort to keep most other patterns running over TCP/IP networks is now leveraged by this pattern as well. Most investment in this pattern should be focused on maintaining service levels and lowering costs. (Renegotiating licenses is one way to accomplish this goal.)

## Looking Forward

This very mature pattern will continue to be used selectively, and it will continue to provide significant business benefits where application fit demands it. The 1-Tier Transact pattern currently is synonymous with OS/390, but UNIX and Windows 2000/.NET Server are also available options.

Many organizations retain a bias to moving off the mainframe entirely. Keeping this pattern viable will require infrastructure developers to create templates or sub-patterns that accommodate specific exceptions. If infrastructure developers do not demonstrate competency in determining which applications should or should not be on this platform, they will face business pressure to get off the host as a matter of course.

The bottom line is that this particular pattern provides significant business benefits where the application naturally fits to these technologies. But users must be very careful about "pattern drift"—attempting to force the pattern on an application for which it is ill suited. Instead, have more than one solution blueprint or pattern to try to match to new requirements.

## The 2-Tier Transact Pattern

This pattern involves a smart PC on the desktop communicating directly with a back-end database server. This definition includes Web servers that intertwine common gateway interface (CGI), active server pages (ASP), and Java Server Pages (JSP) presentation and application logic. This Transact pattern is the quickest and cheapest from a development perspective. However, it has several major drawbacks, making it largely unsuitable outside of a workgroup. Scalability issues limit it to small-scale OLTP workloads. Additionally, the heavy integration of application logic and screen presentation logic make application-to-application integration extremely difficult.

This category includes most traditional client/server applications that became popular in the 1990s and are still popular today, albeit veiled by browser front-end. Common examples of 2-Tier transaction pattern-based applications include those programmed in Visual Basic or Power-builder, and most Web applications using Microsoft ASP or JSP. Figure 3.6 shows typical variations.

These permutations typically locate most application components on a smart PC, or Web server/browser applet, using the database server as a powerful file system. The interaction and associated traffic between these components is frequent and intense. This pattern is most appropriate for application environments that require maximum use of powerful, client-side tools.

A 2-Tier Transact pattern is also best suited for implementation on a LAN or in a campus environment, where bandwidths are high and latencies are low. Unfortunately, Structured Query Language (SQL) statements and database access middleware typically perform poorly over higher latency and lower bandwidth WANs. Remote user response time slows precipitously for these highly interactive protocols. This degradation is particularly true in the case of traditional smart PC 2-Tier. It can be the case for new Java clients if they also do SQL and Java Database Connectivity (JDBC) directly from desktop applets.

One of the key differentiators of the 2-Tier Transact pattern is that the presentation logic is inseparable from business logic, while data access is partitioned to a relational database management system (RDBMS).

While the 2-Tier Transact pattern most often uses smart PC applications, it is also possible to have a thin-client 2-Tier Transact pattern that is either Web-based or terminal server-based. Even though it looks like a 3/N-Tier system, the fact that the presentation logic and the business logic are co-located makes even this thin-client flavor a logical two-tier design, thus a 2-Tier Transact pattern.

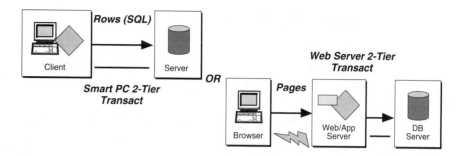

**Figure 3.6** Two Permutations of the 2-Tier Transact Pattern

How can you tell if an application is 2-Tier or 3-Tier? A simple way is to ask the developers how easy it is to create a different front-end presentation. In the past, many people learned that moving Windows applications to the Web was a complete rewrite of the application. Don't be fooled. Many Web-only applications today cannot be easily changed to support multiple points of interaction, such as interactive voice response (IVR) or personal digital assistants (PDAs). Each of these new devices has specific characteristics that have little to do with the Web. Therefore, Web-only design can still be limiting.

Moreover, 2-Tier designs exhibit other failures or limitations compared to three-tier designs. Clearly, this pattern is wrong for many new applications. Still, it has value for some applications, even new ones. So you should keep a standard blueprint for its design going forward.

*Benefits*

Benefits of the 2-Tier Transact patterns are:

■ Speed. The 2-Tier Transact pattern remains the best choice for applications being deployed in a high-risk, volatile business environment, where business cycles are measured in weeks, rather than months or years.

■ Rapid development. Application development time within the 2-Tier Transact pattern is unmatched. Work with the user, application definition, and delivery can all take place at a rapid clip. Even with more years of 3/N-Tier-oriented development tools and experience, the latter applications are still more complex to design. The 2-Tier design remains the easiest and uses the most rapid application design (RAD) tools. If 2-Tier fits the application's function and scope, it is still a viable solution.

*Weaknesses*

Weaknesses of 2-Tier Transact patterns are:

■ Lack of scalability. The 2-Tier Transact patterns are clumsy in their scalability. While Web versions are more easily deployed than smart PCs, they do not scale well from either server or networking perspectives. Generally, database server connection scalability limits total connected clients and/or transactional load, even for the Web server version, which still retains a separate DBMS connection per user. The highly interactive nature of SQL or ODBC interaction middleware is significantly slowed by common WAN networking bottlenecks, resulting in slower response times.

■ Security vulnerabilities. Since 2-Tier designs can show more business logic and even database schema design on Web pages to non-employees, they are less secure than the 3/N-Tier design.

■ Sourcing limitations. This pattern design really doesn't support a mixed outsourcing approach. Since connecting DBMS servers over WANs to Web servers makes the application much more difficult to support and lowers its reliability, you have to give the source everything. You're forced to do forklift outsourcing, or complete outsourcing. This type of outsourcing is not always a problem, but it is a limitation compared to 3/N-Tier, which provides several alternatives.

■ Presentation limitations. The key differentiator that makes 2-Tier less effective was always centered on scalability (see above). Now, however, many people are having difficulties with the way 2-Tier limits presentation choices. Leveraging the same business logic across multiple front-ends or points of interaction isn't easy. New development is required for new views of old apps, which makes this pattern not adaptive. It's fast at first, thanks to highly integrated tools for Web-only or Windows-only development. But it slows down re-purposing application functionality for other front-ends, such as IVRs, PDAs, and wireless devices.

■ Lack of APIs. The worst aspect of 2-Tier design is that it leaves no APIs for reuse between applications, or you may have to develop APIs afterwards, making the applications very difficult to integrate, either initially or later. Since most new applications will need to interact with other applications directly, or via transactional integration solutions like EAI, the key to long-term adaptability is to develop APIs in addition to multiple presentation interfaces. The 2-Tier pattern makes this interaction extremely inefficient; 3/N-Tier makes it practical.

■ Hidden costs. While appealing, use of the terminal server model, for instance, can add licensing costs and network overhead that might not make it a good match.

### Best Practices

So, what should you do?

■ Limit this pattern to small-scale applications offered to users in the same LAN environment.

■ You can solve some networking problems by using products such as Citrix MetaFrame in conjunction with Microsoft Windows 2000 Terminal Server to move the application client to the server, but doing so adds to overhead costs. Many organizations are using Citrix to run widely deployed 2-Tier architecture ERP packages, such as PeopleSoft V6. This sends LANs the highly interactive ODBC protocols that limit user response times on WANs. ODBC traffic goes over the LAN, while Citrix's own terminal emulation traffic runs over the WAN. Yet this approach actually adds to the bandwidth requirements for many applications since it requires 15–20 Kbps per active user. In addition, you have more moving parts to control. Citrix doesn't change the server scalability challenges for

2-Tier or the missing API problem, and it helps with the multiple points of interaction problem only to a limited extent. Citrix can display the Microsoft Windows GUI on UNIX clients, for example, but only if the client has a full-screen display. An IVR or even most PDAs or wireless devices cannot be supported this way.

■ Don't use the Web version of this pattern for large-scale applications. Although the Web makes the client thin and enables running over the Internet, the overall infrastructure is still not scalable.

### Looking Forward

Technology advances won't solve fundamental 2-Tier technology problems of latency and transaction arrival rates, and it is important to avoid developing applications that utilize the 2-Tier Transact pattern if they are going to reach outside the campus. However, prototyping and piloting projects will continue to use this pattern due to its rapid-development, friendly nature. You probably have lots of these examples already, so it's still a useful exercise to get a blueprint together for the individual versions you currently have deployed. You might encounter more than one common approach, and you should determine the *one* of these that you want to use going forward.

The smart PC version of the 2-Tier Transact will wane in popularity and independent software vendors (ISVs) will slowly migrate from this pattern to N-tier Transact. To force a march to the 3/N-Tier Transact pattern, infrastructure developers must establish clear justifications for choosing 3/N-Tier Transact up front. They should also determine appropriate migration strategies for poorly designed, 2-Tier "legacy" applications, and for 2-Tier applications that are expected to scale after initial, rapid implementations. Of course, you can wait for vendors of purchased applications to move to the new infrastructure and force your users to change. PeopleSoft, for example, has a 3/N-Tier Transact infrastructure version of its ERP package, and users will migrate to this over time. For other applications, you may end up waiting a long time.

### The 3/N-Tier Transact Pattern

This pattern consists of a thin client carrying presentation-logic only, communicating with a client-neutral, server-based application, which in turn communicates with a back-end database server. Common examples include PeopleSoft v8 and SAP R/3, especially version 4.6 or later.

With a Web server, the presentation is generated on another Web server tier, but still rendered by the Web browser. This design is truly an

N-tier rather than just a traditional 3-Tier design. Since most applications are using this technique, there is no point in planning 3-Tier separately from N-Tier. Thus, the Starter Kit pattern provided in this chapter is defined as 3/N-Tier.

The 3/N-Tier Transact pattern is the most scalable and flexible client/server transaction pattern. Due to the WAN-friendliness of the client-to-application server protocols, users can be highly decentralized. When implemented correctly, this pattern results in clearly defined interfaces, making it the most flexible to integrate with other applications or points of interaction. Figure 3.7 shows two typical versions.

The 3/N-Tier Transact pattern, with back-end database, client, and any number of application servers, offers the greatest distribution of processing functionality in a transactional environment. Compared to 1- and 2-Tier Transact patterns, this pattern is highly adaptive and is most popular with infrastructure architects who focus on long-term future standards.

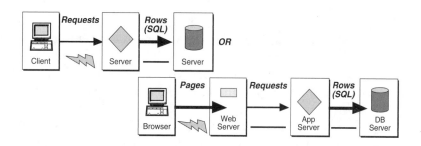

▲ **Description**
  ▶ Presentation, data access, and business logic are all partitioned

▲ **Service Level Matches**
  + Scalability
  + Changing presentation logic
  + Integrating new sources/consumers into the application
  − Speed of initial deployment

▲ **Common Examples**
  ▶ SAP R/3
  ▶ Peoplesoft 8

▲ **Popularity**
  ▶ Most popular with "architects"

▲ **Practices**
  + Designing scalable 3-Tier apps that work well across WANs
  + Designing N-Tier applications to integrate with other applications
  − Limiting support to a single point of interaction

▲ **Futures**
  ▶ Evolution of N-Tier to an Adaptive Services Architecture
  ▶ ISVs slowly migrate to this pattern
  ▶ Better app development tools supporting this pattern

**Figure 3.7** The 3/N-Tier Transact Pattern

While this is the most prominent foreseeable design for future transactional systems, it does not eliminate the need to support other patterns.

Typically, application functionality is deployed on multiple individual servers, while database functionality is allocated according to the required degree of data synchronization across supported application modules. Clients in this pattern tend to be thin, and shared business logic can be supported from multiple points of interaction.

The 3/N-Tier design can fit many transactional applications. It is excellent for geographically distributed operations, since networking efficiency enables putting shared server resources in centralized data centers. This approach provides high-quality support at the lowest cost. It can support multiple business functions and is the best pattern for supporting highly complex, transaction-intensive, or large-scale transaction volumes. However, the 3/N-Tier Transact pattern requires significant customization at the application and tool level, and that translates to a considerable investment of time and resources.

### Benefits

The 3/N-Tier pattern can support large-scale transactional applications across the enterprise, enabling developers to take full advantage of distributed data and application logic. The challenge is to understand data sharing/synchronization requirements as well as network/placement constraints.

What does this mean? Essentially, the distributed approach of this pattern mirrors that of the distributed organization and enables applications to be scaled with a fair amount of precision. If an application requires specific activities to take place in a distributed way across many different locations, the infrastructure can be set up to reflect that business pattern. Within the 3/N-Tier Transact, data can be located close to the application process, minimizing network data traffic. Enterprise software packages have brought this pattern into the mainstream.

The foremost strength of the 3-Tier Transact pattern is its adaptability, particularly with regard to e-Business requirements, where scalability, support for multiple points of interaction, reusability, and speed are all-important. Developers still must ensure they understand the realities of locating and distributing data, and engineer around that. Meanwhile, most application providers are following SAP's lead and instituting the 3/N-Tier model for their applications.

Specific benefits of 3/N-Tier include:

■ Scalability. Distributing the processing load on multiple server tiers provides significant scalability, particularly in offloading the DBMS server. For reliability, 3/N-Tier requires considerably more design effort to partition application functions and limit dependencies. Consequently, if any component of the system changes, the whole system doesn't have to be replaced. (See the related information in the "Stateless Farm Architecture and Scale-Up Design" sidebar.) Proper 3/N-Tier design is also focused on partitioning business logic, presentation logic, and integration logic so that if any one of the three dimensions changes, alternative technology can be plugged in to replace it without affecting the other dimensions. As Web services evolve, this partitioning of functionality becomes virtual, as services can be invoked from a variety of places in the design.

■ Security. Quite often, 3/N-Tier is designed with Web Single Sign-on (Web SSO) products to provide multi-tier security with role-based resource authorization. These new directory-centric products are becoming easier to use, and they avoid the need for multiple authentication procedures in each application. Moreover, the proper partitioning of business logic enables 3/N-Tier applications to be split up with only the presentation portion in the demilitarized zone (DMZ) between the outside world and the internal network, while the application code and data reside in the trusted internal network.

■ Presentation. With the 3/N-Tier Transact pattern, if development is done correctly, all user interfaces leverage the same application logic, both logical and physical. Thus, the problem of rolling out alternative user interfaces—for example, the ability to check the status of an order from a call-center PC, a Web browser, a telephone, and a two-way pager—does not require you to implement "check order" application logic on each user interface platform. Instead, the logic is implemented centrally, which means it is physically located on an application server. And "check order" user interfaces are implemented on a per-client-platform basis.

■ APIs. The ability to use application programming interfaces (APIs) independently of the application's presentation is the key advantage of this pattern. The 3/N-Tier pattern reduces the cost of enterprise application integration (EAI) because sharing APIs between applications reduces the time and expense required to integrate the applications. Since business initiatives such as supply chain management and e-commerce largely depend on cross-business EAI, the ability to rapidly integrate (and de-integrate) applications becomes critical to overall business success. These APIs are prerequisites for the more sophisticated use of Web services through vehicles like UDDI, XML, and SOAP.

### Weaknesses

Known weaknesses of 3/N-Tier are:

■ Needs customization. Flexibility and power comes at a price. The 3/N-Tier Transact pattern requires significant customization at the application and tool levels, which consumes considerable time and resources. Lack of capability or integration at the toolkit level and the tendency to use expensive third-party integrators slows down deployment, sometimes to more than 18 months per application. Support and management offerings in this area are also wanting. The paucity of non-vendor-oriented skills heightens support and management concerns. However, these last issues are expected to be addressed as more organizations gain experience with 3/N Tier.

■ Misunderstood. Moreover, it's just hard to design these most complex systems well. We see many organizations nominally doing 3/N-Tier, but their programmers routinely use large Web-server-based servlets with traditional 2-Tier code mapping to connect Web interface code directly to JDBC or Open Database Connectivity (ODBC) database calls. This coding approach is not really 3/N-Tier, thus it does not provide all the advantages of that design.

■ Expensive. Systems integrators maintain that integration and implementation expenses will exceed hardware and software by a 4-to-1 ratio. According to users, the ratio may be as high as 8-to-1, or even 12-to-1, due to the significant resources and customized tools that are sometimes required.

### Best Practices

For best results with 3/N-Tier, you should:

■ Develop Transactional Integration services to match 3/N-Tier applications. (See Chapter 4 for details.)

■ Work closely with application developers in the early stages, as they build or buy tools.

■ Use scale-out stateless farm architecture.

- Leverage experience from existing OLTP DBMS and server OS/hardware platforms, even if other server tier platforms are different.
- Do not replicate OLTP data to scale.
- Take advantage of pattern benefits.
- Develop a Test Lab, including equipment and procedures for investigating the infrastructure impact of various patterns and services.

Why test 3/N-Tier applications and infrastructure carefully? While you might assume that 3/N-Tier applications operate similarly with similar infrastructure impacts, in practice they vary significantly. Organizations must go beyond simple infrastructure pattern matching, asking who/what/where questions to gain a detailed understanding of a particular application's variance from its pattern's norm.

If this doesn't happen, the 3/N-Tier application can stray far from the ideal pattern and won't exhibit the most efficient network response time or throughput. Failure to perform infrastructure impact assessments results in slower, less successful deployment of applications, with IT groups shouldering the blame for being application ignorant.

Organizations often focus testing on high-profile applications or those that traverse WAN links. While testing is often implemented only for enterprisewide initiatives, offending modules in an otherwise efficient 3/N-Tier suite might be driven by just one line of business. To figure out how applications function, users must combine new skills and tools to better understand and predict specific application performance characteristics, particularly user response time, for enterprise WAN environments.

For example, inefficient database queries can result in a huge number of sparsely filled packet roundtrips, which could affect user response time considerably in a WAN environment. For this reason, the test lab should include some physical WAN components. Some companies have added data channel simulators, which let you easily simulate error rates, latency, and bandwidth parameters. It is then simpler to test applications over a representative set of three to five branch offices or remote access user connections. While some companies install a frame relay link in their test labs, this method offers only a single branch office configuration without much flexibility.

Beyond new skills and tools, the most important best practice is getting applications into a test lab to ensure compliance with infrastructure plans. Besides learning about and simulating the application, more realistic stress testing should be performed in a physical test environment. If infrastructure impact assessment is performed at earlier stages, infrastructure IT groups will already know which applications are likely candidates for acceptance testing, so they can participate in understanding and optimizing their details earlier in the development and deployment process.

Moreover, knowledge of application behavior by tiers can improve post-deployment troubleshooting. But unless new processes are instituted, infrastructure IT staff will continue to be inundated with new applications and unable to make progress in proactively ensuring application success.

### Looking Forward

The 3/N-Tier Transact pattern will continue to be the preferred choice for transactional applications. Organizations will get more accustomed to this pattern, while traditional software vendors will increasingly embrace it. Much volatility and complexity still exists in this immature area, however, so standardizing on your own version of this and sticking with it should improve your success with applications of this class.

## Stateless Farm Architecture and Scale-Up Design

The most significant trends for 3/N-Tier Transact pattern applications concern scalability and availability. These capabilities can be approached using two methods: scale-up or scale-out.

**Scale-up.** The best approach for back-end DBMS OLTP online transaction processing servers, where a single instance database of record must be maintained. An example is centralized application state maintenance.

**Scale-out.** A practical approach for middle-tier application and Web servers. Scaling out is primarily an application architectural issue, creating distributed functionality and presentation services with minimal state maintenance. It does not, by definition, imply any particular physical implementation.

Most IT organizations physically implement scale-out via server farms with large numbers of smaller systems. This preference is primarily due to several factors that include immature or nonexistent partitioning tools, nonlinear server pricing, and human nature. It's simply easier to "rack and stack" numerous Web and applications servers.

## Stateless Farm Architecture and Scale-Up Design (continued)

The capacity upgrade options are more granular, and a larger server typically costs two or three times more than a comparable number of CPUs in multiple smaller systems. Additionally, users seem more comfortable growing server farms.

## Stateless Farm Design

The reason it is now possible to deploy complicated, multi-tier applications with server farms is that application designers finally understand how to build statelessness into Web applications. HTTP makes it possible to use simple techniques, such as IP redirection, to distribute the load to numbers of Web servers and this distribution is easily done for read-only pages. For transactional applications, a requirement still exists to maintain user session information, or state, in the applications. An example is the shopping cart. Each user request for a new page must be redirected to the server that is maintaining the information about previous sessions.

Application state is now achieved using cookies, decorated URLs, or persistence mechanisms provided by the load balancers. State can also be pushed into the database, so it is accessible by all application servers in the cluster, or farm. This last method of storing state in the database is the most safe and reliable design, even if it limits performance.

Such farms or server clusters provide scalability only for certain classes of applications. Perhaps the most common use of clusters for scalability is with Web servers. Data warehouse workloads are another case where cluster-like parallelism can be used, since they are primarily read-only with limited state-maintenance requirements. Indeed, massively parallel processing (MPP) systems are architecturally similar to clusters, and they are able to achieve efficient scalability with numerous processors or nodes.

## Clustering Databases

General-purpose commercial database applications are more difficult to parallelize, given the need to maintain state centrally—just like not selling the same airline seat twice inadvertently. Accordingly, transaction-processing applications using Oracle, SQL Server, and DB2 generally do not scale well on clustered configurations, largely due to the need to maintain distributed state information via lock managers.

Best practice is to use clusters primarily to enhance DBMS server availability, not to extend scalability. Scalability issues will be addressed by new software products, such as Oracle 9*i* Real Application Clusters (RAC), and new hardware technologies, such as InfiniBand server area networks.

The following are several key clustering recommendations:

■ Determine whether clusters appropriately address the problem at hand: extending scalability, enhancing application availability, or both.

■ When business-level requirements dictate higher availability levels, focus initially on minimizing planned downtime and protecting data.

■ Ordering off vendors' preconfigured and pretested cluster configuration menus.

■ Budget for implementation services roughly equal to the cost of the cluster software.

## Clustering Other Servers

To scale Web applications, corporations historically have implemented Web-server clusters with Domain Naming Service (DNS) round-robin load balancing. However, simple DNS policies are not sophisticated enough to avoid unhealthy servers in the cluster, resulting in unacceptable service levels for clients. Vendors have developed server load balancing (SLB) and network load balancing (NLB) products to improve the reliability, performance, and manageability of server clusters, supplanting the use of DNS round robin–based solutions, particularly on high-volume public Web sites.

NLBs intelligently manage traffic into a cluster of servers that support HTTP and other protocols. They distribute the processing load based on various policies, including round robin, least connections, and CPU load.

The three core advantages to NLB solutions are:

- Increased redundancy, including failover and redirection around unhealthy servers.

- Better performance, including better utilization of existing CPU power. This efficiency enables smaller servers to service users, rather than requiring CPU upgrades to handle scale.

- Easier management, including advanced reporting and the ability to add and remove servers without affecting users.

NLBs most often are deployed only at the presentation tier in 3/N-Tier applications (Web servers, for example). Users must ensure that high availability and failover are instituted at each tier in an end-to-end fashion. SLB installation is not a shortcut to a complete design for fault tolerance and usage volume.

For complete redundancy, you should implement parallel network infrastructures to connect users to the database and implement global load balancers across multiple geographically separate data centers to avoid catastrophic outages. These load balancers direct Web requests to the best available site and are available from the same vendors as local SLBs. They employ various algorithms and policy mechanisms, including proximity, response time/latency, packet loss, local server load, local server health, and content request.

Stateless farm scale-out architectures are most common for higher-scale e-Business cases, but they are gradually becoming a key design for other infrastructure. To promote reliability, most recent 3/N-Tier designs incorporate NLB and other DBMS clustering at a minimum. The design is common in other patterns as well, but it is absolutely essential, though hardest to implement, for the 3/N-Tier Transact pattern. To scale Web applications, corporations historically have implemented Web server clusters with Domain Naming Service (DNS) round-robin load balancing. However, simple DNS policies are not sophisticated enough to avoid unhealthy servers in the cluster, resulting in unacceptable service levels for clients.

## Publish Patterns

Publish patterns include most applications that provide read-only and data analysis access. Falling under this umbrella is any application that is designed to allow the user to download, see, listen to, or analyze data. Reporting and analysis tools, Web brochure-ware, and streaming audio are all good examples.

From this basic stance, the definition of a Publish pattern can be expanded to include applications that require a simple query but that don't change the state of the business or don't store the results of user keystrokes for any long-term value. Tracking a package on a shipper's Web site does involve users typing in data such as the tracking number, but this information is not stored. Instead, the system uses it as a unique search key. Of course, user behavior statistics captured from Web sites are stored long term, even for publishing applications, but this is a special consideration that can be included in this otherwise read-only pattern.

Since so little business logic is involved with read-only applications, 2-Tier architectures are adequate. However, N-Tier designs that separate presentation from even such simple business logic (view a document) will evolve over time as publishing moves beyond Web only.

In general, scaling these infrastructures is usually a matter of replicating the data as much as needed to support volume and improve reliability. Since read-only data is *not* changed often, data can replicated easily across many servers or cached closer to the user in a distributed server farm. Thanks to this feature, publish applications are the most easily and thus most commonly outsourced, particularly when the goal is to serve very large numbers of users over large geographies for e-Business.

When defining a Publish pattern, make sure you know what service levels are required for your business and design your patterns accordingly. You might find cases where data changes very often—stock quotes, for example—but the data is still read-only for the users. Such cases might or might not require special patterns with specialized infrastructure. A stock trading floor often requires publish and subscribe middleware that operates in a multicast network mode to make sure stock quotes are received simultaneously at all trader stations without giving unfair advantage. Most users viewing stock data, however, are happy with data that may refresh only once every 20 minutes. In such cases, a simple Web page is fine. For faster refresh rates, many brokerage houses have fancier and yet more costly solutions.

Once an application is determined to fall within the publishing category, it can be subclassified as one of the following three patterns:

■ Client/server Publish, usually leveraging complex GUI analysis tools

■ Web Publish, where the data access is initiated in a browser

■ Stream Publish, an emerging pattern that covers near realtime audio and video downloads

These patterns have only moderate functional overlap between them, thus differentiating between them is easier than it is for the patterns within Transact.

## The Client/Server Publish Pattern

This pattern is defined by the use of a smart PC, such as a sophisticated business intelligence client, with associated session-oriented protocols such as SQLNet inserted between the client and back-end database. This pattern is best used for implementing. sophisticated data analysis capa-

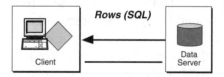

▲ **Description**
  ▶ **Client-based ad hoc query, OLAP, or reporting application that accesses a database over a network**

▲ **Service Level Matches**
  + **Speed of initial development**
  − **Scalability**
  − **Deployability**

▲ **Common Examples**
  ▶ **Business Objects**
  ▶ **Cognos PowerPlay**

▲ **Popularity**
  ▶ **Most popular Publish pattern inside enterprise**

▲ **Practices**
  + **Limiting use of this pattern to LAN networks**
  + **Creating a unified analytic integration service via DW/ODS**
  + **Using publish-specific tools rather than VB or PB**
  − **Allowing direct access to transactional data**

▲ **Futures**
  ▶ **Client-based slicing and dicing of data will remain popular, especially for disconnected users**
  ▶ **Convergence of Web and Client/Server publish with the ability to move transparently between them**

**Figure 3.8** The Client/Server Publish Pattern

bilities for a small, well-defined user base. Figure 3.8 summarizes the characteristics of this pattern

This pattern differentiates itself from the other Publish patterns in terms of the amount of processing that is performed after a query is made to a database. Applications that fit this pattern are online analytical processing (OLAP) tools and reporting-intensive applications, which require a smart PC for post-query processing support. Common examples include products by companies such as Business Objects, Brio, Cognos, MicroStrategies, and SAS Institute. The Client/Server Publish pattern is the most popular Publish pattern inside the enterprise.

Much of the knowledge about this pattern comes historically from the data-warehousing world. Data-warehousing applications have clearly shown the importance of providing access to data in a much simpler, timelier way. This pattern is the one that best deals with the complexities of moving and interpreting large amounts of data, while at the same time trying to retain some consistencies at relatively low cost.

### Benefit

This pattern is highly adaptive. Like the 3/N-Tier Transact pattern, the Client/Server Publish pattern can be fitted to a particular application with a considerable degree of precision, and you can do so easily. This approach is highly adaptive, since it reduces the number of interfaces and the number of extractions that have to be performed on the operational systems. For example, an organization might have its own data store, plus another from a company that it is acquiring. While these data stores support basically the same information, the schema for each is very different. By simply writing an interface for the acquired database into the data store, the data now becomes accessible to all clients.

### Weaknesses

Known weaknesses of the Client/Server Publish pattern are:

■ Resource-intensive. Client code size and bandwidth requirements make this pattern less easily scalable and deployable. Thus, most Client/Server Publish patterns tend to be restricted to LAN use.

■ Unpredictable demand. It is not uncommon for the answer to a query to be 100 to 200 megabytes or more in size. In fact, files of a gigabyte or more are easily found within most data warehouse applications.

*Best Practices*

For best results with the Client/Server Publish pattern, you should follow these practices:

■ Developers must pay close attention to modeling in order to maintain system performance.

■ Both educated and uneducated users may be accessing these applications, and a tiny mistake in an SQL command can bring a data mart to its knees. Data access, then, must be closely managed, with ad hoc query capabilities granted only to the most sophisticated users.

■ Instead of relying on the database server to optimize query results, use OLAP solutions to offer precalculated and stored results for common queries, speeding things up for both the server and the network.

■ Infrastructure developers must also resist suggestions from users to use this pattern anywhere other than in the data-intensive, read-only realm where it excels. Adding even limited write-back or transaction capabilities to applications in this pattern will require much more robust infrastructure and could compromise application performance. Instead, you should use one of the Transact patterns to handle the write-back/change requirements resulting from analyses.

■ Due to the bandwidth requirements, this type of pattern should typically be used in a LAN environment only.

■ Create a unified analytic integration service using a Data Warehouse/Operational Data Store (DW/ODS).

■ Use publish-specific tools such as OLAP analysis tools rather than Visual Basic (VB) or PowerBuilder, which can't take advantage of OLAP rollup data easily or do specialized data visualization. Try to keep the number of tools low, ideally limiting it to one. Also, limit the data warehouse and data mart technologies to a single vendor and product each.

*Looking Forward*

Client-based slicing and dicing of data will remain popular, especially for disconnected uses. Anticipate a convergence of Web and Client/Server Publish patterns with the eventual ability to move transparently between them. With this convergence, the limitations of this practice to the LAN will slowly diminish.

## The Web Publish Pattern

This pattern is defined by the use of an HTML browser and HTTP proto-col to enable read-only access to structured XML or HTML documents. As such, it is more flexible than the Client/Server Publish pattern in sup-porting large, less well-defined user groups. But it is limited in the sophistication of the read-only interactivity and analysis it can support. Figure 3.9 shows the key characteristics of this pattern.

This pattern is best used for read-only Web-centric access to data and content, including documents and pages, while leaving other Publish patterns to deal with other read-only content. Common examples include any type of brochure-style Web site, package tracking for over-night delivery services, and Web-based account review or bill presenta-tion applications. Currently, this Publish pattern is the most popular for applications reaching beyond the enterprise boundaries.

Note that taking keystrokes from a user—not just mouse clicks on Web links—can still be done in a read-only context. When you go to a package-tracking site, you must enter your tracking number for the site

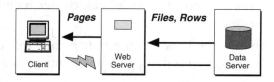

▲ **Description**
 ▸ **Accessing, reading, or querying information via browser-based HTML/HTTP**

▲ **Service Level Matches**
 + **Speed of initial development**

 − **Changing presentation logic**

▲ **Common Examples**
 ▸ **FedEx package tracking Web app**

 ▸ **"Brochureware" sites**

 ▸ **Web-based bill presentment**

▲ **Popularity**
 ▸ **Most popular publish pattern beyond enterprise boundaries**

▲ **Practices**
 + **Scaling out stateless Web farms**

 − **Limiting support to a single point of interaction**

▲ **Futures**
 ▸ **N-Tier publishing based on XSLT, XML, and XQL**

 ▸ **Convergence of Web and Client/Server publish with the ability to move transparently between them**

**Figure 3.9** The Web Publish Pattern

to work. But the site does not store your keystrokes for long-term business use, since it already has the tracking number in its database. Such an application is read-only, even if the end user enters keystrokes. The keyboard entry is used only to query the database and doesn't update the database. In contrast, if the user wants to cancel the delivery, the 3/N-tier Transact pattern comes into play.

Likewise, the same model applies to a sales manager performing analysis on sales data. The manager can pick from a list of territories, specify date ranges, then submit the query. Since the query doesn't update the database, it's still a read-only operation.

Many Web sites today use a combination of Publish and Transact patterns. However, infrastructure planners should separate these distinct functions to get a better picture of the infrastructure that is needed for each activity. Clearly, you will find some opportunities for reuse, but initial planning efforts should split up the functions of the application to clearly understand the fundamental building blocks of each pattern.

The read-only nature of the Publish patterns in general and the Web-centricity of this pattern make wide-scale replication viable. For large, externally focused implementations, it often makes sense to outsource this pattern for hosting so that speed of deployment is maximized and network latency can be reduced.

### Benefits

Due to the maturity of this pattern, many solid tools are available for developing read-only Web publishing applications. Deployment is similarly well understood, resulting in a very rapid initial development phase and wide availability of Web hosting service providers. However, it remains difficult to change the presentation logic from Web to non-Web presentations without completely rebuilding the application.

Scalability is very simple to achieve with scale-out, rather than scale-up, designs using stateless farm architecture with network load balancers and masses of cheap Web servers and file system or database servers. (See "Stateless Farm Architecture and Scale-Up Design" in this chapter.) Moreover, unlike 3/N-Tier Transact, even the file system or database server itself can be duplicated and replicated to scale. Assuming the data doesn't change that often, this is easy to support.

Cheaper hardware and software is supported, because the scale-out design means you can choose database systems that need not be best at OLTP, and therefore are more expensive. Moreover, you can choose economical Intel-based servers and have more of them to scale. At some point, data center rack space becomes important, but the point still holds. For this pattern, you should not be buying a lot of expensive equipment.

Many new Internet-centric acceleration or performance-enhancement solutions work well here, when they are warranted by scalability requirements, such as in applications created for e-Business rather than internal needs. This range of solutions includes:

- Network load balancers and multi-site balancing
- Secure sockets layer (SSL) offloading (for encrypted content)
- Compression
- Caching (for databases, memory, reverse caching in the data center, client caching, intermediate ISP caches)
- Content delivery network (CDN) services like Akamai
- Traffic or rate shaping

Weaker or newer centralized IT organizations can offer this pattern to customers as centralized and shared infrastructure, and in the process, they make most of this pattern into a service, as explained in more detail in Chapter 4.

### Weaknesses

Despite best efforts, it is difficult to manage scale or load on e-Business Web sites that fit this pattern. Many businesses plan for 4x or 10x site capacity, and they are still surprised when the application overflows its capacity.

Publishing to multiple points of interaction is still a work in progress. Web-only approaches are still common, with completely separate portals for voice or mobile devices also still common. Over time, XML-based publishing portals with multiple points of interaction should become available.

### Best Practices

For best results with Web Publish, you should:

- Focus first on availability, then on throughput and response time.
- Design-in at least a two-way redundant solution, even for internal needs.

- Examine Web-hosting service providers for designs and sourcing, or just examples of services to offer to your own organization internally.

- Use Content Delivery Network (CDN) services for static content for very large audiences only.

- Scale-out (duplicate and replicate) Web and data servers with load balancers.

- Support multiple points of interaction (or at least plan on this in the future).

- Manage, limit, or disallow direct access to transactional data.

- Create a unified analytical integration service via DW/ODS.

- Don't use expensive online transaction processing databases.

- Leverage less-expensive hardware and software in general for data storage components.

- Don't neglect security issues, particularly data defacement or tampering—even read-only data can be changed by the malicious, or denial of service attacks can prevent user access.

- Shore up relationships with corporate marketing so you are not surprised by long-planned marketing campaigns that overnight provide 10x spikes in e-Business Web site load.

- Design for outsourcing, even if you never do.

- If an e-Business site is mission-critical, install response time and load-monitoring services to keep track of load more accurately and plan accordingly.

- Take a service-centric approach. You can achieve significant real infrastructure reuse widely within this pattern, not just a blueprint-only pattern value.

## Looking Forward

The pressure to accommodate multiple points of interaction will drive this pattern toward N-tier publishing based on the extensible markup language (XML) and the style sheets and query language associated with it (XSLT and XQL). This advance will allow you to present Web content in a variety of formats, thus broadening the market for Web Publishing applications.

In most cases, users trying to find published information will search for it through some combination of internal or public search engines and portal features. Depending on what is being published, it can be made known to interested parties through the use of Universal Description, Discovery, and Integration (UDDI), Simple Object Access Protocol (SOAP), or Web Services Description Language (WSDL).

### The Stream Publish Pattern

This pattern is used for real-time publishing of streaming content (audio, video, text, etc.) to "multimedia player" clients such as Windows Media Player, RealAudio, etc. Although the Web Publish pattern enables playback of multimedia files, this service is accomplished as a more traditional "file download," as shown in Figure 3.10. Streaming plays the file in near real-time as it downloads. The latency requirements of real-time multimedia delivery are different enough that streaming requires its own pattern.

Common examples of Stream Publish include Internet radio stations and film clip Web sites. Streaming media is a centerpiece of most consumer entertainment Web sites and an increasingly valuable feature of many sites as it enhances the "stickiness" of the site.

The most common tools for stream publishing are proprietary vendor solutions such as RealAudio or Cisco IPTV, which require special servers and players that match. Stream publish components deliver the multimedia content only and are not normally used to deliver the static pages

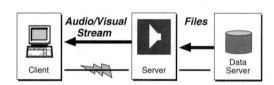

▲ **Description**
  ▶ Accessing, reading, or querying information via browser-based HTML/HTTP

▲ **Service Level Matches**
  + Speed of initial development

  − Changing presentation logic

▲ **Common Examples**
  ▶ FedEx package tracking Web app

  ▶ "Brochureware" sites

  ▶ Web-based bill presentment

▲ **Popularity**
  ▶ Most popular publish pattern beyond enterprise boundaries

▲ **Practices**
  + Scaling out stateless Web farms

  − Limiting support to a single point of interaction

▲ **Futures**
  ▶ N-Tier publishing based on XSLT, XML, and XQL

  ▶ Convergence of Web and Client/Server publish with the ability to move transparently between them

**Figure 3.10** The Stream Publish Pattern

or applications of a Web site. For this reason, multimedia Web sites typically require that the Stream Publish and Web Publish patterns be used in tandem. Over time, these solutions will become more standardized.

Stream Publish is only one-way streaming. It usually isn't live, but involves playing back a canned audio or video file over the network. Some live cases exist, such as multicasting a speech directly, but they are more rare.

Streaming also isn't real-time in the true sense, though the application protocols over IP can provide an almost real-time experience. Real-time streaming requires special networking quality-of-service (QoS) facilities such as multicast, low jitter, or prioritized router configurations. These configurations aren't commonly available on the Internet, with the exception of a special media network called MBONE. The higher bandwidth required for streaming video is also in limited supply.

The main reason most companies are forced to break out streaming as a separate pattern is that it requires a direct focus, a new class of server/storage, and improved network design. Going from simple Web pages with very simple graphics to streaming multimedia requires great changes in user behavior, Web site loads, and network configuration. If streaming becomes common in your environment, it will require close attention by your networking staff.

Even if your Web site is not currently outsourced, adding streaming media makes it even more likely that you will outsource at least the streaming part or all of the publish-focused infrastructure to service providers with much more scalable network designs and connectivity. This need becomes even more critical if you're doing video and not just audio.

### Benefits

Benefits of Stream Publish are:

- Usability. Streaming content is much easier to use simply because little interactivity is involved. The user sits back and watches or listens to a canned media clip. In addition, media players provide stop, pause, rewind, and volume controls similar to a VCR.

- Business value. Streaming content can make Web sites more dramatic and interesting, thus helping increase customer retention. It also provides an extra dimension of information, which people find helpful, particularly in training or e-learning contexts. Audio in particular works well. (See weaknesses.)

- Clear choices. Vendor solutions are coalescing slowly, which makes specifying solutions easier to do.

*Weaknesses*

The weaknesses of Stream Publish are:

- Bandwidth-intensive. This pattern is extremely bandwidth intensive (8 Kbps audio, video much higher), which also can mean expensive.

- Unpredictable results. Unpredictable and variable network performance can make audio or video streams uneven, driving away users in the process. You must monitor service levels, particularly over the Internet, where robust network design cannot be assumed.

- Unpredictable demand. e-Business or consumer-focused sites normally have an unknown external user base, which makes capacity planning of servers and particularly networks difficult at best.

*Best Practices*

For best results with Stream Publish, you should:

- Find qualified service providers to host large-scale content streaming applications, since they are more likely to be able to provide the network bandwidth required quickly and dynamically during peaks.

- Don't use gratuitous streaming content on Web pages, since it complicates infrastructure requirements while perhaps providing little business value.

- Monitor usage carefully. More spikes are likely with this kind of content than with Web publishing alone.

- Use traffic shaping to control the impact of this traffic on other Web applications at this site or on your internal network.

- Internally, use multicasting when possible. This approach involves setting up scheduled releases similar to TV broadcasts for video that many people want to see. Don't always allow on-demand viewing for the most popular material, since it places unpredictable constraints on your infrastructure.

- Internally, consider using scheduled replication of content to servers that are logically and physically closer to large user populations, instead of running streams over bandwidth constrained WAN connections. This approach is essentially what service providers do for external audiences. They can also be used to support geographically dispersed internal audiences.

- Monitor for overuse of streaming media links on intranet sites. Even if the traffic is coming from outside servers, it can affect internal networks and the mission-critical applications that also ride on them. Traffic or content filtering may be required on firewalls.

### Looking Forward

Increasingly advanced compression algorithms, as well as more sophisticated techniques for smoothing hiccups in a stream, generally will improve the streaming quality. Streaming publishing will evolve into multicasting over time, while protocols governing streaming media will continue to evolve. Moreover, content delivery networks are adding streaming support to their distributed caching systems.

## Collaborate Patterns

The Collaborate pattern involves peer-to-peer communication, usually centered on shared documents or groups of documents. Although both the Collaborate and the Transact patterns enable read-write access to information, the Transact patterns are designed to handle read-write access to very structured data, whereas the Collaborate patterns are designed around document sharing, which is a form of unstructured data.

Many people have trouble actually differentiating Collaborate patterns from Transact and Publish patterns. Your company might use the term "collaborate" to refer to *any* activity conducted with a customer, including direct sales interaction and taking orders over the Web. Instead, this book suggests a more useful, focused, and natural infrastructure-specific definition that doesn't lump everything IT builds into the term "collaboration."

The Merriam-Webster Web Dictionary supplies this definition:

> Collaborate: (to labor together). To work jointly with others especially in an intellectual endeavor.

In this definition, collaboration does *not* mean following a script or rote procedure. Buying a soda from a vending machine is not collaboration. True collaboration requires multiple human beings working directly together ("jointly"), though the asynchronous time between their activities can vary from immediate (on the phone) to much longer (trading e-mail messages).

Publishing jointly authored documents is not really collaborating—it's just publishing. Getting feedback e-mail on a published document via e-mail or chat room *is* collaborating. And so is any authorship process that requires trading drafts of a document for editing.

Collaborate patterns arise when users want to share the creation of documents or other data with other users directly. Due to the ongoing globalization of the workplace, person-to-person interactions have become increasingly critical, but ever more challenging and costly to conduct face-to-face. To solve this problem, much of these efforts have been moved online, making it easier to collaborate over long distances or times, thus increasing the popularity of Collaborate patterns within the IT framework.

Telephone, videoconferencing, e-mail, chat, and instant messaging are all collaborative in a simple communications-based way. Other applications, such as knowledge management tools and knowledge exchanges, support collaborative business processes with more intellectual complexity.

Of all the patterns mentioned in this book, the Collaborate patterns have undergone the most change and growth in the last four years. This growth is driven by the need to share and modify calendars, text documents, and design drawings, along with the growth of more advanced collaboration techniques using streaming audio and video.

The growth of collaborative applications will require that you develop new infrastructure techniques, which should be standardized as quickly as possible to ensure the most successful implementation. Indeed, since the very success of collaboration is based on universal access to collaborative tools, it is essential to have unified, highly centralized, and singular infrastructure solutions. Conversely, integrating a wide range of different collaborative solutions has not proven as effective, with some notable exceptions, such as SMTP for e-mail.

The following pages provide an extensive discussion of the individual Collaborate patterns. Differentiated patterns in this category include the network-intensive Real-Time Collaborate pattern for two-way audio and video, Store-and-Forward Collaborate for e-mail and file and print applications, and Structured Collaborate for document management and workflow.

### The Real-Time Collaborate Pattern

This pattern is quite similar to the Stream Publish pattern, because both involve enabling real-time transmission of audio and video. However, since collaboration implies two-way information exchange, as opposed to the one-way flow of Stream Publishing, real-time collaboration warrants its own separate pattern, as shown in Figure 3.11.

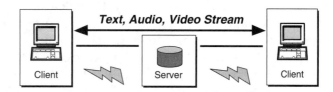

**Figure 3.11** The Real-Time Collaborate Pattern

▲ **Description**

▶ **Streaming audio/video/graphics/text from client to client using real-time streaming protocols, either through a server or peer to peer**

▲ **Service Level Matches**

+ **Usability**

− **Affordability**

− **Scalability**

− **Availability**

▲ **Common Examples**

▶ **NetMeeting**

▶ **Voice**

▶ **Instant Messaging**

▶ **Videoconferencing over the Internet**

▲ **Popularity**

▶ **In its infancy**

▲ **Practice Maturity**

+ **Homogeneous Instant Messaging**

+ **NetMeeting on Intranets**

− **VoIP**

− **Videoconferencing over the Internet**

▲ **Futures**

▶ **QoS support within Intranets and then Internet makes this pattern more available and affordable**

Applications in this category use streaming audio, video, graphics, or text to share information between users. The communication can flow either through a server for scalability and to provide community interaction, or straight from peer to peer. Common examples include Microsoft NetMeeting, Voice Over Internet (VoIP), instant messaging (as on AOL), and any type of videoconferencing (Web-based or otherwise).

Every organization has built or sourced at least one real-time collaborate infrastructure: the voice network. The PBXs, phones, and wires used to carry traffic can all be considered a Real-Time Collaborate system, and a very mature one at that. Most other examples of collaborate infrastructure depend on how the data networks are configured. They either use dedicated networks, such as the dedicated lines use, or video conferencing kiosks or campuswide videoconferencing. Or they ride over a network shared by many other applications, such as the TCP/IP platform.

When these applications ride on existing shared networks, cost savings are apparent, and the services can be provided more easily. Since the data network already connects the business, a new one doesn't need be built. Unfortunately, these same real-time collaborate applications have special network requirements. They demand the kind of capacity or service levels (low latency and jitter) that current data networks cannot provide without significant new investment.

A particular example is running video over TCP/IP through an existing frame relay network with link speeds of 56Kbps. This method not only makes the video erratic—and frankly useless—but it also negatively affects all other applications on the same shared network as well.

Since real-time collaborate solutions can affect other patterns this way, the whole category needs careful watching. Not all Real-Time Collaborate pattern instances are so troublesome, however. Chat and Net-Meeting document sharing are fairly harmless applications, though the latter has significant bandwidth requirements. Others, such as Audio or Voice over IP, may require significant upgrades in network equipment and network management services to support quality-of-service features that prioritize this kind of traffic. Still others, particularly video, will likely require both significant bandwidth increases and multicast features in the network.

If you can run voice over the existing voice network, which is already separate from data networks, though perhaps multiplexed over the same physical circuits at the lowest level, why run the risk of hurting mission-critical applications that *must* use the data network? This issue has slowed the implementation of many Real-Time Collaborate applications in many organizations.

On the other hand, if the business really requires it, you should be prepared to support it. Fundamental business needs are pushing Real-Time Collaborate as a solution. For example, e-Business requirements have led some organizations to use audio (Voice over IP) for customer support on their Internet sites. Since many customers have only one phone line, customers with problems can't stay on the network *and* call technical support. To solve this problem, businesses are delivering customer support audio through the Web interface. This solution provides sufficient quality for some businesses, and it is something they could not do without the new Real-Time Collaborate options.

As new applications of this type are suggested, infrastructure professionals must carefully examine the particular needs and weigh them against the costs required. Many great ideas in this area have proven too costly or have too many problems technical problems—voice or video quality, for example—to implement in the near term.

Certainly, due to its newness, the technology will change and follow the trend of lowering network costs. However, anything that fits this pattern should be examined very carefully for its impact on infrastructure, especially at the network and application service level.

## *Benefits*

Benefits of the Real-Time Collaborate pattern are:

- Lower costs. Running Real-Time Collaborate activities over a shared network can enable significant sharing without significant extra costs. It could also eliminate travel expenses. However, this potential benefit is not necessarily true for all real-time collaborate applications. Examine each one closely in the lab to determine the real impacts and costs to provide these services.

- Better communication. This pattern helps boost the flow of information and ideas, particularly globally, which can increase the speed and quality, and therefore lower the cost, of doing business. This gain in turn makes a strong case for funding Real-Time Collaborate initiatives. In an e-Business context, having Real-Time Collaborate could mean cutting days off of production cycles.

- Customer retention. Some real-time collaborate applications increase stickiness on the Web site and help provide unique or differentiating services to customers in an e-Business situation.

## *Weaknesses*

The weaknesses of Real-Time Collaborate are:

- Bleeding edge. Despite the lure of rich video images, only recently has bandwidth been cheap and available enough, particularly on the Internet, to even consider applications that fall in this pattern. For this reason, the pattern is still in its infancy and does not have a large market penetration, with the exception of traditional voice services. Also as a result, this pattern can raise problems with affordability, scalability, and availability.

- Plug-in requirements. More often than not, real-time interaction requires special players with specialized protocols that are frequently not yet standardized, such as real-time messaging, audio formats, etc.

- Security impacts. Security issues may affect this pattern—this form of access may not be allowed easily through a firewall without creating unacceptable risks.

■ Network issues. While sharing many aspects of the Stream Publish pattern, this pattern also has many of the same drawbacks. It is extremely bandwidth-intensive, therefore both expensive and immature. Unpredictable and variable network performance leaves video and audio streams jittery unless you implement costly solutions. Despite business cost savings, the cost to upgrade shared networking facilities may be prohibitive, especially if you try to provide complete desktop coverage. A careful analysis must be done for each case.

### Best Practices

While user response time is often the key factor in a satisfactory implementation of this pattern, various strategies may be employed to overcome issues associated with it:

■ Implement quality of service (QoS) features of networking equipment and services to reduce latency or overcome jitter or variation of latency.

■ Run protocols over User Datagram Protocol (UDP) without forcing the kind of retransmissions required by Transmission Control Protocol (TCP). Most real-time protocols have adopted this approach.

■ Use scheduled transmissions (broadcast/multicast) instead of allowing on-demand requests. This practice applies even more to Stream Publish.

■ Buy more bandwidth or run applications over separate, better-controlled bandwidth, i.e., separate voice and/or video networks.

■ A more critical best practice is to make sure that you identify applications that fit this pattern early and make sure they are studied carefully.

■ Determine real capabilities—not just application features, but specifically the infrastructure readiness. Use a lab setting to show how the application will work given existing networking and desktop or other infrastructure realities.

■ Determine real costs to upgrade existing infrastructure as a trade-off to expected business benefits, including reduced costs due to less travel, etc.

*Looking Forward*

The value of new ways of doing business and interacting with various constituencies will drive continued innovation in this pattern. Quality of service (QoS) support within intranets, followed by the Internet, will make this pattern more available and affordable. Moreover, bandwidth prices will continue to fall and technology and product options will continue their progress toward cheaper, faster, and better.

Each year, spend time revisiting past rejected projects to see whether they could be supported with a real business case that has significant ROI. A portfolio approach to managing infrastructure plans should document all such requests, not just those approved, but also those rejected, and this approach should allow regular review. History and technological evolution will catch up to this pattern and make it a larger aspect of your business and infrastructure.

## The Store-and-Forward Collaborate Pattern

This pattern involves the basic transfer, replication, and storage of files or documents, as shown in Figure 3.12. Common examples include e-mail attachments, distributed file systems, and print queues. Most

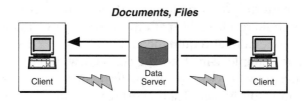

▲ **Description**
  ▸ **Basic transfer, replication, and storage of files or documents**

▲ **Service Level Matches**
  + **Scalability**
  + **Affordability**
  − **Deployability**

▲ **Common Examples**
  ▸ **E-mail**
  ▸ **Distributed file system**
  ▸ **Print queues**

▲ **Popularity**
  ▸ **Most popular Collaborate pattern**

▲ **Practices**
  + **E-mail interoperability**
  + **File and print consolidation**

▲ **Futures**
  ▸ **Directory services decoupled from NOS**
  ▸ **File systems decoupled from OS (e.g., network-attached printers)**

**Figure 3.12** The Store-and-Forward Collaborate Pattern

organizations also put desktop support and software distribution into this pattern, since the same people who support the network operating system (NOS) also support the desktops, or at least the groups are very closely allied. Often, this pattern is managed by the Distributed Systems Group within IT, which may operate under many different names.

Still, this one pattern is where most organizations, perhaps unwittingly, have employed a very pattern-centric approach to planning.

With the exception of traditional voice in the previous pattern, Store-and-Forward is the most mature and popular Collaborate pattern. Many organizations have become very standardized in the products they use, including network operating systems, mail servers, desktop configurations, and connectivity. They've even become standardized in minor configuration details, such as specifying that shared documents go on the F: drive.

Since organizations have been doing this pattern for many years, certain decisions have been made and need only annual review to determine whether key changes must be made.

Any given year could be the right time for a large server or desktop upgrade, such as newer versions of Microsoft Windows, Lotus Notes, or Microsoft Outlook/Exchange.

When tight economic conditions prevail, such upgrades may be postponed, since they won't affect the business as much as investments in other patterns. So, a pattern portfolio approach to prioritizing investments could result in this pattern's upgrade investments being cut. Even so, the operational requirements could still need some budgeted funding. For example, e-mail storage costs grow every year.

Some activities within this pattern, such as centralizing e-mail servers, can result in significant short-term return on investment. Unfortunately, not all the resources in this pattern can be centralized. File servers don't work too well when accessed across slow, high-latency WAN links. Even e-mail should be carefully configured to support replicated interactions with clients when centralized servers are accessed over slower WAN links.

In fact, this pattern should remain the most decentralized in nature. Support investments will include distributed file server and desktop support. Given this extreme degree of decentralization, any level of standardization can cut the cost of supporting it. Thus, standardization has progressed all the way to detailed configurations and full support policies, which even the largest organizations insist upon company-wide in order to keep costs contained.

Applications in this pattern, including MS Office applications such as Word and Excel, often are deployed on every desktop in the organization, so that they become ubiquitous. Moreover, they are increasingly the last vestige of "fat" desktop applications. Even if e-mail is extended by Web interfaces, these do not offer offline capabilities and the full feature set of traditional Windows client applications. Fat clients still rule.

This hegemony is even more true for productivity solutions such as word processing, spreadsheets, and so on. These applications will not be primarily server based with thin Web clients for the foreseeable future. This pattern still will require Windows clients and support for Windows and Windows applications. Getting these applications and clients to be highly standardized is a key goal. Still, these applications will drive most Windows client platform upgrades going forward.

Technical issues in this pattern are fairly straightforward. The most difficult issues here actually are political: setting standards, determining goals and budget responsibility for major systemwide upgrades, etc. Moreover, while implementing applications within this pattern is relatively simple, these applications are the ones that everyone uses, so they are easy targets for criticism from anywhere within the organization.

### Benefits

Benefits of the Store-and-Forward Collaborate pattern are:

- Maturity. Mature standards are common in this pattern: Many organizations already have this pattern well designed, and they can control variety and proliferation within it.

- Collaborative. This pattern offers simple collaboration solutions that are good enough for many needs: While other patterns could be required, e-mail and file sharing on NOS platforms are key services that can be extended and used for many activities.

- Good model. This pattern can serve as a model for maturity in other patterns. You can use your experience and past successes to convince customers of your common goals for other less-mature patterns.

- Undemanding. The nature of store-and-forward makes network impact light, particularly on WANs. Pattern traffic can be slowed down to make room for critical interactive traffic of other patterns. Dial-up networks can be used to support off-net offices or individual offline users.

- Easy component selection. Microsoft products dominate this pattern. They've eliminated most of the competition, making it easy to plan.

### Weaknesses

The weaknesses of the Store-and-Forward Collaborate pattern are:

- Hard to upgrade. Since this pattern is the most distributed, changing standards means changing very many instances of solutions, all desktops, for example. Upgrades must be carefully planned in advance, and in larger organizations, they can take 6–18 months or longer to complete.

- Hard to support. Even though this pattern and its components are well understood, it is still difficult to provide Help Desk support to a vast group of users, especially those working odd hours or working remotely on mobile laptops.

- Data security. Much data can be located on local hard drives. Organizational policy as well as technology can address this practice, but individual behavior is hard to control. Users often store key documents unencrypted on local drives, then the information can be lost because their laptops are stolen or improperly backed up.

- Slow pace of change. Many people have assumed that directory services developed in this pattern would impact other patterns. This hasn't happened, however. The whole Lightweight Directory Access Protocol (LDAP) revolution happened elsewhere, particularly in the e-Business arena. Vendors of directory products closely tied to NOS products, such as Microsoft Active Directory and Novell NDS, have been slow to support new standards. Thus, they have not dominated in directory services or authentication services elsewhere. For now, this pattern's directory and security might only impact some of the other patterns. Conversely, some standards from elsewhere have finally become common in this one; only recently have the major NOS vendors become fully comfortable running on TCP/IP networks rather than their own proprietary protocols.

### Best Practices

For best results with Store-and-Forward Collaboration, you should:

- Establish single standards for e-mail products, calendar products, office automation, and other similar components throughout the enterprise.

- If you can't standardize on a single product, use established standards, such as Simple Mail Transfer Protocol (SMTP), Secure/Multipurpose Internet Mail Extensions (S/MIME), and others, to make e-mail systems interoperable. Naturally, this standardization also is the key to connecting this pattern to other organizations. However, services like strong security (S/MIME standard based) still aren't supportable across multiple organizations.

- Provide a single file, print, directory, and security solution for this pattern. Doing so usually means picking a single product and sticking with it.

- Provide just a few common desktop configurations and stick to them.

- Enhance your cost recovery by charging a per-desktop fee for all investments in all required systems. This fee should cover all your costs to include the cost of network service (excluding WAN but including LAN and remote access costs), hardware, software (OS and applications), and service/support (help desk costs). Many organizations have used this funding approach successfully to help standardize offerings.

- Use centralized planning control to enable strong coordination and standardization across business units. Many no longer see this area as a political battlefield and will follow the carefully marshaled dictates of a centralized planning approach. Even if you can't establish central control in other patterns, you should be able to do so here. This practice includes controlling standard schema for directories in more federated cases, owning the forest in Microsoft Active Directory design, for example.

## Looking Forward

It will be years before traditional file and print services decouple from the OS and become centralized. On the other hand, directory service will be decoupled earlier, even if it doesn't affect the Store-and-Forward Collaborate pattern immediately. LDAP directories, including Microsoft and Novell varieties, will be used separately from this pattern by applications in other patterns. However, as more employee-focused systems support a centralized identity infrastructure, this pattern's approach will become more integrated with other applications in the enterprise.

## The Structured Collaborate Pattern

Structured collaboration, also known as workflow or document management, provides many important integrity-checking features that are missing from the Store-and-Forward Collaborate pattern, including version control, check-in/check-out, and data validation. For this reason, the Structure Collaborate pattern is more scalable, from a business perspective, for business use cases requiring these capabilities. But it also requires a longer implementation cycle and is several times more expensive.

As shown in Figure 3.13, this pattern includes any application that provides shared access and automated, coordinated change to a document, file, or other data structure. Common examples include Lotus Notes groupware and workflow applications (except simple e-mail), document management applications, Web content management systems, many software development environments, and shared groupware calendars.

Structured Collaborate applications focus on more than simplistic workflows, and they are deployed much more centrally than traditional Store-and-Forward applications. In terms of architecture and infrastruc-

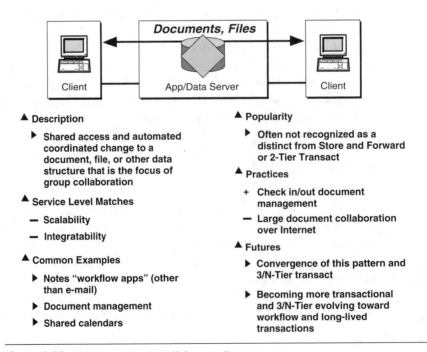

**Figure 3.13** The Structured Collaborate Pattern

ture, applications in this pattern often are a better match to transaction patterns and they are often implemented on the same infrastructures. In any case, these applications provide application controls over sharing behavior while other Collaborate patterns often let users do whatever they want.

You can understand a lot about this pattern by comparing it to the Store-and-Forward Collaborate pattern. While Store-and-Forward Collaborate is a recognizably mature pattern, with an application such as e-mail present on each desktop, Structured Collaborate is not mature or even widely seen in most organizations.

You have good reasons to prefer the Structured Collaborate pattern over the Store-and-Forward pattern, however. Though e-mail and file servers allow ad-hoc workflow and document management, they also require human intervention. Think about all the time you've heard the question "Who has the current copy of this document with all the changes?" for example. By comparison, Structured Collaborate automates the collaboration between users and makes their interaction more consistent. This regulation is done by using services such as rules-based automatic workflow routing, document version control, and check in/check out features with audit trails. With advanced features such as group calendars, Structured Collaborate often more resembles a 2-Tier or 3/N-Tier Transact pattern than a Store-and-Forward pattern.

Structured Collaborate applications are used in many enterprises, yet the pattern is often not recognized as distinct and it is implemented differently from Store-and-Forward or 2-Tier Transact patterns. As vendors of Store-and-Forward products start supporting the distinct infrastructural approaches for Structured Collaborate applications, they compete with vendors who offer solutions tailored to the automated nature of this pattern. This lack of distinction makes settling on a standard choice for this kind of application more difficult. You can use e-mail for some workflow and shared NOS file systems for some document sharing, but beware of scope creep or, more accurately, *pattern creep*. As solutions change, you might need to switch to new applications. And don't be surprised if they require new infrastructure.

Above all, make sure you are clear on which solution the business is selecting and plan accordingly. If they select Store-and-Forward solutions, existing processes will be easy to adapt. If they select Structured Collaborate solutions, completely new process and technology competence will be required.

### Benefits

This pattern is rather new for many organizations. As the benefits and weaknesses are better understood, they will likely mirror those of the other patterns (Store-and-Forward, 2-Tier, 3/N-Tier Transact, etc.). In some cases, however, they could indeed be very different.

In the case of distinct document management and workflow solutions, benefits can include:

■ Automation/integrity checking. These solutions have strong automation features supported by infrastructure: Check in/check out can be rigorously controlled in this pattern, but not so well in Store-and-Forward Collaborate.

■ Good opportunity. Thinking of these solutions as a separate pattern may help clarify infrastructure decisions. Many organizations seem unsure how to tackle these applications. The infrastructure issues could prove to be very significant, and this pattern approach should help make this clear.

### Weaknesses

The weaknesses of the Structured Collaborate pattern are:

■ Uncertainties. Untried solutions require significant testing. Given their structured approach, many will not scale well to large user populations. Document management in a distributed environment is a much more complex case than in a centralized server environment. Yet access to a centralized server can be so slow, particularly for large documents ranging in size from 500KB (PDF files) to 500MB and beyond (CAD/CAM files), that this configuration cannot support desired user service levels.

■ Little leverage. Given product limitations, you might find it hard to get document management systems to overlay and reuse significant portions of NOS or e-mail investments.

### Best Practices

For best results with Structured Collaborate, you should:

■ Employ check-in/check-out document management systems or strong workflow solutions as required. Make sure architectural and infrastructural issues are well understood. (The pattern approach will help.)

- Don't allow large document collaboration over Internet connections. Cross-business security is problematic and networking considerations could make solutions impractical. In some cases, cross-business collaboration can offer significant benefits, but they might need to be offered over existing Store-and-Forward infrastructure, such as e-mail attachments. Another way to implement the pattern is to create a 2-Tier Transact infrastructure that is Web-enabled for check in/check out. Some products are available that focus on this area, using a Web site for document sharing—this approach is especially useful when sharing must occur cross-business. Again, this practice would likely be separate from traditional Store-and-Forward infrastructure.

- Extend ad-hoc Store-and-Forward systems as much as you find to be practical, yet don't hesitate to implement completely new infrastructure to provide structured automation for business units that really need it.

- Keep solutions as small in scope as possible. The more you focus on workgroups, the fewer complications you encounter in providing infrastructure. If only the Legal Department needs strong document management, provide it only to that department. Let the rest of the organization live with the simpler capabilities of their existing Store-and-Forward Collaborate solutions.

### *Looking Forward*

Future trends for this pattern include convergence with 3/N-Tier transact. For instance, where workflow solutions require strong automation and control features, products will trade e-mail exchange for database stored work queues. Structured collaboration will become more transactional as 3/N-Tier evolves toward workflow and long-lived transactions.

Web content management and portals will drive the need for coordinating the various Structured Collaborate and Store-and-Forward solutions. Portals will increasingly become the preferred way to access many different types of content. The traditional content unit of "documents," which is used by document management vendors such as Documentum, will be replaced by the concept of "chunks," as used by vendors such as Interwoven. This change will force least common denominator functionality and information access across content and document management solutions. *Enriching the Value Chain*, in this book series, provides more detail about this change.

From a security perspective, authentication solutions will progress. More of these solutions will offer document or form signing and other features to increase the value of the solutions. These developments will follow the maturing of PKI services in many organizations.

Expect to see more of this pattern in the future.

## Adapting Patterns For Your Organization

You can adapt and use the Starter Kit described earlier in this chapter as necessary for your particular organization's requirements. When developing your own portfolio of patterns, you should consider the issues discussed on the following pages.

### What Patterns Do I Need?

To determine your actual infrastructure pattern needs, first look at your business processes, your applications, and your existing infrastructure solutions and start analyzing where the major patterns lie. As part of this exercise, ask yourself these two questions:

■ Which patterns do I use a lot?

■ Which patterns cover the applications most critical to my business?

Any patterns that answer these two questions should be automatically entered into your list of required patterns.

Some patterns won't be required at all. If you don't have mainframes, 1-Tier Transact probably isn't an option. You may not have structured collaboration yet, but seeing it in our pattern kit can remind you that this might be something you'll run into in the next few years. If you find something very distinct in infrastructure, but you will only do it for a small workgroup or for one simple instance and you don't anticipate it becoming a highly leveraged solution, don't bother making that a full pattern.

Use the 80/20 rule. Include the smallest number of patterns that provide the maximum value toward infrastructure planning. Try to keep below 10 the number of patterns in which you want to excel. The Starter Kit suggests nine. When finished with your analysis, however, you may have only five.

Focus on those patterns that offer significant ramifications for future application delivery, while spending less time on those patterns that are more mature (Store-and-Forward Collaborate) or that should only be kept running without significant new investments or applications over time, such as 1-Tier Transact.

When a pattern is so mature that the primary goal is to squeeze the last drop of return on investment (ROI) out of the implementation, the real ownership and leadership for change will be driven entirely by operations. Less-mature patterns will require more planning and design to drive toward maturity and to handle many new application requirements, though operations must still be involved.

## Extra Patterns Not Covered

In some cases, you might have patterns or versions that aren't listed in the Starter Kit. Since not all businesses are alike, it's very possible that the patterns listed here do not include an important aspect of your business. Other infrastructure patterns not reflected here might include:

■ Supervisory Control and Data Acquisition (SCADA) pattern to cover telemetry needs in the energy, manufacturing, and transportation industries.

■ Private Branch Exchange (PBX) pattern for voice data transmission. This is a separate instance of the Real-Time Collaborate pattern, which should be planned separately from data-network-based solutions, though convergence increasingly will unify these patterns over the next three to five years.

Your choice of representative patterns will be guided not only by different business requirements, but by the different service levels your organization needs to achieve in each instance. For example, does a particular application require high availability on the order of 99.99% uptime? Does your organization have a pilot or prototype program that requires extremely rapid turnaround times for application production? If so, then consider developing a "high availability pattern" or a "pilot/ prototype pattern" for those instances.

## Subdividing Patterns

On the other hand, a large percentage of your business applications might fall into a single pattern, and you might desire to further refine these patterns into sub-patterns or separate pattern instances if the infrastructure needs are significantly different.

Before breaking a pattern apart, consider the following issues:

■ Is the infrastructure different enough to be worth planning it separately? Will it remain different for at least two years?

■ Is the infrastructure highly disruptive to the business as a whole or to other sets of applications? For instance, real-time video applications that slow down all other applications without business justification must be controlled or even eradicated as a class, not one at a time.

■ Do you use the applications, and therefore this infrastructure, a lot? A Web hosting company might distinguish patterns differently from an enterprise. Whatever you do most heavily should benefit most from greater focus on reuse in areas of technology, process, and people.

■ Do you have two parallel product choices that are both commonly used, yet each requires somewhat different infrastructure? For instance, consider implementing an N-Tier architecture through Microsoft versus J2EE. It is not uncommon in larger organizations to see both (bought or built), and it could be well worth your effort creating separate sub-patterns, or at least treating them as instances of a single pattern worthy of separate consideration. Getting just two instances well defined and easily repeatable can keep you from having 10 different choices. Two, while not one, is still very much better than 10!

■ Do you have two instances of a pattern that represent different service-level requirements, such as enterprise 3/N-Tier versus line-of-business 3/N-Tier?

Each organization must base its patterns on its own knowledge and experience. The patterns then become totally adaptable to your own unique business requirements.

## Applying Multiple Patterns

While many applications can be described by a single pattern, it's also possible that large-scale applications will require two or more patterns to describe them fully. From an IT perspective, you shouldn't feel obligated to run every part of an application on a single infrastructure or pattern. Using patterns helps identify when staging of a single application across multiple infrastructures can help maximize efficiency and minimize redundancy.

For example, think of an application that is primarily a Publish pattern; a Web portal, for example. If a business requirement for that application is write oriented—logging on to the portal or updating a profile, for instance—you might put each business process on a different infrastructure. Thus, you might have one infrastructure to support Web portals, another for logon, and another for profile updates. Even if a different infrastructure is not chosen for the each of the application segments, categorizing and maintaining a pattern portfolio correctly is important in the grand scope of infrastructure planning.

To fully understand how to match new applications to existing infrastructure, refer to Infrastructure Pattern Matching in Chapter 5.

## Creating an Infrastructure Portfolio

The idea of an infrastructure portfolio is similar to the way people keep blueprints on file so that the layout of all the electrical systems in a large building might be reused for other cabling needs or just for troubleshooting. Likewise, it's vital to keep a portfolio of patterns that your company will use, once you've identified them. This application-centric, infrastructure pattern portfolio lists all the components in each pattern, so that infrastructure planners can identify all the pieces are when it is time to reuse the pattern. As the pattern changes, they can go to the portfolio and easily update it.

It is not just for patterns that you should maintain a portfolio, but also for platforms, services, projects, processes, and personnel. This section discusses creating and maintaining an application infrastructure portfolio, which could also be called a pattern portfolio.

### What's in the Portfolio?

In Figure 3.14, you see the major infrastructure portfolios, with the pattern portfolio structure broken out.

A portfolio is composed of four parts:

- Standards. This part of the portfolio defines the standards that control both the external and internal structure of the class of entities stored in the portfolio. This part includes:
  - use case matches, specific who/what/where, and additional descriptive differentiators

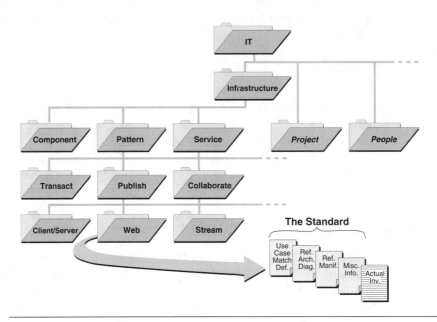

**Figure 3.14** Creating Pattern Portfolios

- a reference architecture diagram, which is a refined version of the pattern thumbnail diagrams in this chapter

- a reference list/manifest of required components or services

■ Historical information. This part includes miscellaneous metrics, postmortems, anecdotal information, lessons learned.

■ Inventory template. You can use a spreadsheet template or database schema to capture information about each application or instance of the pattern. Documentation stored in the portfolio explains the meaning of the fields/attributes.

■ Actual inventory. This part is the collection of pattern instances (i.e., applications). Your inventory should show examples of real cases where the infrastructure is actually used in your organization.

## A Template for Standards

The pattern standard structure includes a template that you can use to describe the nine basic patterns above. For each of the patterns that you have identified in your organization, fill in a template such as the one shown in Table 3.1.

**Table 3.1** Pattern Data Required

| Section | Purpose |
|---|---|
| Pattern Name | The name of this pattern, such as "Web Publish" |
| Description | Brief description of the overall function of the pattern |
| Owner | Name and contact information for the overall owner of the pattern |
| Use Case Match Definition | What/who/where information, plus the service level information below |
| What | Types of business processes suited to this pattern |
| Who | User roles (e.g., employee salesperson, customer prospect) |
| Where | User locations in terms of both geography and network subdivisions (e.g., North American HQ, European Regional Office) |
| Service Levels | Requirements that demand this pattern, and requirements that CANNOT be met by this pattern |
| Conceptual "Reference" Architecture Diagram | A diagram of the technology level only with no products (see pattern diagrams earlier in this chapter) |
| Reference Component Manifest | The list of Platform Components and Services that should be used in implementing the conceptual architecture. For each component, include the current standards, any standards considered obsolete, and any proposed future standards (both immediate and potentially long-term). |
| Miscellaneous Information | Common examples (which may not be implemented in your organization) |
| | Assessment of the popularity of or interest in the pattern in the market |
| | Overall assessment of the maturity of pattern best practices in the market, including descriptions of best practices and worst practices |
| | Key areas of business and technology volatility (e.g., business changes parts suppliers frequently; app server tech is rapidly evolving) |
| | Internal processes, roles, skills |
| | Strategy for change (Short, Medium, Long) |
| | Practical experience with the pattern, post-mortems, enterprise architecture principal linkages, operational process linkages |

### Putting Applications into the Infrastructure Pattern Portfolio

Once you have documented the patterns and opened files under their names, you should catalog existing applications and put them into the correct files. The following path makes performing this task easier.

As discussed before, an application may often be composed of several patterns. To be able to decompose the application, you must first break down application-related business processes into use cases.

1. Inventory major and most common applications into rough "pattern" groups.

    Divide complex applications such as ERP suites into major use case categories based on who, what, where.

    - Match application use cases with patterns.

    - Focus on essential use case and component variations.

    - Capture description.

    - Capture distinguishing service levels.

    - Create new sub-patterns when two sets of applications in a given pattern have sufficiently distinct service levels.

    - A 2-Tier Transact pattern could be divided into 2-Tier Transact Fat Client and 2-Tier Transact Winframe Client.

    - The service levels for the former might be "only employees in HQ" but for the latter it might be "employees anywhere connected."

2. Merge use cases that turn out to have no significant differences in service levels.

3. Analyze results and update draft pattern definitions.

4. Add other descriptive information, conceptual reference architecture.

5. Refine the inventory.

6. Capture all component details, standardize terms, capture component de facto standards, and explain deviations.

7. Recommendation.

8. Fill in de facto and current (exit, maintain, use today, and use in the future) standards for component manifest.

The level of refinement one can undertake with an application-centric infrastructure pattern portfolio is limitless.

## Summary

Creating and developing a basic set of infrastructure patterns will help your organization actually plan or manage a more adaptive infrastructure. Infrastructure patterns deal with business change from the bottom up. Instead of trying to deal with all possible infrastructure variability, the patterns place some boundaries on that variability and give infrastructure developers a framework with which to approach the business. They take hundreds of different application demands and structure them into a fewer than 10 common cases. Then they direct planning skill, plus effort and time, to this smaller set of general goals. Of course, actual implementations will modify these pattern standards to some degree, but in general, using pattern blueprints to govern per application design and implementation activities advances the goal of standardization.

If your organization maintains an enterprise architecture development function (and it should!), the starter set of infrastructure patterns also serves as a reference point for architects and infrastructure developers or planners. The patterns that you choose for your enterprise describe the work to be done in constructing an infrastructure and the systems that need to be created.

On a more tangible level, a good set of infrastructure patterns will help infrastructure developers be active, instead of reactive, in addressing business needs and problems. For example, in many organizations using major ERP or CRM application suites, developing patterns and other pieces of adaptive infrastructure represent an effort to prepare for engaging the business earlier in the change process. They provide a device to enable leverage of experience in planning and building and running real applications on real infrastructure across a larger set of increasingly demanding business conditions and new applications.

Most organizations will have many of these patterns already implemented and integrated into their infrastructure. Your organization may not need to implement every pattern listed above, and you may choose to create new ones. A new business proposal could result in a debate over patterns, but once the concept of patterns is in place, this debate can be lively and beneficial as opposed to fruitless and circular.

The infrastructure patterns are a key component of the adaptive infrastructure approach, as they figure in the infrastructure pattern matching, predictive infrastructure cost modeling, and infrastructure impact assessment exercises that are detailed in the last chapter of this book. They should prove useful in structuring the understanding of other IT groups when doing infrastructure planning. If application developers, architects, operations, and others all understand the basic patterns, discussions between those groups can use a much more commonly understood terminology. Patterns are uniquely suited to simplifying the traditional dialog around lots and lots of components that just have been hard to map easily to applications.

Finally, the patterns should also be used as reference points within an overall IT-to-business discussion, where infrastructure development should be addressed. These infrastructure development decisions are going to be some of the most important that occur within IT during the next few years.

# Chapter 4

# Developing Adaptive Services

By now, you understand the first two building blocks of adaptive infrastructure. You know how to catalog all the *components* into layers that make up a basic technology platform. You also understand how to group these components into common patterns, such as 3/N-Tier Transact, Web Publish, and others.

While these first steps are significant, they still aren't the entire solution. The next part of adaptive infrastructure strategy hinges on the way that you define *services*. Having reusable services that applications can share efficiently is the key element that will make your infrastructure more adaptive and agile. A large part of your effort, then, will be spent defining and designing shared infrastructure services that will make it easier and cheaper to design, develop, and deploy business-centric applications.

You still need to understand many things before you can start developing your own portfolio of adaptive infrastructure services. You need to answer such questions as:

- When is infrastructure a service? What's the difference between patterns and services?

- How do you define appropriate service boundaries?

- How do you create an information portfolio centered on services?

The answer to these questions will help you take some of the final steps toward your goal of a fully adaptive infrastructure.

## Understanding Adaptive Services

To better understand the concept of adaptive services, recall the original discussion of infrastructure earlier in this book. The traditional view of infrastructure is that it is something purely physical, such as the roads and bridges that support our transportation system or the cables, switches, and routers that support our networks. Instead of thinking in terms of physical hardware, however, some of the most crucial components of infrastructure should actually be considered *services*, such as water, electricity, gas, and phone. Figure 4.1 shows the thinking behind this process.

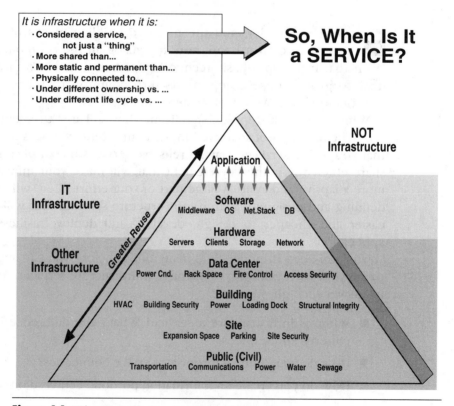

**Figure 4.1** When Is Infrastructure a Service?

Services are distinguished from physical infrastructure by several important features. They are:

- Shared by the structures they support
- More static and permanent than the structures they support
- Under different ownership, with their own distinct lifecycles (plan, build, run, change, exit)

The same criteria apply when you look at adaptive infrastructure services. To be successful, adaptive infrastructure services must provide:

- Sharing. An adaptive infrastructure service is one that is shared by multiple applications. If it's not shared, it still can be considered infrastructure, but it won't be a service.
- Stability. An adaptive infrastructure service should be more stable, more permanent, and less likely to change than the applications it supports.
- Separate ownership and lifecycle. An adaptive infrastructure service is distinct from the structure it supports in terms of its ownership. In this case, the application developers don't own the service. Instead, the infrastructure developers own it and have responsibility for the lifecycle of creating it, improving it, and connecting new applications to it. As a service matures, operations support plays a bigger role, as well.

Adaptive infrastructure services differ from traditional infrastructure services in important ways. First, they allow you to change the implementation of one side of the service interface, without affecting the other side in any way, other than to improve service levels or decrease costs. Second, an adaptive infrastructure service is much more likely to be used by more than one application.

## Benefits of Adaptive Infrastructure Services

The services approach to adaptive infrastructure produces a number of key benefits:

- Reduced complexity. The more you transform yourself to a service-based architecture, the fewer raw components you need to organize to deliver applications. Soon, you will link only a few services together. Thus, you might build an N-Tier application from something like six services, instead of 40 components. That kind of modularity automatically brings with it newfound efficiencies and incredible cost savings.

■ Performance improvements. Defining infrastructure as a set of services helps you keep control of the type of service levels you are providing to the rest of the organization. If designed correctly, you can gradually improve performance for your customers by making sure that service levels are always more than adequate to ensure smooth running of applications.

■ Increased agility. Through more effective use of the API layer, you can decouple important services from the application, freeing each application from the burden of supporting the service itself. This makes it much quicker and easier to design, develop, and deploy mission-critical applications. Instead of having each application perform its own user authentication, for example, that function can be provided by an Identity Infrastructure service, as described in Chapter 5.

## Examples of Shared Infrastructure Services

The best example of an adaptive infrastructure service is the network itself. For many years, the network has been owned and operated separately from applications and other IT-controlled areas. Its lifecycle also has been separate because you could upgrade the network without fundamentally changing the applications that depend on it. Moreover, most IT organizations have created a single image approach to the network, with a single interface for applications.

Not too long ago, many applications were tied to a specific networking protocol, such as IBM's SNA or Novell's Internet packet exchange (IPX) or sequenced packet exchange (SPX). Now, all leading-edge applications assume a TCP/IP-based infrastructure. Decoupling the application from the network has allowed the network to truly function as a service, supporting the needs of a particular application instead of being defined by it. Instead of having to support multiple network protocols, organizations now need to support only one: TCP/IP.

Another shared infrastructure service that many organizations have implemented successfully is credit card verification. By using such a service, any new application that needs the service suddenly becomes easier, faster, and cheaper to develop. You just link the application to the service, freeing application developers from the need to include it in their designs.

If your organization changes the provider of verification services, all applications benefit immediately without having to be modified. The downside is that if the shared service stops executing for some reason, it affects *all* the applications that depend on it. Thus, success depends on how competent the service provider is at running the service, as well as managing upgrades transparently and incrementally.

A final example of a shared service is Identity Infrastructure. Instead of having each application independently solve its problem with user authentication, forward-looking organizations are separating out the entire authentication process, and the infrastructure components it relies on, as a common infrastructure service shared by all applications.

The problem with a new service like this is getting applications to use it once it is developed. Unlike the network example, the easy transparency for applications is not as clearly defined for the security infrastructure. As it matures, the service approach to security infrastructure will become more standardized, but retrofitting existing applications to use such a service will take time.

Chapter 5 will review the goals, benefits, and methods involved in developing an Identity Infrastructure service. It will also explain how to go about creating another increasingly common shared service, a Transactional Integration service, which provides a common way of connecting widely disparate applications.

## The Difference Between Patterns and Services

One of the major conceptual leaps in adaptive infrastructure strategy is shifting from the idea of developing patterns to the idea of developing services. When creating an adaptive infrastructure, you don't really build a pattern. Instead, the pattern becomes a conceptual blueprint that you duplicate when building infrastructure for applications.

Taking a pattern approach alone, without the benefit of a services approach, can lead to the age-old problem of "stovepipes." If you work only with patterns, you can implement the same blueprint many times, like a subdivision with a basic set of 10 home designs. You will have similar infrastructure, which is a benefit, but you will miss significant levels of reuse. For example, you might identify a 3/N-Tier Transact pattern but still have a series of 3/N-Tier applications that are built on separate instances of Windows 2000/.NET Server, SQL Server 2000, or even on distinct unconnected LANs, with no data or process sharing.

In contrast, services are something that you must actively identify, design, build, and implement (see Table 4.1). Ideally, you will build a

**Table 4.1** Comparing Patterns to Services

| Pattern | Service |
|---|---|
| A model of what is common to a class of "business apps" | An actual "IT app" that is used in common by a class of "business apps" |
| Matches business-driven requirements to a blueprint of services and components | Matches IT-driven requirements to the specification of an actual service |
| End-to-end infrastructure | Function-specific infrastructure |
| Minimizes variations in components | Maximizes adaptability, sharing, integration, consolidation |
| Per application funding model | Shared funding model |

single physical instance of a service that many—and hopefully all—applications can share.

Only in rare cases does a service come close to implementing a complete pattern. For example, in some organizations Web hosting is a service implementation of the Web Publish pattern.

The benefits of a service approach are clear. With a pattern approach, you might have to pull together dozens of components to make an end-to-end solution. With a service-based architecture, however, all you have to do is link together a few services. This modularity automatically produces incredible efficiency and cost savings.

It's important to be realistic about what you can accomplish, however. Having dozens of services would be far too complex. Instead, you must focus on the most important ones that are the hallmark of your infrastructure design: the few that you have mapped into patterns, which can be reused by almost everything. By limiting the number of service options, you drastically reduce the complexity of the application, plus you'll actually build some instead of just having them defined on paper.

## How To Develop Services

Different organizations take different approaches to the issue of defining adaptive services. The purpose of this book is to identify some relative definitions, because no absolute definition can state exactly what infrastructure is or what shared infrastructure services are. In fact, almost anything can be a service, including many non-automated operations, which involve no physical infrastructure at all, only business processes performed by people. Physical strata components in the network, storage, and server layers are obviously considered infrastructure, and the decision on sharing these components should go along with the software decisions. With this in mind, you can start looking at what's involved in developing adaptive infrastructure services.

## Shifting Services to the Infrastructure

The most important work in developing an adaptive infrastructure is to make sure that key services with a potential for sharing are shifted out of the application layer and into the infrastructure layer, where they can be more efficiently shared and reused. This process requires a thorough analysis to determine what software is infrastructure and what software is the application.

As key services are identified and moved into the infrastructure layer, they must fit the definition of infrastructure, in terms of permanence, ownership, and lifecycle, or they will be unsuccessful in their role as shared infrastructure services. If successful, they will become more adaptive, manageable, and reusable, saving your organization considerable amounts of money and time, and creating agility in the process.

This is the biggest challenge you will face when developing an adaptive infrastructure. The reason lies in ownership and lifecycle: the way that adaptive infrastructure services shift responsibility out of the application domain and into the infrastructure domain.

You aren't just shifting the physical technology or code; you are reassigning the responsibility for designing it, building it, employing it, maintaining it, and upgrading it. Everything, including technology, people, and profits, must come over the line, as shown in Figure 4.2. Naturally, this tactic will require political as well as promotional skills, as discussed in the closing chapters of this book.

## Decoupling the Lifecycles

One of the greatest advantages of adaptive infrastructure is the ability to change a service without having to change all the applications that depend on it. Conversely, the greatest inhibitor to adaptive infrastructure can be an inability to do this—a tangling of the application functionality and the service functionality so that changes in service functions have unforeseen repercussions in the applications themselves. In theory, you should be able to change your databases, servers, or the network without affecting the applications that depend on them.

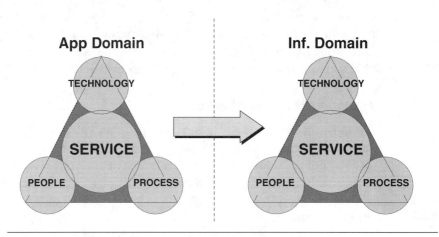

**Figure 4.2** Shifting Service Into the Infrastructure

To get the desired level of independence requires a high degree of *decoupling* between the lifecycles of both the service and the application, at all stages in the lifecycles, including design, build, deploy, and upgrade.

When doing so, you want to make sure you decouple the right pieces, specifically service elements that can be shared by the widest possible audience. When you look at all the pieces of an application, you must ask yourself: What part is the application and what part is the infrastructure?

The idea of sharing and reusability is crucial when developing adaptive infrastructure services. If you remove an infrastructure service from an application, but only that application uses the service, what have you gained? Not much. The idea is to draw out common elements that many applications need to use. That is what makes the difference between a stovepipe infrastructure, with one hardware server per application, and a shared adaptive infrastructure service, where multiple applications access services that run on a single server.

The elegance of your solution depends on how well you can operate the infrastructure below the service interface—if you can't upgrade it transparently and incrementally, problems will become very apparent. However, it also depends on how you design the interfaces between the application and the service provider. Luckily, the TCP/IP stack, which is the interface between applications and the network, has been fairly stable over the past decade and can serve as a model for solving this problem.

The fundamental difference between a component or object-oriented architecture and a service-oriented architecture is that the interface to a service and the implementation of the service must be physically separated by a "network." Although traditional object-oriented and component architectures always stressed the importance of logical separation between interface and implementation, having an interface-enabling component physically embedded in the application required rebuilding, recompiling, or re-linking the application each time you wanted to change the component implementation—which effectively prevented it from ever being changed.

Dynamic link libraries (DLLs) lessened the rebuilding issue to some degree, but since the DLL was still physically incorporated in the computer containing the application, the owner of the computer still had to retain control over changes to the DLLs, such as installing new ones.

## A Decoupled Web Services Architecture

The decoupled approach can be seen in the recent proliferation of "Web services" architectures. Here is how the interface embedded in the consuming application adheres to the "low coupling" requirements of an ideal adaptive infrastructure service:

**Minimal:** The interface hard codes Simple Object Access Protocol (SOAP) over HTTP. This method involves very simple protocols, with minimal non-complex coding requirements.

**Standard/Stable:** HTTP provides a standard and very stable interface. XML will be a widespread standard, while SOAP is also a standard and increasingly stable interface. Universal Description, Discovery, and Integration (UDDI) publish/find/bind will be a standard and is just beginning to become stable.

**Bootstrap Capability:** UDDI's find/bind mechanism and the Web Services Description Language (WSDL) could be used to bootstrap a more complex interface than SOAP for the actual interaction with the service.

Thus, an architecture that most effectively separates control between the use of a service and the implementation of a system is one that physically separates the two over a "network" of some kind. The network should be shared in the sense that it enables the service provider to be physically decoupled from the service consumer so that the service provider never (or rarely) needs to come "on site" to change any aspect of the service. Accordingly, the interface to the service, the physical component that connects the consumer and provider, should be kept as clean and simple as possible.

For example, a wireless connection for television or phone is the most minimal. The adapter and transceiver is on the premises, but there is no wiring. All you need is electricity (or batteries) for a cell phone. It has no plug for the service, unlike landlines and cable TV service, which you must physically plug in.

Consider a more IT-centric example: a managed network service provider installing its own router on the premises. The managed service provider does not let the customer modify his or her on-premises equipment; in fact, doing so typically voids the contract for service levels. Sometimes, such on-premises equipment is locked in a closet or box that only the provider can access. Even here, however, a clear interface or demarcation line, such as an Ethernet port or serial cable, allows customer equipment to plug into the service.

In both cases, the on-premises part of the service has been architected to be as simple as possible. In general, the interface to the service that is embedded in the consumer side should be as minimal, as standard (not customized), and as stable as possible. Any change to the interface should not require the rebuilding or retesting of the application in which the interface is embedded. In a sense, the embedded, hard-coded part of the interface should be a "bootstrap interface." It should have just enough intelligence to plug into a network, access some kind of "full interface" service, perhaps download a more robust interface, and go from there. Everything about the interface should be as dynamic and run-time configurable as possible.

## Potential Ripple Effects

The inability to decouple applications from services can have a wide range of potential ripple effects, if any change is made on the provider side (the service itself) or the consumer side (the user of the service).

In theory, the way the interface is linked to the application doesn't really matter, but in practice it can be very important. For example, if the service provider's service is a static, run-time library, and the group that designed and owns it goes out of business, you may have to migrate (or redesign) your applications in order to free yourself from the service, which can have a major impact.

Another example is if you simply change the implementation of the run-time library. This situation sounds less radical because you don't touch the interface: You just change the interface to make it faster, better, or cheaper. At the very least, however, you will have to re-link it to the application. And many organizations will not let you take an application that is currently running and re-link it unless you also retest and re-deploy everything, then restart the application.

When you have an interface change to something that is embedded in an application, the change should not require you to rebuild or retest the application. Changes that require retesting or rebuilding can have a major impact on the organization. What if you had to retest an entire application every time someone made a service upgrade on the network? You would never get anything done! Instead, network upgrades are transparent. That level of decoupling is needed for other kinds of services that you create as part of your adaptive infrastructure.

## The Role of APIs

Decoupling is aided by the API Layer identified in Chapter 2, where the following points were introduced:

- Infra-APIs make certain low-level services available to developers, such as security, naming, transactional integration, and other Web service invocation. While some prepackaged Infra-APIs are already available, infrastructure developers could be forced to create many of these APIs themselves and provide them to application developers for use in connecting applications to adaptive infrastructure services.

- Inter-APIs contain shared business logic that will be reused by multiple applications. Thus, they also should be defined and managed by infrastructure developers.

- Intra-APIs are used only within the context of individual applications. For this reason, they are best created and managed by application developers.

Notice that the first two types of APIs are specifically developed and maintained by the infrastructure team for use by application developers.

The third type of API is used only within applications by the application developers themselves. Figure 4.3 shows how the API layer architecture works in practice.

## Service Interfaces and Service Level Agreements

Once you decouple services from the application and create APIs, what remains in the application is a *service interface*, shown in Figure 4.4. This interface is more than just an API issue; it is also a contractual issue. Service interfaces involve political and process control boundaries. All of the issues surrounding the delegation of authority manifest themselves when a service interface is created or modified. Questions arise as to who owns and is responsible for this particular function. Many of these issues are addressed in the closing chapters of this book.

Creating a service interface, however, lets you have more control over the *service levels* that you can deliver to the organization. Defining service levels on a per-project basis will help make sure that your infrastructure can provide the quality, speed, and scalability demanded by the business for each deployed application. Likewise, these definitions

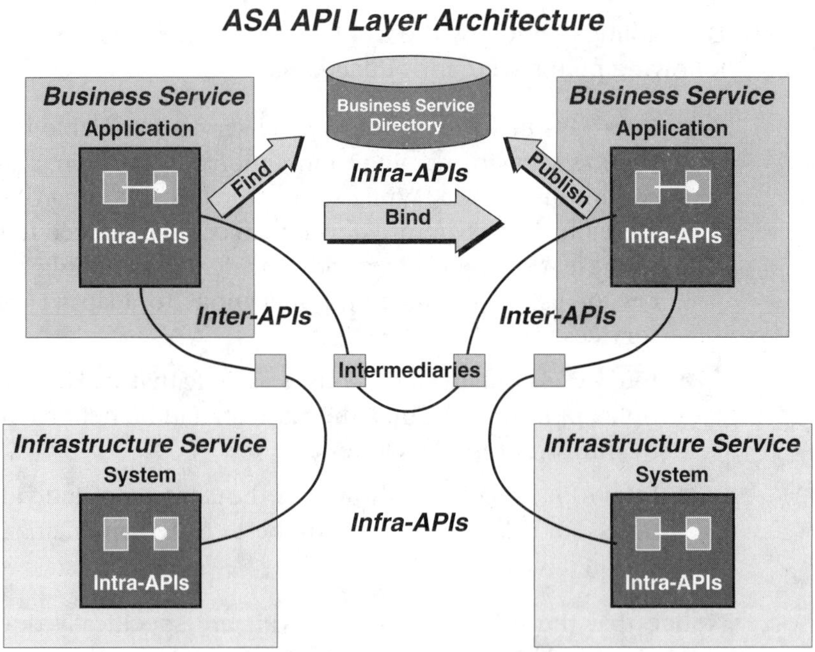

**Figure 4.3** API Layer Architecture

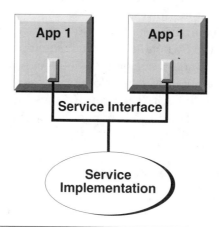

**Figure 4.4** The Service Interface

will help you better understand and communicate the limits of your infrastructure so that application developers, other IT personnel, and even the business are less likely to deploy applications that will overload the system.

The emerging model for this relationship is a contract between the consumers and providers of adaptive infrastructure services that specifies certain "service level attributes" governing its speed or capacity. One part of the contract spells out the functions and information provided under the agreement (the process model), while the other part of the contract spells out the promised performance terms (the service levels).

An example of this in the everyday world is the way a consumer interacts with a vending machine:

1. The vending machine offers a list of sodas available and their prices.
2. The consumer offers payment by inserting a dollar bill.
3. The consumer selects a brand of soda by pushing a button.
4. The consumer receives the soda by taking it from the bin in the machine.

These steps are part of the service contract between the consumer and the service provider, which is the vending machine. The service level attributes, on the other hand, would specify performance metrics, such as the response time between a button press and the soda appearing in the bin.

Once you have established the service contract, the next step is to establish the owner. Even though some part of the business might need a service, if no owner provides budget funding and support, it is never going to work. You can't simply propagate a paper standard and hope everyone follows it. The standard must be centralized by ownership. A more detailed discussion of people and funding issues is included in the final chapters of this book.

## Where to Create Service Boundaries

The essence of infrastructure adaptiveness is to foresee which parts will need the ability to change independently. To do this, look for high rates of change in:

- Component technologies (e.g., server and storage hardware)
- Supply process and suppliers
- Network and middleware
- Policy and implementation
- Service name and location

Knowing what to externalize is the fundamental skill required for adaptive infrastructure. Business, application development, and infrastructure planning teams must work toward adaptiveness and they all must agree on what processes, people, and technologies are involved. Interfaces should be loosely coupled. Proper decoupling among layers enables not only changeability, but also scalability.

For example, in Figure 4.5 and Figure 4.6, moving Step 302 out of the application and into the infrastructure requires that a service interface replace the deleted step. The application developer responsible for the implementation of Step 302 is now simply responsible for invoking the interface to the service, which must still be embedded in the application. For adaptive infrastructure services to work, you must minimize the amount of embedded interface code and maximize the use of stable standards.

Services are difficult because you can have an infinite number of them, with an infinite number of APIs to be consumed. Clearly, that kind of situation cannot be supported. Therefore, keep the number of services (and APIs) as low as possible.

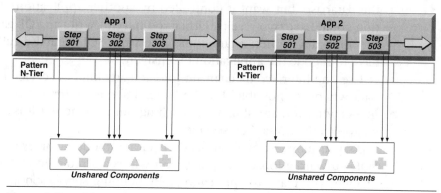

**Figure 4.5** Defining Service Boundaries (Before)

One of the hallmarks of great service design is the ability to narrow down your list of service options to a few major choices. For example, ask yourself, "What are the five things I absolutely have to provide?" Then, focus on the upper and lower ends of those requirements. Furthermore, focus on what can be accomplished realistically in the near term versus the medium or long term. Designing a service that is impossible to build or run is not worth the trouble. The result is a list of services from which you know you will see customers repeatedly obtaining real value.

Another pitfall to avoid is using too many different interface standards. For example, suppose you have an application with hard-coded Structured Query Language (SQL) calls embedded in it. What happens if

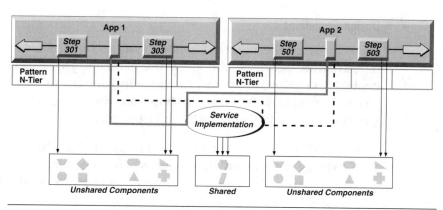

**Figure 4.6** Defining Service Boundaries (After)

the client decides they no longer want customer information directly in the database, but want it controlled by another application? This situation could have two results: Either you have to write an SQL gateway for the application, then retarget and retest the SQL database calls, or you have to recode the application extensively.

Use one interface mechanism to reach any kind of service process or data whenever possible. Build a general service interface up front that masks what you are ultimately reaching out to, whether it is a database, an application, or a Web service.

As you move from a hard-coded service model—for example, static SQL—toward a looser coupling, you will see a reduced impact for any changes you make to applications. By defining service boundaries, you avoid having to retest and recompile the application every time you make a change. All you have to do is restart the application. Sometimes, if you are just changing the implementation of a Web service you have provided, you can even have zero downtime for consumers.

If done correctly, you can completely decouple changes in a service implementation from other changes to the application. However, one thing that you do not want to change is the interface specification itself. If you change the consumer side of the interface or the provider's interface specification, you must then recode and recompile the application, at least to some degree.

Therefore, it is important to make sure you are choosing uses for corporate and interface standards that are very stable and are not going to change much. To avoid these problems, many organizations ensure that they own the interface (at least in internal cases), rather than relying on standard interface specifications.

## Design Guidelines

Now that you understand the concepts and techniques behind adaptive infrastructure services, the question naturally arises: "Where do I begin?" The following guidelines will help you start finding logical service opportunities, then turning those into real services that will move you closer to the goal of adaptive infrastructure:

■ Snapshot the current state. Conduct an inventory to portfolio existing services and determine where some services might prove useful. You will find a template for doing this on the following pages.

- Create interfaces. Put interfaces in place, including both APIs and people-process workflow handoffs, that better insulate the consumers of the service from implementation changes on the service provider side of the interface.

- Define service levels. Upgrade and expand the service provider side of the interface to improve service levels.

You must do a thorough job of assessing the current application inventory to get a good feel for the API issues. You need to understand both what standards are available and what calls are being made. You should also have a good record of what integration has occurred versus what services are implicitly fragmented and not factored well.

For example, you could potentially choose between hundreds of methods for conducting file transfers. If you find yourself in this position, you should seriously consider upgrading to a Transactional Integration service that handles bulk inter-process communication, not just single transactions.

Your inventory of integration applications should tell you how much opportunity you have for improvement. You could end up with a very clear map with a few well-defined interactions, or you could end up with a map that is extremely complex with no unifying threads at all.

Along with the functional interfaces defined in your interaction map above, you should also capture the use cases: How reliable is the current FTP service? How quickly can I change or add a new application into the FTP flow? What is the latency between generating a request and getting a response? Capture that, because you can use it to design the new unified transactional integration service and illustrate its values.

## How to Portfolio Existing Services

As part of your inventory process, you should develop a portfolio of existing services, including the different types of information listed in Table 4.2.

When collecting information on potential users of the service, be sure to capture all of the data listed here:

- App Name
- App Owner
- Scribe
- Integration Provenance
- Interface Use Case Match

**Table 4.2** Information to Be Collected for a Services Portfolio

| Information to be Collected | Description |
| --- | --- |
| Service Name | Name of the service |
| Description | Brief description of the overall function of the service |
| Owner | Overall owner of the service |
| Type of Service Consumer | The type of application or service that would use the associated service interface(s): application, application pattern, or other service |
| Service Levels | Explicitly define offered service levels, as well as service levels that are NOT being offered |
| Service Charge | Price of the service per consumer for both use and provisioning/on-boarding (price and time) |
| Interface/Process change authority | Person who has the authority to approve interface design and change it in the future. For example, small suppliers to a large manufacturer might find implicit in the service level agreement that the manufacturer can mandate a change to the interface with only limited advanced notice. |
| Use definition/description | The interactions between the consumer (actor) and the service (system under design). This information will often be highly service-dependent (e.g., the use description of a Transactional Integration Service interface might distinguish straight-through processing [STP] from reference information synchronization from broadcast). |
| Service Programming Interface (a.k.a. API or SPI) | Formats, protocols, bindings, or transports to be used by the service (e.g., function call vs. message buffer) |
| Conceptual Architecture | The architecture for the automated sub-processes of the service |
| Component Manifest | The list of platform components used in the conceptual architecture |
| Examples | Common examples |

**Table 4.2** Information to Be Collected for a Services Portfolio *(Continued)*

| Information to be Collected | Description |
| --- | --- |
| Potential Users | Assessment of the popularity of or interest in the service |
| Maturity | Overall assessment of the maturity of service best practices in the market |
| Best practices | Descriptions of best practices and worst practices |
| Internal processes, roles, skills | Details on business processes, roles, and skills |
| Change strategies | Strategies for change (near, medium, long term) |
| Volatility | Key areas of business and technology volatility |
| Case studies | Practical experience with the service, post-mortems, enterprise architecture principal linkages, operational process linkages |
| Provenance and hosting | See Pattern portfolio |

- Service Levels
- Use Definition
- API

Keep track of this information each time you create a new service and start taking requests for it. Service levels and use definition are particularly important. You should capture the expectations, even if you are certain you will offer only one level of service.

## How to Apply Services to New Applications

A complete discussion of two major services is provided in Chapter 5. Once you create a service, however, some art is still involved in applying the new service to new applications.

First, you must redefine patterns to use services where applicable. While not all implementations of a pattern may use the service, at least this redefinition gives people an idea when the service should be used. For example, you might insist that all Web Publish applications use the Identity Infrastructure Service, but not insist on this for other patterns.

You probably wouldn't welcome its use with all applications, but insisting on limited use for one pattern can help application developers get accustomed to it, thus increasing the chances that they might use it voluntarily on other patterns. Figure 4.7 illustrates services being applied to new applications.

Over time, some application patterns will increasingly evolve from component architectures, which involve a batch of components tied end-to-end into service architectures, with just a few key services invoked by application code that use infrastructure already deployed. As this happens, services will increasingly be used in the assimilation process and become like a component in application pattern inventory. When this happens, assimilating a new application becomes more a process of mapping onto a set of services via interfaces with service levels. The most evolved case of a pattern using services is the Web Publish pattern, which is almost entirely composed of just a few major services or provided by a single Web hosting service.

With this approach to services, a whole pattern can be easily outsourced. Web host service providers can do almost everything after you give them the HTML application code and data itself—everything except run your customer's browser. While these vendors have experienced significant viability issues due to recent fluctuations in their market value, they will increasingly price these services closer to their actual cost structure in order to stay in business. For e-Business needs, these types of services might be quite appropriate.

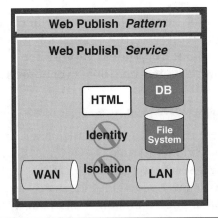

**Figure 4.7** Applying Services to New Applications

For internal needs, you could adopt a similar approach. Find any outsourcers offering any service you want to build, and then learn from them how to provide the service and how to charge for it.

If you run a Web hosting service internally, for example, you can adopt many of the same practices as Internet service providers and alter them as necessary. Later, if asked to benchmark your service against outside vendors, you'll find it easier to differentiate your service offering or compete with outside vendors. While competing with outside vendors sounds challenging, doing so will become an increasingly common requirement as the business requires more of IT. Furthermore, the mark of a truly mature infrastructure organization is to know when to utilize outside vendors, instead of competing with them.

The adaptive infrastructure services approach should help you excel under these conditions. By establishing a service-oriented approach, you have set yourself up to leverage such external services as much as possible. You must examine the outside world for precedents as you design your own internal services!

Over time, a service-focused approach helps make application development and infrastructure planning easier. When fully realized, a services approach makes it as simple as inserting the appropriate code and data into existing services, then flipping a switch to make it run.

Some operations controls will be needed to verify service level issues. For instance, does it break anything else running on the same infrastructure? (Remember the network case!) Design will be much simpler and it will still be possible to implement non-shared infrastructure for service-level issues, if necessary.

## Summary

In general, to best execute an adaptive infrastructure service, you should:

- Use the network as a guide in designing, applying, and pricing services.

- Be prepared to deal with the shift in power over the service from the application realm to the infrastructure realm.

- Keep accurate inventory of service users to gauge impact of service changes.

- Strive for loose coupling.

- Look to outsourcers for models and service suppliers.

# Chapter 5

# Services Starter Kit

To help you better understand the process and the value of building adaptive infrastructure services, this chapter lists a set of services many organizations use or are trying to build now. It also looks in more depth at two of the most common services that agile organizations are developing: Identity Infrastructure and Transactional Integration. To get a quick start in moving toward a service approach, you might consider borrowing heavily from these models.

## Identity Infrastructure

Identity infrastructure is a relatively simple concept. It is a way to provide a single service for user authentication that many different applications can use interchangeably. This approach implies having a single user attribute store, with simple authentication at a minimum and with hooks to enhanced authentication services as needed. In addition, the user attribute store will contain more information about each user than just a user name and password; it might also include a phone number, department name, or other information. All of this information must be managed, both by the individual user and by IT staff, as a support function. User administration tools are required for such an infrastructure service—otherwise the service will not work well.

The benefit of an Identity Infrastructure is that it helps minimize the widespread proliferation of user names and passwords. It also frees application developers from having to constantly grapple with the issue of user authentication. Instead, it provides a single unified approach to user authentication that can easily be reused by any application developer needing an authentication process.

An Identity Infrastructure offers many benefits to users, as well. For example, since it supports a single sign-on, users can traverse a set of Web or intranet sites without having to repeatedly enter different user names and passwords. Having a single logon that works for a wide range of sites helps cut down on help desk calls regarding forgotten passwords or password resets. It also avoids the problem of users pasting stick-on notes to their computer monitors with passwords written on them, which can pose a significant security risk.

When developing an Identity Infrastructure, it's important not to think of it as a cure-all or a panacea. The Identity Infrastructure will not solve every problem for the applications that are already built; just the ones you are planning to build in the future, and perhaps only a subset of those. In particular, this service will be especially useful in an e-Business context where security is particularly critical and complex. Over time, as applications and infrastructure realities change, the service could be expanded to service more requirements, but at first, it should be structured in a fairly narrow way to service only some applications and with specific service levels. As a general matter, the best practice is: "Show that you can make the service work, then think about extending it."

## Basic Components

The basic components of an Identity Infrastructure include:

■ Directory Service, for storing credentials. Example products include the iPlanet Directory Server, Microsoft Active Directory, Novell Directory Services.

■ Web Single Sign-on (SSO), for retargeting Web-based authentication calls to use directory service credentials. This component also helps manage authentication state using methods such as "cookies." Example products include Netegrity Siteminder. As the challenge becomes single sign-on across the Web sites of multiple organizations, other products will apply such as Microsoft Passport, which is an example of an outside party providing an infrastructure service.

■ Delegated Administration, a utility used to administer user authentication data. Typical products include Siteminder and iPlanet DS.

Some of these components should already be well defined in your component catalog. If not, you will need to add them.

Figure 5.1 shows a simple diagram of the required components and how they are separate from, yet connected to, the main application components. Components inside the circle are the core elements of the Identity Infrastructure.

In this model, Web servers can directly access a directory server, Web SSO middleware, and servers that identify authorized users via a simple user name/password logon. This middleware component might be adapted later to provide more advanced solutions, such as Public Key Infrastructure (PKI), with strong authentication via digital signatures. The directory server stores permissions, authorization or policy data, as well as other user attributes such as department name, phone number, and more.

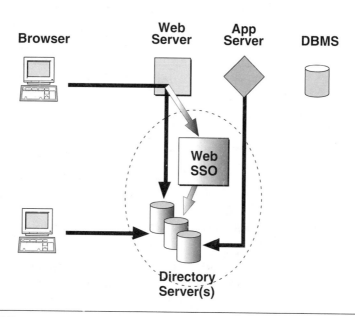

**Figure 5.1** Basic Components of an Identity Infrastructure

## Designing Service Transparency

A well-designed Identity Infrastructure service is totally transparent, both to the application developers and to the users, but especially to the application developers. For this group, transparency is accomplished by providing APIs that make it easy to connect to the service without having to incorporate the service itself into the actual coding of the application.

Separating applications via APIs not only enables you to externalize your data store and the authentication functions that go with it, it also makes it easier to change solutions without having to re-code applications. For instance, if your Web SSO today relies on Netscape and Netegrity, you could change it to Microsoft Active Directory and Netegrity tomorrow without affecting the functionality or integrity of the applications that use the service. Figure 5.2 shows API standards use in Identity Infrastructure.

As shown in Figure 5.2, the best practices for building an Identity Infrastructure leverages a number of important API standards:

■ Lightweight Directory Access Protocol (LDAP) for programmatic data access and API, and perhaps later, for server-to-server replication when the technology is more mature. Although LDAP is a standard protocol and API to access user authentication data across a network, many organizations hide low-level LDAP APIs in a higher-level API, using tools such as Visual Basic to help application developers be more comfortable.

*Note* | X.500 is an older technology being replaced by LDAP, which is actually based on the X.500 Directory Access Protocol (DAP) standards.

■ LDAP Data Interchange Format (LDIF) for bulk data load and transers.

■ Web HTTP header variables and authentication exits. Applications can exchange information included in the header fields of the HTTP protocol, which can serve as an API if properly documented. Web SSO products often use this method to automatically log users on to applications they support. In addition, Web servers make it easy to support LDAP or other authentication calls just by marking a page with access control information. The Web server will ask automatically for a user login to verify whether the current

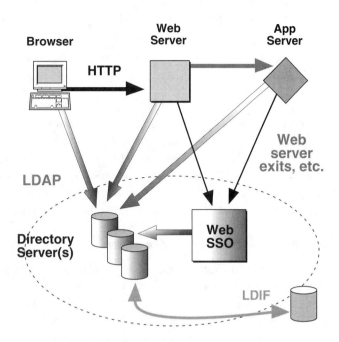

**Figure 5.2** API Standards Use in Identity Infrastructure

user is authorized to see that page. The Web SSO products then pass user credentials to the Web server, which services the application automatically (auto-logon). Using preset standard APIs, Web SSO products can perform authentication services without having to modify applications, and it can also transfer other information to an application in header variables. In actual practice, Web SSO products even hide most of the direct LDAP interaction an application might need—these can be passed to an application using Web SSO middleware.

■ Extensible Markup Language (XML), Universal Description, Discovery, and Integration (UDDI), Simple Object Access Protocol (SOAP), and Web Service Description Language (WSDL)—all have emerged as increasingly important interface standards over the past few years. This collection of API standards promises to enable Identity Infrastructure as a set of Web services that can easily be called on and accessed from any location, which makes it likely that portions of Identify Infrastructure will be offered by outside parties such as Microsoft and VeriSign.

- Microsoft Active Directory Services Interface (ADSI), a de facto, yet proprietary, vendor interface.

- General Security Service Application Programming Interface (GSSAPI), the most commonly used API for legacy application integration.

LDAP APIs supply most of the basic transparency for today's Identity Infrastructure services, along with Web SSO header methods and Web server authentication calls. Without these standardized APIs, Identity Infrastructure would be hard to implement for many applications. In fact, the lack of standardized APIs has kept applications from providing single credential (directory) and single sign-on for many years. Now, thanks to the Web revolution, we finally have some transparency to leverage.

## Selling Use and Reuse to Your Customers

A key benefit of developing adaptive infrastructure services is that you will have an easy way to provide value and to estimate the costs of supporting applications. This situation in turn makes it easier to get the funding you need to support the work required to develop the service.

When developing services, however, you must stay focused on what you will be selling to the users of that service. For example, people often say, "You can put anything in a directory." Yes, you can—but don't. Your directories should have only user data. You might be tempted to include application data, network device data, or asset management data. But you must keep it simple and build something you can actually deliver in a reasonable period of time. Otherwise, you could run into trouble delivering a useful service and just add complexity to the tasks that lie before you.

The main purpose of an Identity Infrastructure service should be to simplify user administration. If you want to sell this particular service, however, you might need to offer the ability for customers to manage their own data, not just on a personal level by allowing John to change John's attributes, but also on a departmental level by allowing the help desk or a departmental support person to change John's attributes, particularly for internal applications.

You also might want to allow lines of business to control their own employee data, but not anyone else's. The Human Resources department might need to control each employee's U.S. Social Security Number, preventing individuals from changing their own numbers without HR approval. Even if it's a centralized utility, you have to offer decentralized or distributed administration. Doing this was a problem for

Microsoft Windows NT initially—domains did not scale well in large organizations, and many third-party products arose to fill the gap.

## Keys to Success and Reusability

The key to success for any new service is to identify up front what realistic set of service levels and features you can successfully implement, and then promote *only* this predetermined package to potential users. Once you have a set of users paying for the initial service offering, you can focus on the next realistic steps to make this service actually reusable:

- Identify compatible patterns. Establish a close mapping of services into patterns. In this case, Web Publish will probably be the heaviest user of the Identity Infrastructure service. Other patterns might not be heavy users of the service at first. The service might be leveraged by some 3/N-Tier Transact or 2-Tier Transact patterns, but not necessarily. Initially, you should think this way: For which pattern is this service required rather than only recommended?

- Identify a champion. Identify the person who will take the time to make sure that the service is well known and understood by the development community. This evangelist must do the marketing.

- Market and sell. It's not a case of "build it and they will come." If your champion doesn't sell the service, you could build it and no one will ever use it. Use brown bag lunches and developer's conferences to promote the service. Giving the service adequate publicity will help make sure people know about it. The next time someone plans a new application, this service will be on the list of things to be included. The pattern mapping should also help because it will assist application developers in understanding the proven solutions that are available.

***Note*** | Marketing is an even bigger challenge for public versions of Identity Infrastructure, where Microsoft has to convince companies to use its Passport services and VeriSign has to market its public key infrastructure services.

## Determining Realistic Scale

One key in designing a reusable service is to pay close attention to scaling performance to higher service levels. With Identity Infrastructure, whole sets of issues revolve around how you offer scale within the service.

Scaling issues will be different, depending on whether you are using the service for internal applications to authenticate employees or for external applications to authenticate customers and partners. LDAP directories have limits on:

■ Traffic type (bind, single row, sets, sub-string search, write, etc.)

■ Proper ratio of read/write events (95/5)

■ Data latency induced by replication frequency (scheduled common)

Web SSO solutions have their own limits, as well.

When dealing with issues of scale, make sure you're using the service in the way it is intended. First, focus on cases where the level of write access is less than five percent. As soon as the writes go above that level, you should consider taking out some of the data or using a different pattern.

In such cases, the service is becoming too transactional and not static enough, and it will start overwhelming the ability of the service to function properly, given the use of read-oriented infrastructure components such as directory servers.

Be certain—very early in the design process—that you're putting mostly sharable, mostly read-only data into your directory. For example, something like a current bank balance is probably not appropriate to store, because it will change every day. Identifying whether a user is a "gold customer" could be a different case, since that status probably doesn't change every day.

Inappropriate uses of this service would be a real-time personalization data store (use DBMS instead), private key store, and storage of highly private Human Resources data. Use a relational DBMS only in the largest configurations.

To actually scale the Identity Infrastructure service, you must take advantage of the read-only, mostly static nature of the data and the capabilities of the directory server components. You *must* replicate to scale—both for availability and for performance.

As shown in Figure 5.3, replication supports having many copies of the same credential data available for applications, particularly when all the applications are centralized, as is common for e-Business and many intranets. Directory services are designed to handle this using built-in replication. Interestingly, most implementations can work well with simple replication solutions based on a master-slave concept, so the more often touted feature of multimaster replication might not be needed, at

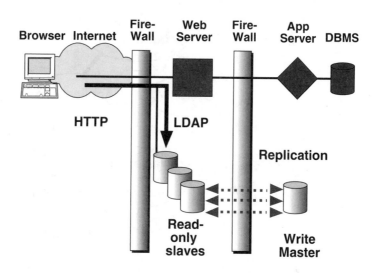

**Figure 5.3** Using Replication to Scale the Service

least initially. Over time, however, a five percent write activity will create a sheer load that may require multimaster capabilities.

There is much more to discuss on scale, but this one best practice is the heart of the issue for this type of service. The final design of an Identity Infrastructure service must address scaling the Web SSO solution using some run code on each Web server, yet still have centralized components that must be carefully planned. The design must also address other important issues, such as storage, networking, firewall integration, and more.

## Policing the Directory Schema

Once you put a service together, it's difficult to change it on the fly. User directories are often based on customer records and employee records, and you may end up fighting battles over those issues. Figure 5.4 shows some of the user dependencies involved in an Identity Infrastructure service.

Since a standard schema doesn't apply here, the role of a "directory schema police" should be centralized in your organization, not distributed. In Windows 2000 Active Directory environments, for example, those who design and police the directory schema should have authority at the forest level (above the domain level). And, make sure you always design for the entire organization, even if you adopt independent

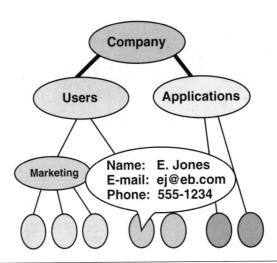

**Figure 5.4** User Data Dependencies

instances of a particular server platform. The same schema everywhere, even if managed and deployed separately, will allow for easier consolidation or integration later.

On the other hand, you might have a completely different schema for external customers. Don't be surprised if you have to use completely different trees in your directory, with two separate file structures or two completely different products.

As with all services, ownership is an important issue. Be very clear about what the attributes are, who owns them, and who is responsible for maintaining them. In the end, if you ever want to integrate directories, having a well-designed, well-policed schema will make this easier.

## Avoiding Scope Creep

You can do many things with an Identify Infrastructure, but at some point you must do a rigorous cost/benefit analysis to determine the most desirable options.

Some people might think that cost is no object. However, some features can be quite costly, so it's important to be realistic about the functional services you will offer. Even if you want an Identity Infrastructure that focuses on every application, you could find in some cases that the costs outweigh the benefits.

An incremental approach often works better than trying to create an Identify Infrastructure project that attempts to solve every problem.

Certain features can be valuable for a specific set of Web applications your organization is planning. Later, you might want to apply the Identity Infrastructure to your entire network operating system. The idea is to become very focused on what your specific use cases are for this service. Since everyone will assume that your service offers everything they want it to do, you should be clear in telling them what it actually does and what its limitations are.

It's like scope creep on a consulting job or when you're trying to get a contractor to build your house. You ask for more features and the contractor says, "No, that isn't included in the scope of the job," or "We can do it if you give us more time and money."

If you really want to build services, you have to be very concrete about the service's functional features and the use cases they actually support, and stick to that concrete definition.

For Identity Infrastructure, stick to simple Web-only services for the first year or two. If you are successful with this, add more. But don't promise more than you can deliver, and be very concrete and realistic about what you can achieve.

## Transactional Integration

Transactional Integration is another high-value adaptive infrastructure service you might want to consider as part of your Starter Kit. Many organizations call this Enterprise Application Integration (EAI) when used internally, or Inter-Enterprise Integration (IEI) when it supports outside business partners rather than just internal needs. Eventually, Transactional Integration will become a subset of Web services offered through application servers such as BEA WebLogic and IBM WebSphere or frameworks such as Microsoft Windows 2000/.NET Server, although some aspects of traditional EAI and IEI solutions will probably remain.

Transactional Integration fits the classic definition of an adaptive infrastructure service. From an application point of view, it lets you transfer business data to or from other applications in a common manner, while making transparent the locations, formats, protocols, and other components that are part of the service. From an infrastructure point of view, it provides a common set of technologies and a unified management facility that forms the foundation for all communication of business events between applications.

Another way to view it is as a set of technology services, typically built using the following components.

The list of technologies used to build a Transactional Integration service can take different forms with various levels of sophistication and complexity, depending on a number of factors, such as the nature of the business and how thoroughly processes will be integrated. To keep this set of best practices simple, we will not consider adding semantics and workflow to support durable transactions across multiple applications.

In general, the best practice technology solution is based on a hub-and-spoke architecture, as shown in Figure 5.5. The message broker hub is a centralized location where you can easily control all the complex formatting, routing, and higher-level functional configurations. Existing application integration solutions are difficult to maintain because they were designed one application connection at a time, resulting in a huge variety of code and internal processes that no single individual in IT can accurately map. When something in this system breaks, the problem can be very difficult to trace and the symptoms often show up all over the place. A centralized approach provides a much more stable and maintainable solution.

When you examine the features shown in Figure 5.5 and Table 5.1, you start to see a pattern emerging. Transactional Integration follows the classic model of an adaptive infrastructure service by moving highly complex functionality out of the application layer and into the infra-

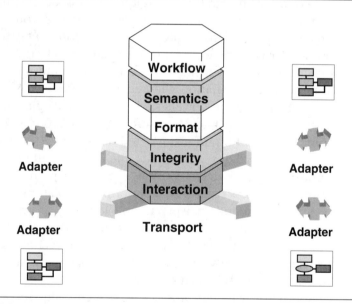

**Figure 5.5** The EAI Stack

**Table 5.1** Components of a Transactional Integration Service

| Component | Purpose | Benefit |
| --- | --- | --- |
| Adapter | Provides application interfaces to send/receive business events (i.e., place/change/cancel order) | Applications don't need to know what APIs and/or protocols other applications use |
| Transport | Moves business events around the network | Applications don't need to perform transport functions |
| Formatting | Transform business events from one application specific format to another | Applications don't need to know what format another application is using |
| Routing | Define which applications receive which events | Applications don't need to know where other applications are located or even which other applications need to get their data |

structure. Having a Transactional Integration service makes it easier for your organization to develop applications, because it relieves the applications of the burden of locating and talking to other applications. Transaction Integration service also creates a set of reusable code (or at least reusable access to that code) that can be shared between all applications, making application deployment and integration easier and quicker, and making your business more agile.

## Defining the Business Problem (Use Cases)

Whenever you start defining a new adaptive infrastructure service, you should first define the business problem by creating a carefully researched set of use cases. This process is where you can make or break the architecture. Your efforts could fail if you don't narrow down the scope and capture exactly the finite set of business processes, partners, and applications involved.

You cannot build a generic Transactional Integration infrastructure that allows you to plug anything into it for any reason. It sounds good in theory, but it can't be done. Instead, you must determine what processes are involved, who your internal or external partners are, and

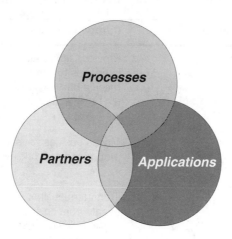

**Figure 5.6** Areas of Design Focus

what kind of applications you are dealing with, as illustrated in Figure 5.6. This focus makes all the difference in the world when it comes to how you build, what you build, the service levels you can provide, and how much it will cost. Exploring the three issues of processes, partners, and applications is the first step in planning the overall service. You should take this step even before you start thinking about the technology you will use. The three issues are discussed in more detail below.

### Processes

In terms of business processes, you need to understand who owns the processes and how much you can change them. You need to ask questions such as:

- What service levels are currently being offered?
- How many transactions are currently going through your FTP, batch file, or EDI infrastructure?
- If you want to replace your existing system with more message brokering and message queuing, what is the best way to achieve your goals?

You also need to look at regulatory requirements. For example, U.S. government regulations already require financial and healthcare institutions to encrypt all transactions on many networks.

Your use cases should be very specific. For example, a use case might say that if any application changes a customer name, address, or phone number, that change should apply universally across all applications.

Detailed use cases will help you identify design and service level issues, because each business process will have different request/response characteristics. So what the use cases are, and what the response time will be, depends on which business processes you're trying to integrate. For example, you might find that the acceptable round trip from a point-of-sale to a back-end system takes 11 seconds between the request and the response. When updating a customer record, however, this 11-second lag might be unacceptable from a business standpoint.

## Applications

Once you've nailed down your business processes and the scope of what you are trying to accomplish, you should examine the applications that you know are touched by and participate in the processes. An inventory approach can help.

If you have already captured the API level information for your applications, you will know what interfaces exist. For example, does the application support just the database APIs, such as ODBC or JDBC? What technical infrastructure does it run on: Windows 2000/.NET Server, mainframe, or UNIX? The answer will affect whether or not you can support the adapters on a particular platform.

Pay attention to the scale of the application itself, as well. Would it be possible to saturate this application with too many requests from other processes and bring it to a standstill? One organization, connecting its mainframe payroll system to a Web interface using a rudimentary EAI architecture, found that they were bringing the mainframe to its knees with month-end inquiries from 50,000 employees trying to find out how much their paychecks were going to be. These scenarios will help you determine how to scale appropriately.

## Partners

You need to look both inside and outside your organization and determine whose interests will prevail when the time comes to choose between standards. Partners with clout may insist that you adapt to their standards, rather than adapting to yours.

Keep in mind the expected duration of the business relationship, as well. If it takes six months to build the infrastructure, the problematic partner could be playing a different role by then. It will be a complex task to design each integration connection and the overall Transactional

Integration service that supports it. You don't want to do that for a partner who will only be around for five weeks. If you switch suppliers every six months, you don't want to spend six months plugging them into your infrastructure. So the weight of the interface will also be affected by the duration of the partner relationship.

All too often, the process of analyzing business requirements then determining appropriate solutions happens exactly backwards. Most people think first in terms of "Which tool will I buy?" Then they go back and do all the hard work of building use cases, trying to make their requirements fit the tool. Or they try to do things piecemeal as they go along. This is exactly backwards. You must get the use cases right, in sufficient detail, before looking at a list of products.

### Understanding the Costs

With all of your planning done, you can start looking at solution products and get a rough idea of costs. For Transactional Integration, as well as most other services, cost is an issue that you should address at initial meetings between the business, the application developers, and infrastructure team. Some rough costing metrics should be used, even given the extremely complex and volatile pricing environment for Transactional Integration. You will need to consider three types of costs when designing any infrastructure service, not just Transactional Integration.

| *Note* | These are good rules of thumb as of the publication date, but will change somewhat over time. |
| --- | --- |

#### Cost to Acquire

Look at the basic components that go into the Transactional Integration service (see Figure 5.5). For adapters, you can choose packaged solutions or you can leverage existing in-house conversion routines, at a cost ratio of about 5-to-1 for packaged versus in-house, assuming the in-house conversion routines already exist. Message brokers and business process automation software are available on the market. Messaging transport components are sometimes bundled, or sometimes included in the cost of the message broker, and they often follow a capacity-based pricing model.

Users can expect vendors to charge 50 percent of operational licensing costs for test and development instances of software. With this information in hand, you should count the number and types of applications, and do the arithmetic.

Most entry-level EAI projects initially integrate anywhere from three to five applications, with costs ranging from $100,000 to $700,000. This starter set of components can then become the foundation for much larger projects later. And of course, because it is an adaptive infrastructure service, the main benefit is that it will be reusable, meaning that it pays more to spend the money up front in order to get it right.

### Cost to Implement (People Costs)

Costs to implement your new service will typically run two to five times the software costs. The final price tag will be a function, primarily, of the quality of the interfaces in the existing applications. In other words, how difficult will it be to pry open the stovepipes and bolt in this new integration service?

If you have up-to-date applications that are designed for integration, with good XML-based interfaces, the cost will be somewhat less, in terms of the people and time required to do the interface plugs. If it's a total stovepipe, where you have to re-code applications or go in through the database level with database staging tables, the job will require a lot more developer time.

Again, if you've already done an application inventory and know what APIs you are working with, you can more quickly estimate software costs on a per-application basis. If you're creating business process automation on top of general integration services, your costs will be even more expensive.

### Cost to Change

Other costs will arise if you need to modify the core application, to open it up and create an API, which you may have to do in some cases. In terms of funding and who pays for it, try charging those costs back to the application owner, not to the infrastructure. Sometimes they're paying for mistakes made in the past, when they took shortcuts or created stovepipes. Now, they should be paying to create new APIs instead of the new service provider paying for them.

Naturally, your new Transactional Integration service costs more than conventional methods. The first-time charges are more than just building in the same old point-to-point file transfer, or whatever method you've been using. However, the true payback will be in reducing the cost to change. The cost of adding new applications will go down and deployment speed will rise, because the Transactional Integration infrastructure that you've created can be reused for each new application.

## Getting the Funds

You might be successful convincing the business to "pay more now for better infrastructure, so you will pay less later for new applications." But sometimes that doesn't work, so what other techniques might work? First, push for integration as part of a bigger initiative.

**ERP and supply chain initiatives.**   A big enterprise resource planning (ERP) or supply chain project, for example, might provide a good impetus for developing a Transactional Integration infrastructure. If the package will touch dozens of other applications, it makes sense to focus on integration and repeatability.

**e-Business architecture.**   Another good opportunity comes when you are building an e-Business architecture. Integrating a Web front-end with a complex back-end is a common situation where people find it pays to create a new Transactional Integration infrastructure.

**Mergers.**   Companies that do lots of mergers and acquisitions, such as banks and services companies, may be able to justify a Transactional Integration infrastructure based on the need to constantly integrate physical systems and data. This justification applies to divestitures as well.

**B2B initiatives.**   Some of the business-to-business (B2B) market initiatives demand easy integration between disparate systems.

**CRM initiatives.**   Developing customer relationship management (CRM) systems requires a unified view of customer data, which in turn demands some level of transactional integration to make it happen. One touch point from the customer can touch many applications.

## Calculating ROI

As always, when you ask business managers to spend money on a big infrastructure project, they want to know how quickly they can get a return on investment (ROI). First, make sure you know which ROI information should be supplied by which constituency—IT or the business—as indicated in Table 5.2. For Transactional Integration services, you should examine the following benefits.

**Table 5.2** Benefits to be Examined and Source of Cost Information

| Benefit Being Examined | Cost Evaluation Provided by |
| --- | --- |
| Doing integration in the first place | the business |
| Event vs. batch | the business |
| Decreased "time-to-change" | the business |
| "Brokered" versus "point-to-point" | IT |
| One vendor versus another | IT |

Vendor selection is listed last for a reason. Correct vendor selection lowers the risk associated with building a Transactional Integration service, but it *does not* guarantee success.

There is a value in comparing service levels. You should provide a value analysis, or you should work with the business to articulate it. In one sense, laying out a Transactional Integration infrastructure is just a different way of using familiar techniques, such as traditional EDI, file transfer, or batch processes. The value in doing things the new way is it is faster, better, and ultimately cheaper, which simplifies application development and speeds time-to-market.

With this new approach, much of the benefit comes from changing the value of the service level. Faster and cheaper, for instance, are actually service level metrics, so many value equations will center on the service level side of things. This is why it's so important to capture service level benefits and expectations in your use case analysis. Defining service levels happens during the initial negotiations—very early in your first discussions with the business. In terms of developing expectations, you should talk in terms of service levels provided, value and ROI, not which technology to use to make it happen.

## Alternatives and Trends

As mentioned earlier, this example was not intended to cover every potential variation of Transactional Integration, particularly not the semantics and workflow to support durable transactions across applications. Consider leveraging publish-and-subscribe middleware, such as Tibco products, in addition to the hub-and-spoke, message broker approach used in the example.

As Web services and frameworks such as Microsoft Windows 2000/.NET and J2EE become more sophisticated, they will play a larger role in Transactional Integration. XML was already mentioned as a standard that can increasingly be counted on as an interface into and out of applications.

The emergence of Universal Description, Discovery, and Integration (UDDI), Simple Object Access Protocol (SOAP), and Web Service Description Language (WSDL) will add yet another layer of transparency and enable more sophisticated integration services. These standards could blend to support Transaction Integration, the previously mentioned Identity Infrastructure, and many other types of integration and adaptive infrastructure services.

As standards and products mature, the key to infrastructure service success is to keep in mind the scope issues mentioned earlier. Jumping on the latest bandwagon for standards or products is unlikely to lead to infrastructure success. Success is more likely when you focus on the capabilities that will provide the most value to your organization, especially developers and operations staff.

## Other Common Services

Transactional Integration and Identity Infrastructure are two services that many organizations are struggling to plan right now. Others have been planned and are running already, while still others are just blips on the horizon. Figure 5.7 shows a more complete range of potential starter services. These services are increasingly used together, making application development easier as increasing levels of functionality are provided by reusable services.

Each of these service types is discussed on more detail on the following pages.

### Network Service

**IP.** The Internet, a worldwide, IP-based inter-network, is now a universal standard. Consequently, the Internet Protocol (IP) can be considered a universal service for communication between applications. Many organizations split network services into LAN, WAN, remote access, and a few other service options that are planned or purchased differently. This service includes other functions, such as TCP/IP protocol support on routers, domain name services (DNS), and dynamic host configuration protocol (DHCP).

**Voice.** Another network or communication service, voice is usually provided in the form of a dial tone, and charges are based on minutes of

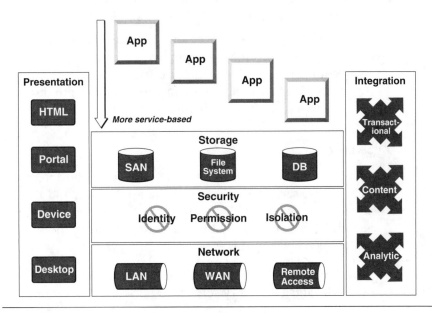

**Figure 5.7** Starter Services for Adaptive Infrastructure

usage. Convergence promises to eventually integrate voice, data, and video over IP, making this a subset of the IP service.

## Presentation Services

You can provide a number of different presentation services:

- HTML. The combination of a standard Web browser and Web server can be treated as a single service by applications. The application defines the code, the Web server executes it to generate HTML, while the Web browser renders it on the client. A more evolved version of this service would include additional devices or techniques to improve service levels, including HTTP caching, Content Delivery Network (CDN) services, ISP link bandwidth, network load balancers, on-the-fly device-specific compression, and encryption services.

- Portal. This service adds profile, personalization, search, analysis, and custom application access services to the HTML service.

- Device-specific. Various presentation services are available for non-standard browsers and mobile devices. For example, see 3GPP's

Open Service Access Generic User Interaction Service Capability Feature 3GPP TS 29.198-5 at www.3gpp.org.

■ Desktop. Some organizations consider the desktop itself a service, but it is not literally implemented once for all applications and with many locations. Still, the standards for infrastructure technology, along with help desk and applications, are often bundled into a service IT offers to the business.

## Security

Security involves some of the first services to be intermediary based. That is, the service sits between the application and the network; the service is not explicitly invoked by the application. This book has already discussed Identity Infrastructure as part of the security category, but other aspects to this service are:

■ Identity includes authentication and nonrepudiation; it can involve SSO and a directory service.

■ Isolation includes encryption and anonymity; it can involve secure sockets layer (SSL) or virtual private network (VPN) capabilities, firewalls, network address translation (NAT), and intrusion detection.

■ Permission includes access control and authorization. It is closely tied to Identity Infrastructure, but is not as easily separated from each application as authentication alone.

## Integration

This chapter has already discussed a Transactional Integration service, but you might consider other services as well.

■ Content. Some portals include the ability to integrate content from many back-end sources. New approaches such as Web Distributed Authoring and Versioning (WebDAV) and Internet Content Exchange (ICE) are focused on greater content standardization.

■ Analytic includes processes related to extracting, transforming, loading, and managing information, as well as operational data stores, data warehouses, data marts, and enterprise reporting.

### Storage

You might consider providing several typical storage services:

- Storage Area Network (SAN). This is a major example of the evolution of an IT component from internal subsystem, to external subsystem, to LAN service, to WAN service, to full-service provider model. All of these phases of evolution were enabled by using a network to separate the client and service interfaces.

- File system. Network-Attached Storage (NAS) is an example of moving the implementation of a service (file system) out of the operating system using a network. Network Operating System (NOS) provides printing and other services on the local device as well as over a network.

- Database. A final example of a service that is network-based.

As you can see, the list of potential adaptive infrastructure services is quite extensive. Instead of getting too ambitious, however, remember to start small with high-value services that you can deliver in a way that meets customer expectations for service-level performance and ROI. Then build on them over time.

## Summary

While the details of building any service are numerous, the following principles will guide you when developing any of the services discussed so far:

- Scope the service carefully, taking into account the most important value and features it can deliver, the likelihood of success, and the interest levels of your audience.

- Pick the best combinations of components to make a service work. Not all combinations will work best.

- Design interfaces with minimal coupling to enable change.

- Use the Web or the network as an architectural guide.

- Implement service automation as much as possible to make it fully automated.

- ∎ Make the service funding strategy a clear priority in planning.
- ∎ Market the value of the service.
- ∎ Establish an evangelist or champion to market or sell the service.
- ∎ Organize over time around services to improve process modularity.

# Chapter 6

# Processes and Methods

**B**y now you've heard plenty about adaptive infrastructure concepts. You understand all about components, platforms, patterns, and services. You've laid the technical foundation that will make your business more successful, agile, and adaptive in a fast-paced, high-technology world.

Now you need to start thinking in a different context. It's great to be able to understand the fundamentals of adaptive infrastructure, but how do you make it all work on a daily basis? What is the process by which you apply these concepts to make the activity of infrastructure planning an ongoing success within your organization?

This chapter will provide you with a set of best practices for infrastructure planning, along with a set of methods you can use to do your job better. It will help you understand why process is important and explain some of the strategic and tactical concerns related to the infrastructure lifecycle.

## Understanding the Process

Technology expertise alone will not solve the infrastructure-planning dilemma. As stated before, what's truly required is a balanced focus on people, process, and technology.

In particular, structured, repeatable processes will make a difference in terms of the speed, quality, and the ultimate cost of developing infrastructure solutions. Although this chapter discusses particular process models, all process models (including this one) must be adapted to the individual requirements of your organization, and those processes will evolve naturally over time.

## What Types of Processes Are Needed?

You need to understand and handle correctly at least two main process areas:

- Tactical, or "per-project" planning, is conducted for each new application development or infrastructure-driven project.

- Strategic, or "periodic," planning is conducted on an annual basis.

You also need a bootstrap process to handle the initial overhaul of processes within your organization. These concepts are explained in greater detail in the following sections.

## Modeling the Process

Many common methodologies are used to describe business processes. The basic model structure shown in Figure 6.1 was developed by META Group. This method uses the terminology of Inputs, Tools, Outputs, Services (ITOS), which is a variation on the well-known IDEF0 process modeling.

For any process, these four ITOS issues (inputs, tools, outputs and services) should be carefully deliberated and documented. You should also record the actual functions of the step.

How does this work? Each step in the process requires Input, which includes anything that is needed to generate the Output. What's in the step, of course, is the actual work that needs to get done. Here's a closer look at each element:

- Inputs include any information necessary to complete this step, including physical items such as guidebooks, documentation, and templates that you can use to fill out data. Templates are formats for documents that need to be prepared during the step's activities.

- Tools are automated aids that help to perform the work, such as word processors, spreadsheets, and so on. One special tool is added to this list: the Predictive Cost Modeling (PCM) tool intro-

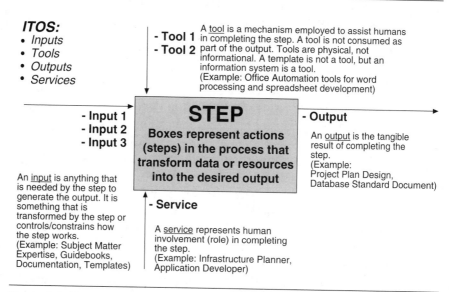

**ITOS:**
- *Inputs*
- *Tools*
- *Outputs*
- *Services*

- **Tool 1**
- **Tool 2**

A <u>tool</u> is a mechanism employed to assist humans in completing the step. A tool is not consumed as part of the output. Tools are physical, not informational. A template is not a tool, but an information system is a tool.
(Example: Office Automation tools for word processing and spreadsheet development)

- **Input 1**
- **Input 2**
- **Input 3**

**STEP**

**Boxes represent actions (steps) in the process that transform data or resources into the desired output**

- **Output**

An <u>output</u> is the tangible result of completing the step.
(Example: Project Plan Design, Database Standard Document)

An <u>input</u> is anything that is needed by the step to generate the output. It is something that is transformed by the step or controls/constrains how the step works.
(Example: Subject Matter Expertise, Guidebooks, Documentation, Templates)

- **Service**

A <u>service</u> represents human involvement (role) in completing the step.
(Example: Infrastructure Planner, Application Developer)

**Figure 6.1** The Basic Model Structure

duced later in this book. Blank forms are not considered tools; they are just more inputs to the model: They do not do any work by themselves and are not automated, per se.

■ Outputs include designs, plans, or standards documentation produced as a result of a step in the process. For example, an output might be a specific deliverable for which you have a template.

■ Services represent anything required to actually perform the process. For example, human beings might do some work to complete a step. So, the services step includes defining the roles of those who will be involved in executing the process. In this case, the word "service" does not refer to the adaptive services discussed in the previous chapter—it refers to people or things that provide a service for this step of the process.

The goal of this process model is to be *complete, actionable*, and *modular*. To be *complete*, it must completely describe critical infrastructure planning functions. To be *actionable*, the model must describe particular outputs (specific deliverables) of each step, and provide practical value immediately. To be *modular*, it must describe discrete steps that can be adopted incrementally and independently. These characteristics should also allow you to make the process as light or heavy as the situation requires.

The diagram in Figure 6.2 shows the highest-level view of the model adapted specifically to infrastructure planning.

In this case, the step portion of the model (the central block in Figure 6.2) is the process called "Plan Adaptive Infrastructure." The diagram in Figure 6.2 shows examples of Inputs, Tools, Outputs, and Services related to this process. Traditional architecture concerns, such as architecture domains or application development, are outside this box. Many people consider operational "build" and "run" processes to be outside the box as well.

Governance is another aspect not wholly included in this model. However, any planning model must consider governance as part of what executes the work. The infrastructure planning model helps you get through all the approval cycles and related activities, but it doesn't explain how to do great project management. However, it does show what documents you need to produce, and what documents need to come from other people.

Here's a closer look at each category of ITOS specific to infrastructure:

■ Inputs may include any of the items listed under this category in Figure 6.2. Generally, the best inputs for infrastructure planning are business vision, technology, skills, and process innovations.

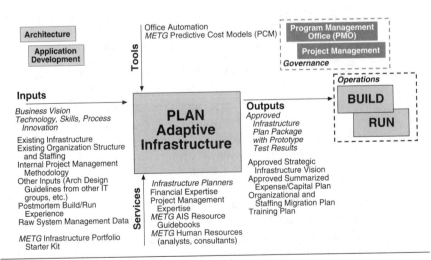

**Figure 6.2** The AIS Infrastructure Planning Model

- Tools include using the Predictive Cost Model. Many of the steps can be completed with Microsoft Word and Excel, tools commonly used during infrastructure planning.

- Outputs would include approved plans that are ready for the build group, such as plans for a specific infrastructure project, prototype test results, training plans, organizational ideas, tactical plans, full strategic infrastructure visions, and so forth.

- Services include infrastructure planners, who should have the skills to handle all the steps in the entire model. Later sections in this book discuss other service roles, including stakeholders, financial experts, analysts, consultants, and project managers.

## A More Detailed View

The previous diagram (Figure 6.2) showed all the processes that were *outside* the infrastructure step itself, and how they are related. Figure 6.3 shows what's *inside* the infrastructure model one level down from the top view, including all the major steps involved in planning adaptive infrastructure.

For example, two major aspects of infrastructure planning involve a set of key "periodic processes" called Managing Infrastructure Strategies and Standards and a set of key "per-project processes" called Assimilat-

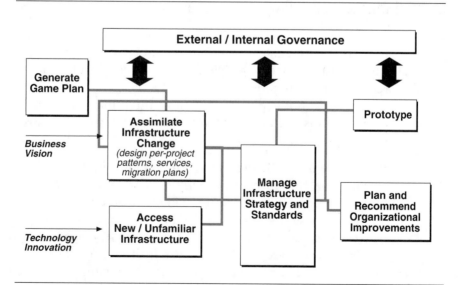

**Figure 6.3** Planning Model: Top Level View

ing Infrastructure Change. Aside from these two major issues, you might assess new and unfamiliar infrastructure, which can be independent of the other two activities. Also, you could be involved in the work of generating game plans, prototyping, and planning or recommending organizational improvements. These high-level steps in the infrastructure model are usually referred to as "stages." The next level down would be "activities," and below that "tasks," making the names of each level consistent with traditional terminology defined by the Project Management Institute. Keep this terminology in mind as you proceed through the discussion on the following pages.

Notice that governance sits above the diagram. The relationship of governance is not examined too closely here, but it will be detailed in subdiagrams. In various steps, output is generated for review by governance including technology steering committees, program management offices, budget committees, and the like. Most organizations employ governance oversight before moving between major stages. For example, before project plans go into prototyping, governance should approve new budget expenditures.

The next few sections explore some of the major boxes of the diagram in detail. This discussion is limited to a summary view of key steps, because explaining them all would take too long.

## Managing Per-Project Processes

The stage called "Assimilate Infrastructure Change" in Figure 6.3 is the process used to manage per-project processes. Figure 6.4 shows how this consists of specific activities you must conduct for each project that requires infrastructure support.

In the per-project stage, you have three major activities. Only one activity seems like infrastructure planning, but the other two are important for producing best results.

**Business Vision Refinement.** You must understand the client's vision to be able to plan properly. As part of this activity, you collect business vision information to use in other process steps.

Business Vision Refinement documents the goals of the particular initiative being planned. A good approach is to leverage application development's use case analysis research. Detailed statements of user behavior are easier to map to infrastructure patterns than vague business formulations such as "business-to-business." Outputs of this activity

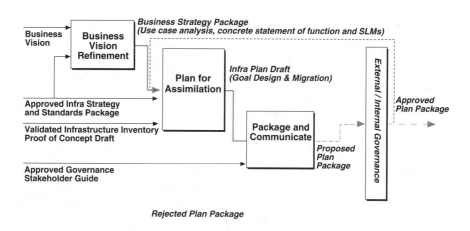

**Figure 6.4** The Assimilate Infrastructure Change Stage

could include a use case analysis, a concrete statement of functionality, and service level metrics that the business specifies up front.

**Plan for Assimilation.**   You must plan for the project and determine what infrastructure will be required. This activity is discussed in much greater detail later in this chapter.

**Package and Communicate.**   This activity is required to secure management approval. Your packaged plans should be based on realistic vision requirements. The packaging process can include finding champions and funding for the project, preparing presentations, and having casual, face-to-face meetings to explain your plan to key participants. The goal is to get the plan approved so that you can move to the next stage. Packaging issues are discussed more fully later in this chapter and in Chapter 7.

To help you fully understand the detail work and the challenges involved, the rest of this section explains specific details of several key areas of the per-project processes to help you understand what's involved in designing patterns and services.

## Assimilation Planning

Figure 6.5 details the "Plan for Assimilation Activity" discussed earlier. This activity lets you get more specific about the process of designing patterns and services. The basic work here is a sort of gap analysis. Assuming you already have an inventory of current infrastructure, you

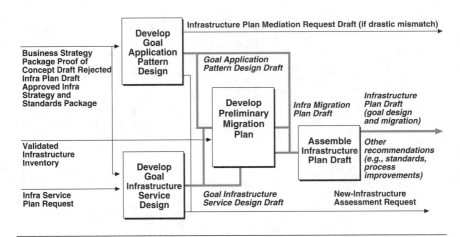

**Figure 6.5** The Plan for Assimilation Activity

should define a goal, then plan your migration toward that goal. The final task, Assemble Infrastructure Plan Draft, helps make sure the migration plan and the initial goal plan are in fact unified and communicated effectively.

During this planning activity, you're essentially trying to use your knowledge of the patterns and services you've developed elsewhere to formulate a solution, both on the pattern side and on the services side.

Once you have defined your design goals, you can develop a preliminary migration plan and assemble a preliminary draft of your infrastructure plan. Here, you must understand the base cases and describe in detail how you plan to address them. Full refinement of your design should wait, however, until you have had a chance to communicate with the customer and obtain budget approval.

## Designing Patterns

The task of designing patterns, first shown in Figure 6.5, involves much more detail, as shown in Figure 6.6. This task involves using your previous business vision and strategy approach to develop a preliminary set of pattern choices, then create a more refined set of pattern designs from them.

As this diagram shows, pattern design consists of five major steps.

First, you must take your portfolio of patterns and use it to do Infrastructure Pattern Matching, a technique detailed later in this chapter.

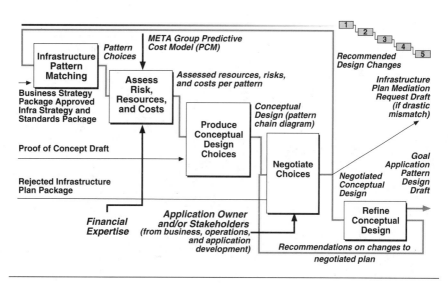

**Figure 6.6** The Develop Goal Application Pattern Design Task

Essentially, you match the use cases or project details to the set of infrastructure patterns that best serve the purpose.

The next step involves assessing risks, resources, and costs. If you have long experience with this pattern, you should have your own internal model already defined. If not, you can use the Predictive Cost Model (PCM) tool described later in this chapter to make an assessment. Also, it is prudent to have a financial expert help determine the costs of a pattern.

Once you've thoroughly analyzed the risks, resources, and costs, you can make your first conceptual design choices. The conceptual design should not take a lot of time to draft. It should provide a quick look at infrastructure patterns, tools, and the simple use of pattern design choices, as suggested in Figure 6.7.

Then, when you have settled on a preliminary set of design choices, you can begin negotiations with customers and other stakeholders. Your negotiations should include an explicit discussion of service levels and the use cases that will be addressed. The main point of negotiation is to determine whether a pattern design will fit your customer's needs and budget. If customers disagree with your design choices, you can backtrack and find other ways to bridge the gap. When you encounter a significant disagreement, try to document as many of the problems as possible, then ask management to break the impasse. If customers are asking you to violate a fundamental policy or security concern, successful negotiation will require management attention as well.

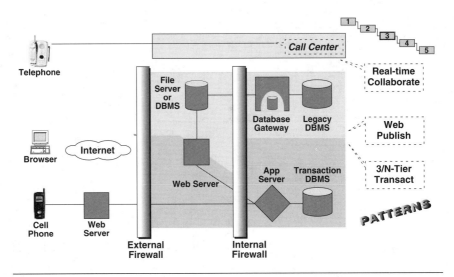

**Figure 6.7** The Produce Conceptual Design Choices Subtask

When you finish negotiating and come to agreement on the basic design choices and service levels, you can develop a much more detailed design. At this point, you might need even more negotiation to further refine service level issues, such as mapping the number of concurrent users that must be supported to the projected number of servers needed and the capacity of those servers.

Pattern planning will be directly addressed in the next book of this series, which describes this pattern goal design process in more detail by giving more detailed technology refinement guidelines and best practices.

## Designing Services

The task of designing services, first shown in Figure 6.5, involves much more detail, as shown in Figure 6.8. Services can be planned in a manner similar to patterns, but they require no intermediate negotiation with the business. In fact, unlike patterns, services are usually driven by the infrastructure organization directly. On the other hand, you could end up spending time making sure your goals fit the business's goals in order to get funding, but this is a packaging issue fully described in Chapter 7.

To plan services, you must assess the risks, resource requirements, and costs, using whatever models you might have. Then, you create service designs. Based on these designs, you can develop appropriate mod-

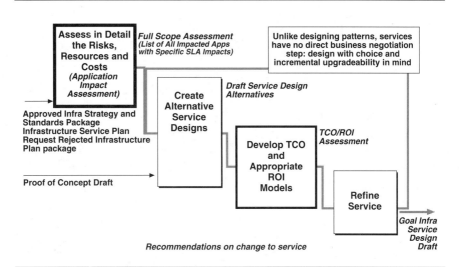

**Figure 6.8** The Develop Goal Application Service Design Task

els for total cost of ownership (TCO) and return on investment (ROI), which are greater concerns for services than patterns. Finally, you will refine the service design based on the realities you encounter when it is actually tested and built.

## Managing Periodic Processes

The other critical stage in the infrastructure planning model is the "periodic process" listed under "Manage Infrastructure Strategy and Standards" in Figure 6.3. The periodic process involves three major activities, as shown in Figure 6.9. These activities include assembling information, analyzing it, and then packaging and communicating it. Each activity is discussed in more detail later in this chapter.

### Assembling the Information

Figure 6.10 shows a more detailed view of the Assemble task listed in Figure 6.9. To assemble information, you must take whatever current standards you have and package them. The goal is to generate a proposed overall infrastructure strategy, as well as to define and document infrastructure standards (patterns and services), for management review and approval.

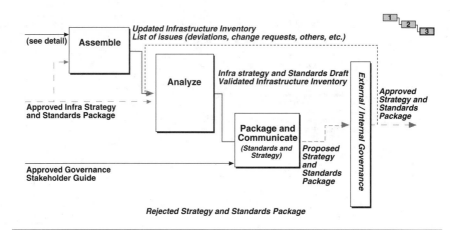

**Figure 6.9** The Manage Infrastructure Strategies and Standards (MISS) Activity

The first step is to assemble all relevant infrastructure documentation and other information currently available in your organization. You have many sources for this information. Current project plans may reveal new components and patterns being introduced into your organization. Suggestions for improvement could come from any part of the business. Details on other people's experiences using a particular technology might be relevant. An updated inventory of patterns and services is certainly a

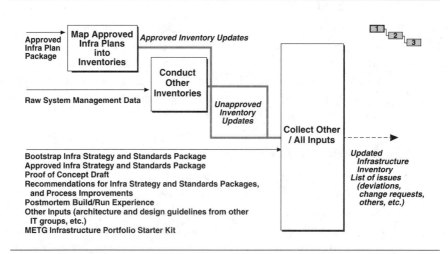

**Figure 6.10** The Assemble Task

key input, as well. Create a virtual "in box" for all such data as it arrives, then use it for reference as you update your strategies and standards.

While updating the infrastructure inventory is important, it doesn't have to be extremely detailed—at least not for overall planning purposes. For example, do you have 5,000 desktops or 10,000? Of these, do you have only five desktop configurations, or do you really have 37? You don't need the same kind of line-item detail that an asset manager requires; you just need to know the major categories and rough quantities.

The same idea applies to a network inventory. If you are in charge of a retail network of 1,000 or 5,000 links, you don't need all the detail at your fingertips for major strategic planning. But you do need a *summary* of the data—for example, the five or 10 basic network types that you deploy. When you start the Analyze task, this information can help verify whether you are testing or designing properly, or it can help determine what additional service changes might be required.

Other data that you gather might include proof-of-concept drafts, starter kits, and various architecture and design guidelines from other IT groups. Collecting and assembling this incoming data from various sources makes it simpler to update and track without becoming a huge effort every year.

In fact, you should assemble and update this information often—not once a year at an annual strategy session. If you wait too long, you're going to be overwhelmed with the data collection and organization. Keeping your map of the world continuously updated is half the battle.

### Analyzing the Information

Once you have finished the Assemble task shown in Figure 6.9 and Figure 6.10, you are ready for the Analyze task shown in Figure 6.11. While many issues can be addressed during the analysis phase, it is crucial that you perform two basic steps shown in this diagram.

First, you must evaluate individual strategies and standards. Look at every system component and pattern to determine whether the decisions you made with the component or pattern are still working. Are all services working well? Do you need to upgrade the services in some way?

Make a list of specific updates or developments you'll ask your team to design. The design work itself is part of the "Assimilate Infrastructure Change" stage, with new component research taken from the "Assess New/Unfamiliar Infrastructure" stage. (See Figure 6.3 and Figure 6.4.)

Second, you must analyze everything in a more holistic way. Compare and judge the total infrastructure picture with the services, patterns,

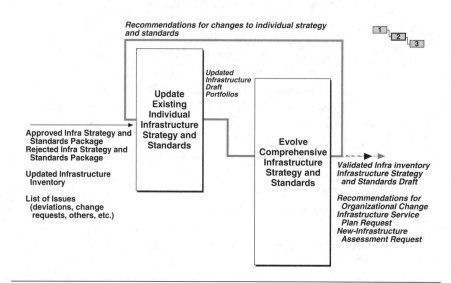

**Figure 6.11** The Analyze Task

and components. Make sure that any individual standards that are created will work with the entire infrastructure. A broader analysis should define realistic goals for the current year. Various constraints, such as budget issues, could narrow your list of planned changes.

After evaluating your infrastructure inventory, standards, and strategies, take time to evaluate any recommendations for change in your organization. Will you be successful at managing services with your current team? Is your team organized in the most efficient and effective manner? Any organizational changes you identify should be moved quickly to appropriate management review levels, if the decision must come from outside your group.

If analysis identifies that a new service is needed, consider sending this request back to the per-project team for further design. While it may seem logical to design a service within the group that envisions it, it is often more effective to let people who design per-project services handle the design work because they are used to dealing with regular project-oriented deadlines. Most standards group work is done on quarterly or even yearly deadlines.

The Analyze task may occur at different times, depending on the organization. Many do it quarterly or yearly. The most important thing is to make sure that you do it at all. In fact, more frequent analysis is often required for more volatile areas of the infrastructure.

Standardization can start at the architecture level or the base technology level. For example, you might architect a new a design element, such as using network load balancers in the Web Publish pattern. Or you might make basic technology decisions, such as using SOAP over HTTP for cross-business integration.

Later, once you've implemented a few instances or actual applications using those standards, you can get down to the level of standardizing on specific products. Finally, after many iterations, you should have developed full configuration standards, particularly in patterns like Store-and-Forward Collaborate. For example, your definition might state that files should be on the F: drive, certain login scripts will be used, and so forth. These deeply standardized and stable patterns need less frequent periodic review, as indicated in Figure 6.12. In contrast, some patterns, such as 3/N-Tier Transact, may need quarterly reviews.

Some standards will not be as clearly defined as others, simply because they are not as well tested. The basic goal is to define standards, but it is also crucial to test these standards as often as possible for their applicability and relevance.

Overall, this assembling, analyzing, and recommending next steps is managing the infrastructure portfolio of components, platform layers, patterns, and services over time.

## Packaging and Communicating the Product

Once the infrastructure standards and strategies have been defined and the infrastructure inventory has been validated, you must prepare a communication plan for your management or stakeholders. After all, communication doesn't happen by accident; it must be planned. Once you

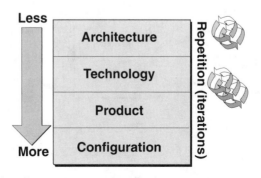

**Figure 6.12** Defining Standards In Practice

have finished the Analysis task shown in Figure 6.9 and Figure 6.11, you are ready for the Package and Communicate task shown in Figure 6.13.

The communication plan spells out the proposed infrastructure strategy and standards packages, so that individual stakeholders or managers can approve or reject these standards. It should speak in terms stakeholders can understand, not just in technical terms. That is why this completely distinct step appears here and elsewhere in the infrastructure model: It must be a separate step if you want each planning or strategy document to have any chance of being approved. To do the work, you should find someone who is good at speaking the stakeholders' language; you need the groups who must approve these documents to understand your standards. First, come up with a general communication plan for standards approval and then use the best communication method to present it to each stakeholder, whether through formal presentations, informal outings (such as golf games), short documents, long documents, a series of e-mails, or even voice-mail messages.

In summary, your standards and strategies require a methodical, periodic process with regular reviews. Detail what each process must do and repeat the steps required for that process. The portfolio approach gives you a framework to manage these standards and strategies.

## Integrating Your Planning with IT Processes

No process can execute without people doing some work, at least not in infrastructure planning. So, who are these people, and where do they

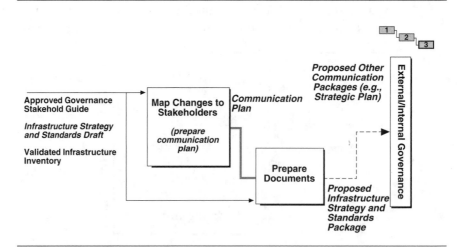

**Figure 6.13** The Package and Communicate Task

come from? And, even more challenging, how can current team members find time to create good infrastructure planning processes like the ones defined above?

We believe the first key step from the people perspective is to get the process defined—don't assemble a team and fail to assign roles. Thus, the discussion in Chapter 5 is key.

Moreover, you should organize the team only after clearly understanding which processes actually work inside your organization. Then you can decide which centers of excellence should exist and reorganize staff to assure even more excellence and efficiency. Meanwhile, you can get team members from different organizational entities to work together without making them all report to the same group.

This is a virtual team (or matrix) approach, but one key strategy to make it work is to have *at least one* full-time equivalent (FTE) assigned to lead key processes. Depending on the size of the organization and volume of work, you may need more than one FTE. These full-time infrastructure planners can assemble teams to complete the work, inserting appropriate experts in specific technology areas as needed. The infrastructure planners also do much of the physical documentation and other tasks themselves between team meetings. It's important that the infrastructure planners be dedicated resources. They should *not* be on a beeper or have too many other responsibilities to deliver. Otherwise, they will not have time for important new infrastructure planning processes and the work will never be finished.

Eventually, infrastructure planners should report to management separately from application development and operations, precisely because their job is to make sure work gets passed efficiently between the two groups: that applications are deployed and successfully operated by virtue of better planning. Reporting to neither group lets this infrastructure planning function make more independent decisions to best connect these two major IT constituencies.

Similarly, infrastructure planners might best be separated from traditional architects in order to move them closer to day-to-day operational planning, which will assure that plans are very realistic. Figure 6.14 depicts this relationship.

People are crucial to getting a correctly balanced infrastructure planning process. Details on specific roles would require another book, but it's worth summarizing a number of characteristics for an infrastructure planner as shown in Table 6.1.

To cope with future challenges, the infrastructure planner should have strong skills in networking, security, and middleware. These skills

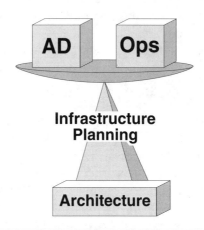

**Figure 6.14** The Role of Infrastructure Planning in the IT Process

are critical compared to more traditional skills in servers or other physical infrastructure strata components. You should hire people who have a larger view of infrastructure and are not going to concentrate on simply holding up the goals of their particular technical area. A few traditional architects do very well with this, but they must be willing to plan for implementation and compromise some of the long-term architectural goals to prepare something that will work in the short term as well.

## Useful Planning Methods

As part of the infrastructure planning model, specific methods are used to accomplish steps of the process faster and with greater repeatability. This section provides much more detail on several of these methods.

### Infrastructure Pattern Matching (IPM)

Infrastructure Pattern Matching, or IPM, is a method used in the per-project processes described earlier (see Figure 6.6). Typically, infrastructure professionals jump into detailed design/implementation work as quickly as possible. It's familiar, it's interesting, and it's what they are paid to do.

The problem is, as the technical design gets deeper, it becomes more difficult to engage the business. Design problems are encountered and tradeoffs must be made; yet the business usually is incapable of participating in discussions at the technical level. What you need, then, is a way to plan infrastructure without asking overly technical questions.

**Table 6.1** Sample Job Description for an Infrastructure Planner

| Title | Infrastructure Planner |
|---|---|
| Job Description | This person provides per-project infrastructure planning support to move applications into operations while researching new technology and working with architects to determine standards periodically. |
| Job Responsibilities | The infrastructure planner will work with application project teams and operations to plan specific, per-application infrastructure designs. They will leverage as much existing infrastructure as possible, and infrastructure standards and processes where innovation allows. The infrastructure planner must research new and unfamiliar technology to determine its value to the enterprise for project use and as future standards. This person must understand existing infrastructure and regularly plan for overall standards that can directly affect day-to-day tactical planning and operations. Furthermore, the infrastructure planner must test new applications and technologies appropriately for proof-of-concept, as well as extensive stress and integration requirements. |
| Skills | The successful candidate must be able to communicate, both verbally and personally, as well as in presentation or written form, with other IT personnel (and often with non-IT personnel). Financial and project management background is a plus. Logical and detailed thinking across multiple disciplines within infrastructure is required. |
| Experience | Background in application development, operations, and architecture, or at least extensive experience with the requirements of these IT groups is required. Should be well versed in middleware, networking, and security, as well as a wide ranging set of infrastructure as necessary. |
| Education | Requires bachelor's degree. |
| Reporting Structure | Reports to VP Infrastructure Planning (or VP Operations or Infrastructure Planning Team Leader) |
| Salary Range | (to be determined) |

**Table 6.1** Sample Job Description for an Infrastructure Planner *(Continued)*

| Title | Infrastructure Planner |
|---|---|
| Measuring Success | Specific improvements in speed, quality, and cost efficiency of per-project application delivery will be measured. On-time delivery of budgets and standards will be considered as well. |
| Judgment | Must decide recommendations on per-project infrastructure plans as well as standards. |
| Accountability | Role will be accountable for those deliverables (plans, designs, standards, etc.) as defined by process steps and in success measuring section above. |
| Contacts | Must know exactly which people to consult (both internally and externally) for more detailed infrastructure expertise (years in IT will be considered as appropriate experience). |
| Process Steps | From the infrastructure planning model, this person may be required to do ALL stages of work (assimilate infrastructure change, manage infrastructure strategies and standards, prototype, and assess new/unfamiliar infrastructure, etc.). Larger organizations might divide these roles by major stages. |
| Job Description | This person provides per-project infrastructure planning support to move applications into operations while researching new technology and working with architects to determine standards periodically. |

IPM helps keep the discussion at a level high enough to get infrastructure planning started and yet keep the business engaged in the process. Using IPM, infrastructure developers, working with the business, can highlight business-critical design tradeoffs and adjust infrastructure investment priorities, as shown in Figure 6.15. The essence of the IPM process revolves around three basic questions:

■ Who is the user? Answers might include employee, customer, or business partner.

■ Where is the user located? Answers might include headquarters, branch office, or remote.

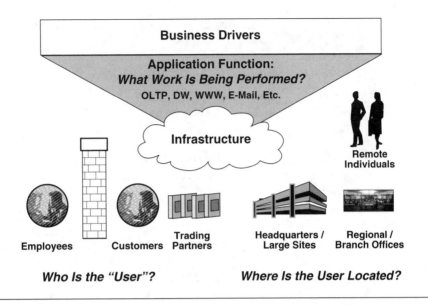

**Figure 6.15** The Basics of Infrastructure Pattern Matching (IPM)

■ What work is being performed by the user? Answers here map to the specific categories of patterns defined in Chapter 3.

These three business-friendly questions can generate the information necessary to predict which basic infrastructure will be required for new business initiatives very early in their lifecycle—even before a product has been selected by the IT applications development group.

The starter kit of infrastructure patterns defined in Chapter 3 provides established sets of infrastructure that can be described or differentiated by who the users are, where the users are, and what they're doing. For example, the three pattern categories (Transact, Publish, and Collaborate) are a simple set of "what" answers to use. Using simple answers to simple questions will help you identify the right pattern(s) for the current initiative or application program, as indicated in Figure 6.16.

## Predictive Cost Modeling (PCM)

Predictive cost modeling (PCM) techniques can help you put a price tag on infrastructure development projects, by helping determine what resources are required and what it will cost to develop those resources. PCM also takes into account the complexity involved in creating an application or business function.

| INFRASTRUCTURE PATTERN MATCHING (IPM) | | | | |
|---|---|---|---|---|
| **PATTERN** | **IPM Primary** | **IPM Secondary** | **IPM Tertiary** | **Use Case** |
| *Publish* — Web Publish | Document | Read-Only | None | Advertising Online Catalog |
| *Publish* — Client/Server Publish | Record | Read-Only | None | |
| *Publish* — Stream Publish | Stream | Read-Only (one-way flow) | None | |
| *Collaborate* — Real-time Collaborate | Stream | Read/Write (two-way flow) | None | |
| *Collaborate* — Store and Forward Collaborate | Document | Read/Write (sequentially) | COORDINATION Manual | Push Notification |
| *Collaborate* — Structured Collaborate | Document | Read/Write (sequentially) | COORDINATION Automated | |
| *Transact* — 1-Tier Transact | Record | Read/Write (simultaneously) | PARTITIONING Monolithic (Host) | |
| *Transact* — 2-Tier Transact | Record | Read/Write (simultaneously) | PARTITIONING Date only (2-Tier) | |
| *Transact* — 3/N-Tier Transact | Record | Read/Write (simultaneously) | PARTITIONING Date and presentation (3/N-Tier) | Ordering, Registration |

**Figure 6.16** An Example of Infrastructure Pattern Matching

·   PCM differs from most current cost models, and with good reason. Most total cost of ownership (TCO) models used today are not structured to analyze new applications. The rapid proliferation of business application choices has expanded infrastructure complexity and cut the life span of cost models to about 6–12 months.

Making assumptions about future applications using dated cost models—especially while application development cycles continue to shrink—simply institutionalizes existing thinking, both good and bad. Thus, you might find yourself repeating earlier mistakes when assembling applications and their requisite infrastructure.

Most current TCO models are resource-based: accounting for the number of servers to be used, the number of database licenses, and so on. These resource-based measurements offer little that you can use in negotiations with business users, since there is no easy way to tie the application benefits and complexity to resource-based costs.

Savvy business users today tend to think of application infrastructure in terms of the user base and service levels. They shouldn't care how many servers are required. Thus, unless you can demonstrate some link between business drivers and resource requirements, you will have no common ground for talking to the business users. You need a way to predict what costs will be, as well as to tie service level tradeoffs to specific investment and cost alternatives.

Also, existing TCO models don't reflect the benefits of infrastructure reuse practices. The models are hard-coded to resources, making it difficult to analyze tradeoffs or the effect of different architectures. Current

TCO models are too labor intensive to apply, as well. People may spend half a year analyzing costs of an application, only to have it all thrown away when minor factors change.

The PCM technique, on the other hand, is a coarsely grained model that is quick and easy to use, which will help you select the most cost-effective infrastructure option within a number of days while still accounting for total system costs.

PCM moves the Infrastructure Pattern Matching process from simply matching a pattern to providing more detail on risks, bills-of-materials, and costs. To reach this next level, you need more than just three simple questions; you need a structured and repeatable questionnaire.

### PCM Components

There are three components used in PCM: cost drivers, cost buckets, and the complexity mappings between the two.

- A cost driver is a characteristic of a business initiative or application that affects complexity. For example, how many users are expected, what response time is required, and what availability is required? These sound a lot like service level metrics, and many are. Part of the PCM tool's job is to document these common service level goals early in the design process, and it uses these questions to generate cost estimates.

- Cost buckets help the PCM tool define costs for each particular item that consumes resources and costs money, such as a server or a person.

- The tool subsequently maps or establishes the link between the complexity of the cost drivers and its effect on any possible resources.

Modeling can be complex and not all mappings work the same for vastly different applications. PCM models costs using the concept of patterns as defined in this book, using sets of similar infrastructure to solve particular types of application problems. In this way, it doesn't create a single massive model for everything—which would be impossible; it stays focused on particular models for patterns and services.

For example, there are 28 cost drivers within the 3/N-Tier Transact pattern. These can be expressed in the form of simple questions.

- How is data being shared?
- What is the transaction load?

- What is the security requirement?
- What is the business volatility?

These questions serve as interview tools. Infrastructure developers can sit with customers—including application developers, business users, or the operations group—and gather information. The answers to the questions are multiple choice and help divide the technology into seven ranges that can be used to capture the overall complexity associated with the application being modeled.

The validity of this model isn't found in mathematics, but rather in the research that goes into creating the answers. There is a tremendous amount of value in using this list of cost drivers. Working through the questionnaire with business users helps determine what will be required in terms of infrastructure. If you interview a business unit manager using PCM, and consistently discover extreme risk, you will know immediately that he or she is dealing with bleeding-edge technology. More important, so will the business user. In such a situation, the business people will hopefully realize the potential pitfalls of their desired courses of action.

### Applying PCM to Service Level Agreements

You can also use the PCM process to negotiate service-level agreements. The negotiation process will provide you with a good sense of the response time, recovery, and availability users are willing to pay for.

Infrastructure developers can offer options to the business in the form of scenarios, and then attach a dollar figure to each of these scenarios, as well as predict the likelihood of successful completion. An extremely risky scenario, for instance, might carry a substantially higher price tag, while the chance of successfully completing it is very low.

Since most PCM models generate a "green field" estimate that assumes no existing equipment, the gap between the model and what is in place must be addressed through gap analysis, as indicated in Figure 6.17. A grasp of the difference between existing infrastructure and the model will help both short- and long-term planning and budgeting efforts.

In short, PCM should be a tool that fosters realistic budgeting discussions. As the model becomes more refined, the TCO expenses it generates may seem high to the business users. However, PCM will help outline the level of complexity, a suggested infrastructure pattern, the refinements that particular application will require, and some general cost characteristics for the project.

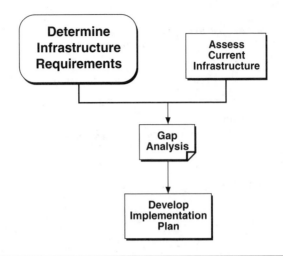

**Figure 6.17** Steps Involved in Predictive Cost Modeling (PCM)

PCM is also the key to shifting the cost decisions to business users, an important concept in the adaptive infrastructure process. Instead of coming back to business users with costs in a matter of months, now it can be a matter of hours. This rapidity should help business people understand what they gain or lose (in terms of service levels) when they change budgets.

## Infrastructure Impact Assessment (IIA)

Once the concept of adaptive infrastructure has been established within your organization, people will tend to develop and reuse specific infrastructure patterns. For this reason, if you start thinking about changing these patterns, you need a way to test the impact of your proposed changes on the existing infrastructure *before* making the changes.

Infrastructure Impact Assessments (IIAs) are a set of techniques used to make sure that patterns are planned, built, and run well. Apart from the need for planning, these assessments focus on measuring how well patterns (and infrastructure planning as a whole) align with the real world during project prototyping and operation.

### IIA and the Implementation Cycle

IIA can be applied throughout the application development lifecycle, as shown in Figure 6.18.

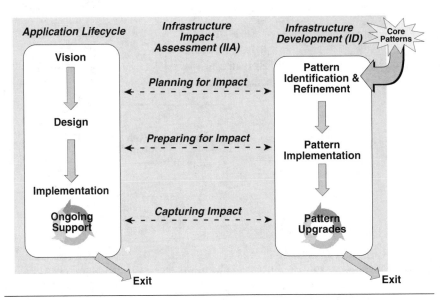

**Figure 6.18** IIA and the Application Development Lifecycle

This diagram shows how IIA matches steps in the application development lifecycle to steps in the infrastructure development lifecycle (plan, build, run) with specific activities in between.

■ Vision phase. Even before you start choosing products or building infrastructure, infrastructure planners must try to get in sync with the business strategy, map the initiative or application to an infrastructure pattern, and determine the key business drivers that will affect cost and delivery the most. This can be done using the Infrastructure Pattern Matching (IPM) and Predictive Cost Modeling (PCM) techniques discussed earlier in this chapter. Much of the infrastructure planning model concerns activity during this planning stage.

■ Design phase. At this point, a mock-up of the application probably exists, which means you can work with it in the test lab, examining how it consumes server resources (among others) and how it behaves. Not only does this test a particular application with a particular set of infrastructure, but it should provide a reference for future efforts based on that same infrastructure component, pattern, or service. The infrastructure planning model provides detailed steps (not covered in this book) that help you do this prototyping work. However, a key requirement for this kind of work is a lab, as explained later in this section.

■ Implementation phase. Once the application is rolled out, you can step back and look at some of the earlier assumptions. Did you deliver on the service levels that were targeted in an earlier stage? What should you have done differently? What kinds of new things are going to happen? This activity must happen to assure that infrastructure patterns and services are working as planned. Naturally, it will require great assistance from operations personnel in your organization.

IIA works a lot like an environmental impact study. But instead of deciding which trees need to be saved or what natural habitat must be protected, it gauges the potential repercussions of a certain course of action in infrastructure development. In particular, it may indicate which infrastructure-planning activities need to be performed. Specifically, you will research how applications "fit" a given infrastructure pattern and you will test them in a lab to see if you are right.

## The Value of Infrastructure Impact Assessment (IIA)

Why is this valuable? When infrastructure users approach you with a new proposal, you must ask them three things:

■ What will the application look like from an infrastructure perspective?

■ How much will it cost?

■ What is the likelihood that it can be successfully implemented within the organization?

The first two questions are answered by Infrastructure Pattern Matching (IPM) and Predictive Cost Modeling (PCM), as discussed earlier in this chapter. IIA answers the third.

## Benefits of a Testing Laboratory

A key aspect of IIA involves developing a testing laboratory. If you already have a lab for data, servers, networking, and so forth, it will work well as part of the IIA effort. Instead of experimenting with technology, however, you must use the lab to actually prove (and improve) the chances of success of application and infrastructure projects.

That is, it must be used to verify the performance impact of particular applications on the infrastructure and to verify that a particular pattern will suit a particular application well. This is what the infrastructure planning model calls "prototyping," and many other people call integration or stress testing.

Performance measurements that you will test in the lab include capacity, response time, availability, and so forth.

While measuring these conditions can be challenging, certain tools can help in a lab environment. However, no single tool or framework provides the "holy grail," which is end-to-end response-time measurement that can be broken into its constituent parts for diagnostic purposes. Collections of tools are available for separate functions such as metric collection, performance monitoring, data correlation and summarization, detail diagnostics, capacity planning, and modeling. You should also remember that performance measurement, especially in terms of Web Publish or 3/N-Tier patterns, is still an emerging specialty.

With these considerations in mind, the first question to answer is "Where do I begin?" Start with the areas that are easiest to measure, and with the largest potential impacts. For instance, you can find lots of tools and services to measure WAN performance, an area where problems can have a major effect on overall performance. Keeping an eye on network performance also helps ensure that wide area networking service providers are complying with predefined service levels. Network monitoring tools can look at bandwidth utilization/capacity, latency, latency variation (jitter), and availability.

Other tools work at the server level, where the application is actually running, to monitor the performance of the server operating system as well as the database. These tools capture information relating to transaction rates, CPU utilization percentage, disk and network I/O, and overall performance.

Stress testers (i.e., scripting tools) help with server and network-centric impact modeling. Application performance measurement tools capture data transaction rate/volume, response time, availability, and so forth. Desktop performance measurement tools cover metrics such as display refresh rate, CPU/RAM/Windows resource utilization percentages, and disk/network I/O.

Ideally, you should model each application before implementation, then measure its performance during testing or after it has been installed. Lab testing should include stress tests to check the limits of your configurations, as well as normal operations tests to ensure your configurations meet agreed upon service levels and are manageable within your existing operations automation, processes, and skill sets. Document your application traffic patterns as a baseline for IPM and post-implementation troubleshooting. Your testing should continue after implementation to compare application performance to an established baseline and to defined thresholds for normal and peak operations.

## Components of a Test Lab

To be most successful, your test lab should have certain characteristics:

- It should have at least one example of each infrastructure component.
- It should be isolated from production facilities.
- It should be able to simulate multiple sites, even if it exists at a single location.

The idea behind this kind of lab testing is not to figure out if one server, switch, or router is better than another. The goal is to simulate different production environments so that you can tell how applications will perform under different circumstances. Traditionally, application developers haven't used labs because they haven't given these infrastructure issues much thought, or because they're only testing in their Quality Assurance (QA) lab the functionality of their application (not the service levels). Moreover, many people with infrastructure labs haven't made their capabilities readily available to developers.

Funding a lab can be problematic, however. Some organizations just make lab testing a component of major infrastructure projects and include money for testing in the project budget. This has worked well for very large projects, but typically there are only one or two projects a year, such as an ERP or CRM rollout. Otherwise, you may need to allocate some portion of the overhead IT budget (as discussed more fully in the section on packaging in Chapter 7).

Many organizations have built IIA labs using leftover equipment from Year 2000 test labs, or from older servers and other components that have been replaced. Still others have commanded key vendors to supply test equipment as part of their relationship. Regardless, you will still need additional funds to purchase monitoring tools.

The hardest part of funding a lab is not the equipment—it's the people. If the lab is to succeed, someone must manage it. Then as application developers or per-project infrastructure planners start using it, you will need someone who knows how to operate the monitoring tools and who can make the testing as fast and yet repeatable as possible.

If your organization doesn't have the resources to support this kind of effort, there are third-party alternatives available. Unfortunately, these can be quite expensive, and suffice only for a few projects.

Finally, if you've ever had an application deployment failure due to mismatched infrastructure, compare the cost of the failure to what the cost would have been if it were tested and implemented properly. This makes it more imperative to find business leaders who understand that you're trying to achieve success for their goals and get them to associate the cost of a lab with the cost of specific projects.

Senior executives may understand that inconsistencies or mistakes can ruin the reputation of your organization. When that sort of message is broadcast from the top of the organizational pyramid, it has a way of getting your message heard, which gets the lab funded.

### *Applying Infrastructure Impact Assessment (IIA)*

Maintaining an IIA process is actually an exercise in credibility. It is a crucial part of your effort to maintain a level of post-implementation responsibility.

Also, the IIA effort should help tie the application and infrastructure development teams together more consistently, reinforcing the type of interaction described throughout this book.

IT policy should include use of IIA at appropriate times in business, application, and infrastructure lifecycles. Thus, infrastructure developers will actually get involved in the vision phase, early in the development process, instead of being involved at the last minute during pre-implementation activities.

Infrastructure developers must have an open approach that reaches out to the various constituencies. This openness, in turn, will prompt people with potential infrastructure issues to seek them out. This is why you should publicize service levels on a Web site so that people know whether the service levels are being delivered (and if not, why). Publicizing success and failure will help you ensure that customers understand the reason for infrastructure problems and respond quickly.

Application certification procedures should enforce the use of IIA resources, including the infrastructure development team, the lab itself, and the tools. However, when enforcement does not work, IT must supply alternative scenarios. Finally, infrastructure developers and other constituencies within the organization must realize that, like PCM and IPM, IIA is a critical component of an adaptive infrastructure strategy.

# Chapter **7**

# Packaging and People

In the adaptive infrastructure strategy, packaging and people issues are two of the most critical issues involved in making new infrastructure successful.

- Without skillful packaging of your services, people on the business and application side will never understand the true value of what you have to deliver. This, in turn, will stymie your efforts to get funding and management support. Packaging is a communications effort that requires savvy marketing skills.

- Without careful attention to staffing issues, you will find your infrastructure planning and development efforts lacking the basic resources needed for success. Make sure you fully understand both the types and number of human resources, as well as the best way to organize teams.

While you have read discussions of packaging and people earlier in this book, this final chapter gives special attention to the issues of packaging and people to ensure your success in developing a fully adaptive infrastructure.

## Packaging and Funding Infrastructure

When the time comes to sell your infrastructure initiatives, there are several issues you must address.

### Dealing with Funding Challenges

First, is funding a problem? When you are dealing with patterns and services, some things are easy to fund, while others are much more difficult, as summarized in Table 7.1.

For instance, individual active projects are easier to fund than longer-term upgrades in service. Projects are initiatives directly sponsored by a business stakeholder that are directly driven by business value. Project work is pretty straightforward, so it is usually clear whom to charge for your work. You will also find it easy to get funding for infrastructure that supports a single application and which is *not* shared across applications.

Most infrastructure professionals are comfortable bundling needed work into a project budget. If it's required for the particular project, you will put it in the budget. On the other hand, bundling makes it harder to get project budget funding for some of the larger shared infrastructure service implementations you're trying to do. Project stakeholders think they're being asked to pay for something someone else would use, not just them.

Associating them with large-scale initiatives such as CRM can fund certain infrastructure upgrades, but that typically won't cover all the work you want to do. It's difficult to get shared infrastructure paid for by projects, although you can try by dividing the whole cost into 10 chunks, and charging 10 percent to each of the next 10 projects that use it.

**Table 7.1** Funding Challenges

| Easier to Fund | More Difficult to Fund |
|---|---|
| Projects | Services |
| Infrastructure NOT shared across applications | Shared infrastructure |
| Infrastructure costs easy to directly charge back (voice minutes) | Infrastructure costs that are difficult to charge back (requiring extensive new infrastructure simply to measure it and figure out how to allocate it) |

Some organizations take a tax approach where all application projects have a 15 percent fee for infrastructure costs, no matter what infrastructure the particular project actually requires. Bigger projects thus contribute more. Yet this approach still doesn't guarantee that you'll have enough money for all the service projects you want to do.

In the end, you'll have to directly justify the value of the service projects on your list, rather than hiding them in some other per-project or overall IT budget allocation. Some service projects are just too big to hide.

Some infrastructure costs are easy to expense, including traditional voice minutes and mainframe resources, such as DASD. In general, if you can directly allocate something, you probably should, but business cultures differ on this.

## Thinking Like Your Clients

When you try to get funding, you must ask yourself these questions:

- What does the client really value?
- What does the client really want?
- What is the client's biggest problem with the infrastructure?

If you start by answering these three questions, the proper positioning and selling approaches for shared infrastructures will become evident.

Of course, if you aren't having problems getting funding, then you don't need to make any drastic changes in how you approach the client for money. If you're doing fine, don't upset the apple cart.

Occasionally, you may have to consider getting one person or full-time equivalent (FTE) funded for work that you already have a team set up to do. Persuade the client to agree to fund one person up front. This team member can be the champion for the changes, and can add virtual resources later without having to go through any major budgeting discussions.

Next, you must determine the complexity of the job, the service levels needed, and the risk involved. In general, if you're going to handle the funding, you must account for all of your costs. This is true both early and later in the lifecycle. A tool such as Predictive Cost Modeling (PCM) helps you define costs quickly and do it in a repeatable way. Getting this assessment done quickly is crucial. If it takes weeks or a month to complete, you are significantly impeding your service levels to the business, as well as losing the initial momentum to address an issue.

## Analyzing Complexity

When analyzing complexity, make sure you approach it from the basis of functionality and service levels being provided—not in terms of the components being manifested. If you focus on the hardware and software costs, which can total in the millions, the client will question the need for the components. Even worse, the client may step into the infrastructure realm and start specifying his own preferred vendors and products. Instead, sell funding to cover the functions or service levels you are performing, which are harder to question in terms of cost. Table 7.2 provides an example linking business drivers with complexity.

You should determine the risk and also show your plan, build, and run-time costs, splitting these up into major categories. Make sure that personnel costs are included.

Most of all, if you can associate these numbers directly to a service level discussion or answer set from the client, then you should be able to get a direct connection between what they value and what you're going to provide for them. You need a concrete linkage between value and cost.

To make things easier, you might try to provide the client with three options for funding enhancements: small, medium, and large, as shown in Table 7.3. If you just give them one set of costs, and they don't want to spend that amount, you'll have to go back and do more cost analysis.

**Table 7.2** Analyzing Complexity Associated with Various Cost Drivers

| Driver | Medium Complexity |
| --- | --- |
| E-business volatility | E-business cycle measured in 12–24 months |
| Speed to deployment | 4–6 months |
| Hours of operation | 98% availability (7–8 days/year downtime) |
| Recovery time | 4–12 hours |
| Peak page request rate | 75,000–150,000 page requests/hour |
| Degree of dynamic content | Web-page content is roughly half static and half dynamic. There is little user personalization. |
| Transaction response time | 2–3 seconds |
| Transaction complexity | Single table record inserts and deletes |
| Transaction rate | 2001–5000 transactions/minute (35–85 TPS) |

Worse, they might do budget changes right then—slashing needed improvements by line item.

A best practice is to *never* give only one answer to clients. Instead, give them a set of choices, but make sure that the choice most palatable to you from an infrastructure standpoint actually looks like the best choice to the buyer.

You'll have to make a serious effort in the communications plan and other marketing material to get this done. And, you'll have to do it more than once for multiple constituencies or stakeholders. Your client may want to see the costs, while others may want to see your arguments for the technical architecture, especially application developers who are line-of-business based. You'll need marketing plans for all—and some of these will require detailed funding work.

Whenever possible, avoid showing the client a line item cost for every feature you plan to provide. If you do this, the client will unfailingly try to cut line items to reduce the budget.

Finally, make sure you show a *complete* cost picture. It is important to show the initial or first-year run costs at this stage, not just the costs to plan and implement. You'd be surprised how many budgets have *no* run costs in them. Some of the best architecture plans are the ones that initially cost the client the most to build. But these are the plans that will have the lowest run costs in two to three years. If you don't include the initial funding strategy, which estimates the run costs, then your clients are going to choose poorly. Worse, you'll end up getting stuck with the run costs since the client might say, "Isn't that already paid for in that big budget allocation I see on my financials?"

**Table 7.3** Analyzing the Cost of Complexity

|  | Very Low Complexity | Medium Complexity | Very High Complexity |
|---|---|---|---|
| **Personnel** | $310 | $981 | $2,614 |
| **Hardware** | $140 | $856 | $18,859 |
| **Software** | $376 | $2,157 | $8,991 |
| **Supporting Services** | $172 | $431 | $894 |
| **Totals: (in thousands)** | $998 | $4,425 | $31,358 |

Obviously, the PCM tool can help with this kind of work—it makes sure you can:

■ Give choices.

■ Show complete costs.

■ Do it quickly.

You can use your own costing methodologies as well; just make sure your estimates are complete, ideally showing multiple scenarios.

## Preparing a Communication Plan

Once you assess the costs and resources for the project, you should create a communication plan. One of the keys to understanding how to successfully secure funding is to understand what people value so that you can deliver a funding strategy that matches their goals and value drivers. You obtain funding from particular individuals in particular roles.

Moreover, there are often other stakeholders (sometimes even inside IT) that will need to "sign off" on the plan, even though they won't actually have funding authority—you'll need to market to them also. So you must know who these individuals are and why they care about you spending this money, as indicated in Figure 7.1.

In general, when you're mapping stakeholders to traditional infrastructure values, ask yourself what these individuals typically care about. What will get these individuals a promotion or a bonus? Then, when you're working on a particular infrastructure project, you can refine this to what you should highlight.

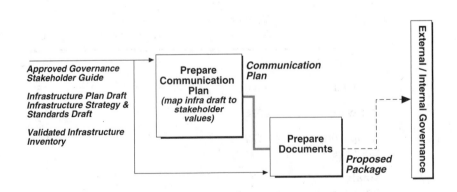

**Figure 7.1** The "Package and Communicate" Step

Business focus changes over time. It is important that you can easily modify your communication plan for business conditions and changes. That is why it is important for management to assist or provide you with a stakeholder analysis regularly. You must understand who needs what in your organization. When significant business events change, you should be able to quickly modify your funding strategies based on the changes.

The last step is to prepare specific yet reusable communication plans or packages for each of your different stakeholders up front. These can be used for periodic overall budget cases, then you can modify them as needed for particular project needs. Ask yourself how each stakeholder would like to hear about your plan. Often, you must alter and adjust your communication plan to best communicate with the various stakeholders.

When you customize your communication plan for specific stakeholders, make sure that you don't change the overall architecture or meaning of what you are building. You still must build for adaptiveness and flexibility, but you may not want to sell this capability to the stakeholders.

Instead of totally changing your plan, just change the marketing strategy you use and put a different spin on what you're selling. For example, a prior marketing message might have been that your product features a faster time-to-market response. Now you can change that to focus on how the project can save money. Nothing about your product has physically changed, but you have changed how you approach the stakeholders with it. Since their values have changed, your marketing must follow suit.

Think of your communication plan as a box with six sides—each of which can be viewed by one stakeholder. How do you describe the surfaces of the box to these stakeholders? You are building the whole box, but each surface is different depending on who uses the box. It is all about perspective. There isn't just one funding strategy. The funding strategy must accomplish more than one stakeholder analysis.

## The Customer Service Culture

What do users seem to value most? The answer is customer service. So don't build technology just for technology's sake; do what is right for your business.

The business must lead, not the technology, so focus on customer service. The infrastructure planners in your organization must have the ability to focus beyond technology and be able to communicate with their stakeholders. This attitude must be realized in other key groups in the organization too, including operations.

To some degree, you don't have to be great at keeping your systems running, but you must be great at ensuring that everyone knows what you're doing. This is especially true when things aren't going well.

In a traditional example, one organization had a recurring problem with a mainframe controller that would crash and interrupt service to some of their mainframe users. The group would replace the problem controllers *in only five minutes* through the help of hot standby controllers. Yet the end users were unhappy and felt the service was poor because they noticed five minutes of downtime and never received communication about it.

Eventually, the IT organization decided to handle the problem differently:

■ They notified users immediately when a problem occurred.

■ They told users how long it would take to fix the problem.

■ They fixed the problem and informed users when everything was normal.

Stopping to communicate with users actually slowed their response time, but customer satisfaction went up because they were doing a better job of communicating. They were talking with their users instead of hiding from them.

## Value as the Critical Issue

Do you know what is important to your users? When you buy a car, the salesman lets you walk around and look at the car, and carefully watches what you do. But he doesn't immediately try to talk to you. Why? Because he's trying to observe what it is you are looking for in a car.

What do you do first? Do you look at the sticker price? Do you look under the hood? Do you sit in the leather seats? Or do you immediately want to go for a test drive? Those are all signals indicating what you value most in a car. Good salespeople observe their clients, and then create a focused sales pitch based on what they have learned.

Even better, the salesperson understands that there may be other constituencies as well. If the whole family is there, the salesperson will mention other features to those family members. Or, if the buyer is alone, the salesperson will ask about the family and recommend arguments to use on the rest of the family.

All too often, infrastructure planners make the mistake of listening to their clients and then responding with a list of the technologies that they can produce. This is like a car salesperson actually telling you that a certain car produces the highest commissions! Poor marketers try to sell users on what they spend all their time thinking about, instead of selling users on what they really want. It is important to focus your plan around your users' needs and not on what you can produce.

If you haven't talked to your clients, you may not have a clue what they value. This is why the process model for per-project planning (see Chapter 5) explicitly involves the stakeholders in an early negotiation session. This is your opportunity to ensure you know what they care about.

Also, be sure to remain focused on what they value, and match your goals to their ideals, because they won't value yours. Sometimes you can use service levels to focus in on what the client values, in terms that are meaningful to the business.

## Packaging Models To Consider

One effective way to get funding is to divide your important business items into categories that you think the business will value. For example, if you're selling Identity Infrastructure, you might divide the costs by the number of people in the directory. That lets you tie cost to a variable that the client values and controls.

The client wants many customers, so the cost of your services will increase as the customer base grows. This explanation should sound reasonable to your clients, because their primary goal is to expand their customer base. They should understand that your costs increase as their revenue increases.

Another funding model that many businesses use to help them gain funding from a client has four categories, as shown in Figure 7.2.

**Behind-the-wall services** include features that are less tangible or visible, or features that are easily broken into other categories, which makes it very difficult to get funding for them in any certain or direct way. These services could include building a new, shared infrastructure or creating subsidy programs.

**Project services** are a bit easier to fund, because they are tied to the actual projects under construction. Examples of infrastructure planning

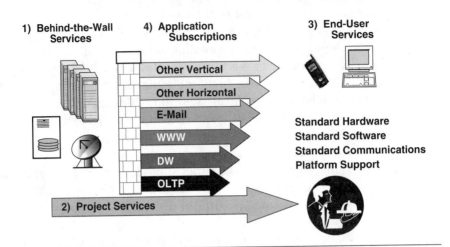

**Figure 7.2** Packaging Strategies

project services could include anything from the per-project set of processes, including requirements analysis, design of infrastructure patterns and applications, customization, development, testing, deployment, and integration. Of course, a project budget can include the full cost of software, hardware, and other components for plan, build, and perhaps run.

**Application subscriptions funding** might take the form of a "per-user, per-month" fee to run the specific applications that business leaders find most valuable. This could include lumping plan, build, and run costs together, as Application Service Providers do, or just charging for run costs after getting the up-front costs paid for as a project. Subscriptions work well for applications that control server/database provisioning, server management, user administration, backup/recovery, and performance management.

**End-user services** include standard hardware, software, network, and technical support. Many organizations have set this up for desktop services, and have a standard "per-year, per-user" fee to charge for this part of the infrastructure budget. Such end-user services should not just include the physical hardware. They should also account for things such as: desktop PC provisioning, desk-side support, Common Off-the-Shelf (COTS) applications, Moves/Adds/Changes (MACs), and LAN access. You can bundle a lot into this kind of charge.

While this approach to bundling your funding is worth considering, you can bundle funding in many other ways. You should entertain the

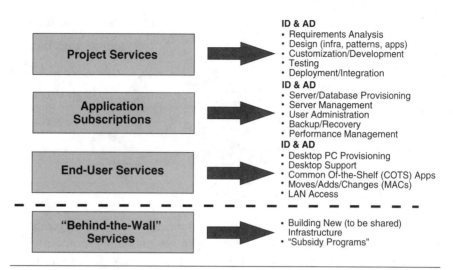

**Figure 7.3** Examples of Packaged IT Services

idea of being somewhat eclectic or diverse when accounting for services. Not everything needs to be charged the same way, yet many organizations try to oversimplify. Try different approaches, because one may work. If it doesn't work, try another. Figure 7.3 shows an example of packaged IT services.

## Mapping Categories to Stakeholders

Once you've categorized your funding, think of the categories in terms of the stakeholders to which they map. This is the start of your communication plan.

If you are selling a project, it's easy to sell it to the application group and line of business that is driving the initiative. However, if it is a behind-the-wall service or asset, you must sell it at the highest level in the organization that you can. It must become a capital expense. Shared resources, such as the corporate WAN, are usually the most difficult items to get funded. Figure 7.4 shows the relationship of projects to organizational levels.

The more shared the item, the more it falls into the behind-the-wall assets category, which means you must try to fund it as a cost to the entire business.

Interestingly, the level of sharing and target audience directly affects which service levels and metrics you should emphasize in your discus-

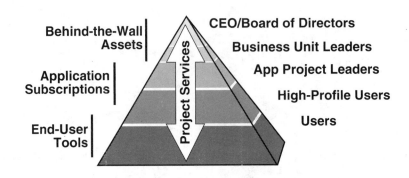

**Figure 7.4** Mapping Infrastructure Packages to Buyers

sions. Typically, project services tie directly to value propositions of the project sponsor. Thus your marketing messages should include details of the new capability in the context of the overall project and the time it will take to deliver these capabilities.

In contrast, discussions related to behind-the-wall assets could also focus on new or improved capabilities, but the detailed messaging often works better when it focuses on response time, availability, and the speed at which problems can be resolved. In this case, the financial metrics that tend to work best are those that emphasize unit cost reductions, such as a decrease in the cost of a megabyte of storage, or a minute of voice traffic. These kinds of metrics help the stakeholders understand that overall budgets will need to increase if storage volume or traffic rises faster than unit costs fall.

Know the language of the stakeholder and speak it when you divide the categories into things you want to sell. You may have traditional stakeholders involved in funding your projects, but other stakeholders may have veto authority.

### Speaking the Language of the CFO

Another model for portfolio management and funding in Figure 7.5 shows you can drive business by learning to "speak CFO." What do CFOs talk about all day long? Investments. This financial management model is often used at the highest level in organizations.

Here are some typical CFO terms with examples:

■ Non-discretionary costs are items that you must fund to keep the business going.

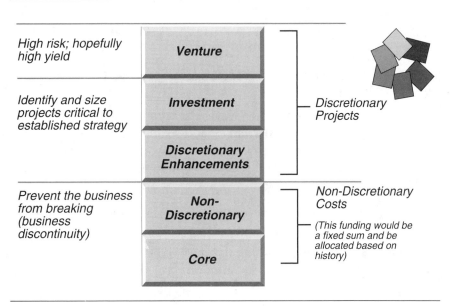

**Figure 7.5** Speaking Like a CFO

■ Discretionary enhancements are those that can be implemented at the business's discretion. For example, if there is a budget crunch and you have 10 enhancements planned, you might only execute two within this category.

■ Investments are long-term costs that will have future payoffs. At first, putting together Transactional Integration infrastructure might be considered an investment. However, over time this will become a non-discretionary cost to keep it running. Interestingly, the management techniques and metrics change when the status of a project changes this way.

■ Venture funding is comparable to a particular client wanting to fund a group of business and technology research projects with a big budget to support it. You can divide the work into 10 enhancements and get 10 projects going. Of these 10, the investors might expect five or six venture activities to fail, two or three to break even, and the two successful ones to more than pay for the others.

Using these categories, along with the categories described earlier, can provide an ideal context for budget decision-making.

### Getting It Right

In conclusion, to effectively package your infrastructure changes to the stakeholders, you must do several things, including:

- Determine the costs faster and earlier—or (even better) at the right time.

- Instill a customer service culture into the IT organization, regardless of what packaging and selling are actually implemented. Knowing your client, marketing, and communicating well are all techniques that will keep you looking good.

- Develop infrastructure communication plans.

- Identify buyer constituencies (stakeholders) and values long before pricing and packaging anything.

- Package according to buyer value, not IT organization, vendor, product, or cheap solutions.

- Remember that pricing and costs do not have to be related.

- Consider outsourcers good sources of packaging and pricing methodologies, and learn from them.

Always remember that you need to know your cost, value to the buyer, and the street price, to properly price any costs back to the business.

## People: Roles, Skills, and Organizational Issues

Another key area that deserves your attention is integrating infrastructure planning processes and personnel with other processes and structures in your IT organization. These might include processes and groups such as operations, applications development, and architecture. This section explains the skills and roles needed for good infrastructure planning, as well as a skills sourcing strategy for both internal and external resources.

Infrastructure planning (also called technical architecting or engineering) has two major goals with regard to other IT constituencies.

- First, it should take higher-level architecture planning and focus it into standards that are realistic in the near to mid term, with specific product and other technical details fully fleshed out. This should help the architectural work, which is highly theoretical in nature, be visible and practical enough for the operations group. For example, infrastructure patterns could be viewed as templates for applying architectural standards to actual application deployments, thus clarifying the decision about which standard to use.

■ Second, the infrastructure planning group must balance the needs of applications development and operations on a per-project basis to make sure that applications are deployed successfully and that the two teams work together successfully.

For example, if the Applications Development team held all the power, and Operations has no early impact, then the company's operational excellence would not be very good. All projects would be optimized for application development goals, and probably would not be optimized for operational excellence. Many things would be done differently each time, and operational costs would not be considered in creating project budgets.

Conversely, if the organization has strong operations but lacks applications development leadership, the organization might have trouble changing very quickly or moving to the next level. The natural inclination of operations toward less variety and more stability would make innovation a difficult proposition.

If you are an infrastructure planner, you must find the best middle ground between innovation and stability.

To do this, you must have an adequate staff to handle infrastructure planning, a good budget, and the time to focus on doing the work. Many organizations try to use existing resources to fill these roles on a temporary basis. It is crucial that someone on your team can focus on this important planning role, without being called away to do other work.

## Strategic Versus Tactical Roles

The new role of the infrastructure planner works on two levels, as shown in Figure 7.6. At the strategic level, the infrastructure planner deals with periodic reviews and standards updates. At the tactical level, he deals with per-project work.

Many roles fall between these two levels as well, and they must be filled to support the entire team.

**Tactical Roles.**   These roles deal with the "per-project processes" identified in Chapter 6. The main tactical roles are infrastructure designer, business requirements negotiator (or relationship manager), infrastructure auditor, and an effective project manager. While many architects and engineers do not excel at project management, it is important to find someone who does in order to support your team. There must be some-

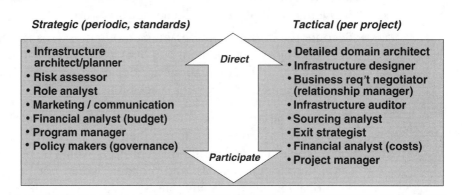

**Figure 7.6** Strategic Role Versus Tactical Role on the Infrastructure Team

one outside of the designer role who can make sure the work is finished on time. Likewise, most people with a technical background do not have the talent or an interest in being a financial manager. Yet the financial analyst role is very important on a per-project basis.

**Strategic Roles.** These roles deal with the "period processes" identified in Chapter 6. On the strategic side, there must be infrastructure planners and architects, as well as policy makers and managers who make the overall decisions. There should be a program manager for issues related to the Program Management Office (PMO), so you can ensure infrastructure projects fit into the overall project goals of the organization.

Risk assessor is another important role in the organization, and there should be a few focused on highly infrastructural issues. At the strategic level, there also needs to be a role analyst, who plans out the human resources in the organization; a financial analyst, who works on the overall budget; and a marketing and communications specialist, who handles communications issues for the organization.

At the strategic level, there will likely be multiple teams.

- A project design team would be composed of many technology experts to fill in the details of the infrastructure planner's pattern and service plans (during the "refine" steps in the infrastructure model). This team will need help in the financial and project management areas.

- A strategy team would include infrastructure planners, architects, application developers, operations leadership, and others. This team also will need financial and program management help.

The Adaptive Infrastructure Model can help guide you through all the various roles involved in infrastructure planning. For every step in the model, there must be a person or function that performs the step. The model guides you through detailed process modeling, which generates the requirements needed for which you must have roles. So the process model and the role definition go hand-in-hand. If you know the process steps well, you can describe the role much better.

## Key Infrastructure Planning Skills

When organizing an infrastructure planning team, make sure that you have the right people with the right skills for the job. For the infrastructure planner role itself, the following skills are critical:

- Leadership. Infrastructure planners should exhibit certain leadership skills and have the ability to move the group forward to success.

- Expertise. They must also have some broad technical expertise, with particular emphasis on middleware, network, and security technology.

- Business skills. The infrastructure planner role requires a solid understanding of the business. The business training you might give such infrastructure planners is education on the significant business concerns of their users.

- Communication. Planners should have strong marketing communication skills. The planners focus on doing the detailed analysis. However, marketing professionals will later take the analysis and use it to fully market the product or service. Therefore, planners need to have a basic knowledge of marketing to perform their job effectively. If you do not have the luxury of having separate people for infrastructure marketing and infrastructure planning, the planner will have to do the marketing as well. Planners will need to be convincing, both verbally and in writing.

It is not realistic to expect infrastructure planners to be highly knowledgeable in all necessary areas for successful business (or even infrastructure planning). Often, outside resources must work with the planning team to assist in areas such as management, finance, and auditing. Infrastructure planners will need deep technical expertise in areas such as networking, middleware (application servers and integration), security, and content distribution. In fact, it is advisable to have several people who have some expertise in these areas working directly with the planning team. It is the infrastructure planner's job to keep this level of expertise available and directly applied to tasks such as managing infrastructure strategy, assimilating infrastructure change, prototyping, and so on.

Sometimes a traditional technical architect is repositioned to handle the infrastructure planning role. Other times, organizations have been successful using staff members from more specific and focused technological roles, who change jobs to handle the complete range of infrastructure planning duties.

## Finding the Correct Resources

The infrastructure planning group will need to look externally to find other skills needed for the planning process. Your choices include internal resources, strategic suppliers and vendors, tactical suppliers, and advisers. The following discussion explains more about each.

### Internal Resources

You must interact with your internal stakeholders. Key roles may fall inside or outside IT, but they typically include those listed in Table 7.4.

Some roles do not involve infrastructure planning, but are crucial to the whole organization, such as the CTO. When preparing to present to these leaders, ask yourself what will appeal to them. This will help you sell your infrastructure plans and investments to the right audience.

### Advisers

These people provide strategic IT guidance and leadership. They understand your users' key business application demands and they can leverage existing resources to help users make the right decision. They also act as facilitators and should be able to make recommendations free of any vendor bias.

The advisers' relationship with the infrastructure planning team can vary from a one-on-one coach, to serving as part of the extended infrastructure planning team, to a long-term relationship with the planning team. When you need to bring skills into your team, you don't always have to hire someone from outside your organization. You can bring in advisers to give you some of the needed skills and training.

**Table 7.4** Internal Resources for Infrastructure Planning

| Title or Position | Role |
| --- | --- |
| Business Partner Manager | Works with the business partners at a technical level to ensure project focus. |
| Vendor/Sourcing Manager | Manages relationships with vendors and outsourcers. |
| Internal Partner Manager | Supervises relationships with internal resource groups (legal, accounting, HR, marketing, and so on). |
| Chief Security Officer | Coordinates security activities and determines policies. |
| Chief Technology Officer (CTO) | Executive-level people who will be reviewing your infrastructure plans. |

### Strategic Vendors

These include infrastructure vendors and systems integrators who can provide you with industry-leading capabilities in key areas. The list should be short, focused on a few key providers who are fundamental to the success of your key infrastructure projects. These vendors must be financially secure organizations that complement your planning skills in critical technology domains. (Obviously, in areas their own products and/or services are available.) They may not have the best product, but they should have one of the best. More important, they should be best-in-class at support. Choose a supplier who understands that your group needs support, not just a product sales pitch. Your clients don't want products; they want solutions. Good suppliers will want to know your long-range goals to do their job effectively.

However, keep in mind that the supplier/customer relationship is a two-way street. You should communicate your future business plans to your suppliers. Continue to urge your suppliers to change their products, so that the services, which are critical to you, become part of their architectures. There should be constant knowledge transfer between these suppliers and your group.

While strategic suppliers do not need to be involved with the internal core strategic planning in your organization, they should be members of the extended planning team, or they should perform other roles. Typically, the relationship between the strategic suppliers and your organization is a long-term one, with a high level of integration.

### Tactical Suppliers

These are groups with which you may not have a long-term relationship. These suppliers assist more with project-level vendor needs. Tactical suppliers should fit in areas where either best-of-breed technology or lowest cost is the key requirement—they may not have great support or be extremely strategic to your overall plans.

With the current business world constantly in flux, many tactical suppliers find themselves running out of money and closing their doors. For that reason, you should place these businesses on your list of tactical suppliers, where you can easily replace them if they go out of business. However, if the supplier's technology is fundamental to your organization, you may put them on your strategic list. Always prepare yourself for the possibility that they may not have the same kind of long-term viability as your strategic supplier relationships. In most cases, you should design your infrastructure to easily substitute tactical suppliers.

### Next Steps

Once you define the core planners from your internal resources—the advisers and the strategic and tactical suppliers—you can quickly pinpoint the correct group to contact when problems occur. Once you've identified these key players, you can begin to draft your basic information plans.

You can then use these key roles as a system of checks and balances. Telling your advisers, suppliers, and others about your plans allows them to confirm whether they think you are moving in the right direction. This can be a reality check for any plans and strategies, including patterns and services, which are offered by some of the infrastructure vendors or systems integrators. These groups can act as watchdogs for you.

## Planning the Planning Team

There are several recommendations for organizing your infrastructure planning team.

- Ask yourself how many people should be on the team. Your answer to this question should be based on the size of your organization and the complexity that occurs when your business meets infrastructure.

- There must be at least one FTE allocated to be a full-time infrastructure planner. Teams alone are not enough.

- Determine the necessary processes before you pick the team, and then designate people to do those processes.

- Organize the team to minimize any confusion with project hand-offs, overhead, and complexity.

Virtual teams must have a nonvirtual team leader. Keep in mind that teams don't get the work done, people do. At some level, it must be clear who is going to get the work done and when. That is the job of an actual team leader, not a virtual one. That is also why project and program management disciplines are critical.

The team leader job should be assigned to an infrastructure planner. If someone isn't showing up for meetings, the team leader will track him or her down. If a deliverable is due at the end of the week, the team leader is responsible for getting it done, even if all the team members bail out due to other commitments.

Next, ask yourself what will motivate the team to finish their work. If your virtual team has members who belong to other departments, will they take the time to stop their other work and finish your team's work on a daily basis? Experience suggests that the answer is often "no."

When organizing your infrastructure planning group, consider some of the metrics that will be applied to the activities of the team. Can the team improve service levels to have the greatest customer satisfaction? Can they optimize processes better? Can they increase the reuse percentage?

These kinds of issues should be considered early on, particularly if you're setting up an infrastructure planning organization. As you get these role definitions, staffing, and process refinements well structured, you have created a new Center of Excellence (COE) for infrastructure planning. The next question is: To whom should these people report?

## Organizational Models

There are many ways to organize your infrastructure planning team in relation to other IT constituencies. However, it pays to make a few observations first about the impact of organizational change, which can be tragic.

First, there is no such thing as a perfect organization. Politics often drive organizations, as much as great ideas or reality does. Moreover, finding the right people for your team usually makes the biggest difference, often making or breaking a troubled organization. A talented manager can make a big difference in a troubled organization. A bad manager can sabotage the effectiveness of a group within a good organization.

There are pros and cons to each available organizational model. In fact, no matter what the model, you must ensure the process is strong enough to overcome the inevitable frictions and miscommunications within any group.

**Report to applications development group.**   The team planning the infrastructure could report to the applications development group. One positive feature of this arrangement is that the application level work is most likely to be easily integrated. In this plan, infrastructure planners may be more focused on API work.

This type of organization model, however, does not work well for infrastructure planning teams that are heavily middleware oriented. They are not separate enough from per-project application decision-making to truly take an adaptive infrastructure approach, and they will not be able to sufficiently reduce variation to capture efficiencies at the infrastructure or operational level. In addition, operational costs can be vastly simplified, or simply ignored in all infrastructure planning projects when using this model.

**Report to IT architecture/planning team.**   Another possibility is to have infrastructure planning as a part of the IT architecture/planning team. The integration of infrastructure planning and architecture in itself could be very beneficial to the organization. The group can leverage its skills, have more of a panoramic perspective of the business, and have stronger management practices.

A downside to this model could be the negative perspectives that sometimes exist in operations and other IT constituencies regarding the architecture team. Namely, that architecture is not connected enough with reality, and that it places unrealistic demands and plans on application development and operations for future work.

Furthermore, the interaction between infrastructure planners and operations or application development team members could suffer with this plan. Because infrastructure planners and architects often deal with the same problems, the day-to-day problems of the other groups could go unnoticed by infrastructure planning. Also, there could be conflicts between how architecture and infrastructure planning measure success, as compared to other groups in the organization.

Infrastructure planners usually plan for things that can be completed immediately. Architects tend to plan for the future. So, if the infrastructure planning group reports to architecture, the team could begin to focus more on the future goals and ignore the more immediate work. Finally, infrastructure planners in this organization model might not be as effective in project management.

**Report to engineering/tech support.** Another option is for the infrastructure planning group to report to the engineering/technical support team or even the operations team. The logic behind this organization model is that engineering/technical support people do much of the application building, which is closely aligned with technical management.

Other positives of this model include a smooth integration with the operations team. This means that the technical experts in infrastructure planning are directly accessible to the people in operations, so their skills can be more easily leveraged. An infrastructure planning team in this model would have a more task-oriented focus.

The downside to this organization model is that the infrastructure planning group might start to function in a more tactical or reactive way. Infrastructure planners might be more technology-driven, rather than business-driven in their planning goals.

Engineering and technical support groups are often focused on the short term, versus medium and long-range goals. Infrastructure planning might lose its ability to focus on quarterly or yearly goals, and might focus only on immediate problem resolutions.

There is also the perception, and sometimes the reality, that the engineering and technical support teams are averse to change. Infrastructure planning groups reporting within this model might start resisting change, which can drastically affect the business.

**Report to IT management.** A preferred model of organization for the infrastructure planning team is not to report to any of the previously mentioned groups. Instead, the group reports directly to IT management, at a peer level with these other groups. This model makes it easier for management to measure what the infrastructure planning team does, in contrast with the other teams.

Here, the infrastructure planning team is more focused and more likely to be process-driven, because it isn't located inside a project-oriented or operations-oriented group. Infrastructure planning can be more program-based, with a more panoramic view of the business because the group is not buried inside another team.

However, because this is a fairly new approach to organizing business, management may be reluctant to organize the business this way.

They might also balk at using this model because it increases the number of direct reports to management.

When you separate one team from another, you invite communication problems. In this new model, there are three other groups with which infrastructure planning must interact, rather than the two groups in the other models. Thus, our focus in infrastructure planning is on connecting to these different groups with specific processes (e.g., goal pattern design) and technology models (patterns, services).

## Summary

The bottom line is that you must define your infrastructure processes and map the actual resources. Determine your skills-sourcing strategy across your internal resources, advisers, and strategic and tactical suppliers. Choose strategic partners that complement your internal resources and skills. Clearly state your infrastructure planning mission, as well as the roles and responsibilities associated with it, which you can document in an official charter document, if needed.

# Appendix **A**

# Component Catalog

This appendix lists some of the primary components contained in the adaptive infrastructure platform. Many of these components were discussed in detail in Chapters 5 through 8 of this book. However, this list provides additional information, including vendor/product examples, key patterns, and key services related to each component.

This list was current upon this book's publication. Change in representative vendors and products should be expected, given continued market volatility and the normal pace of technical innovation. Vendor and product references in this appendix, as well as those appearing in the rest of this book, are intended to be used as examples for understanding more clearly the general points being made. Sometimes, seeing a familiar product makes a discussion much more clear and useful.

However, the use of any vendor and product names in this appendix (or the entire book) should not imply endorsement of any particular product. Such references are made for illustrative purposes only.

## Index to Components

## Infra-API

*Purpose*

Exposes low-level technology services, including security, naming, transactionality, and object invocation. Application and infrastructure developers consume these services during the creation of business logic. Increasingly, Infra-APIs and the services they encapsulate are provided off-the-shelf within application servers (J2EE/EJB/Java-based, CORBA, Microsoft COM+/.NET, and so forth). Infrastructure developers still need to augment application servers with higher-level frameworks, and then provide them to application developers for use during the development process.

*Examples (Vendors and Products)*

**Technologies:**   J2EE Enterprise Java Beans, Java Transaction Service, Java Messaging Service, Object Transaction Server, CORBA Messaging Services, and J2EE/EJB, Microsoft .NET, CORBA, and even DCE security services.

**Products:**   Container servers (provide off-the-shelf infrastructure services) and container server IDEs (used to invoke off-the-shelf services and create new infrastructure services).

**Containers:**   BEA WebLogic, IBM WebSphere, Microsoft COM+/.NET, Sun iPlanet/ONE, IDEs, IBM Visual Age, WebGain (a.k.a. Symantec Visual Cafe).

| | |
|---|---|
| Layer Number | 1 |
| Component Layer | API |
| Priority | 9 |
| Key Infra Pattern | 3/N-Tier Transact |
| Key Infra Service | Transactional Integration (EAI, IEI) |

## Inter-API

### *Purpose*

Used in inter-application communication to expose application business logic for use by other applications. Since Inter-APIs affect other applications, they should be defined and managed by infrastructure developers.

### *Examples (Vendors and Products)*

**Technologies:**   X.12/Edifact EDI interfaces, user developed APIs into business process functionality, and ERP vendor provided APIs into packaged application functionality.

**Products:**   Container server IDE, visual modeling tools (such as UML tools), and adapter SDKs.

**Containers:**   BEA WebLogic, IBM WebSphere, and Sun iPlanet.

**IDEs:**   IBM Visual Age and WebGain (a.k.a. Symantec Visual Cafe).

**Modeling Tools:**   Rational Rose, Visio.

**Integration Servers:**   IBM/New Era of Networks MQ Series Integrator (MQSI), SeeBeyond (formerly STC) e-Gate, and Active ActiveWorks.

| | |
|---|---|
| Layer Number | 1 |
| Component Layer | API |
| Priority | 4 |
| Key Infra Pattern | 3/N-Tier Transact |
| Key Infra Service | Transactional Integration (EAI, IEI) |

### Intra-API

*Purpose*

Used in intra-application communication to expose application level business logic that is used only within the context of a single application. Since Intra-APIs are not reused outside a given application, they are created and managed by that application's developers.

*Examples (Vendors and Products)*

**Technologies:**  COM IDL, EJB IDL, CORBA IDL, RPC IDL, and Function calls.

**Products:**  Container Server IDE, visual modeling tools (such as UML tools).

**Containers:**  BEA WebLogic, IBM WebSphere, and Sun iPlanet.

**IDEs:**  IBM Visual Age, WebGain (a.k.a. Symantec Visual Cafe).

**Modeling Tools:**  Rational Rose and Visio.

| | |
|---|---|
| Layer Number | 1 |
| Component Layer | API |
| Priority | 9 |
| Key Infra Pattern | 3/N-Tier Transact |
| Key Infra Service | Transactional Integration (EAI, IEI) |

## E-Mail MTA

*Purpose*

SMTP messaging (another POI) that is commonly used by e-mail response solutions for customer interaction or instant messaging. SMTP message transfer agents (MTAs), or gateways, are used to relay e-mail outside of the organization.

*Examples (Vendors and Products)*

**SMTP gateways/MTAs:**   Exchange, Notes, and SendMail.

**Response vendors:**   Kana, BriteWare, Egain, and Mustang/Quintus.

**Instant messaging:**   AOL and ICQ.

| | |
|---|---|
| Layer Number | 2 |
| Component Layer | Presentation |
| Priority | 9 |
| Key Infra Pattern | Store-and-Forward Collaborate |
| Key Infra Service | N/A |

## Integrated Voice Response (IVR)

*Purpose*

Also called Voice Response Unit (VRU), a device that pre-answers calls, asks for an account number or personal identification number (PIN), and enables the caller to access information, make transactions, etc. IVRs are another point of interaction (POI) whereby a server translates telephone Touch Tone (and going forward, speech) requests into data queries, which are then returned to the IVR with the result spoken back to the caller.

*Examples (Vendors and Products)*

Lucent Conversant, IBM DirecTalk, InterVoiceBrite, Edify, and Periphonics.

| | |
|---|---|
| Layer Number | 2 |
| Component Layer | Presentation |
| Priority | 9 |
| Key Infra Pattern | 3/N-Tier Transact |
| Key Infra Service | Voice |

## Interactive TV

*Purpose*

TV networks that run over cable, satellite, and broadcast, as well as Web networks. This interactive component should have bandwidth.

*Examples (Vendors and Products)*

BSkyB, Premier, etc.

| | |
|---|---|
| Layer Number | 2 |
| Component Layer | Presentation |
| Priority | 9 |
| Key Infra Pattern | Stream Publish |
| Key Infra Service | N/A |

## Streaming Server

*Purpose*

Software that is used to stream out audio and video content to player clients, which may be proprietary protocols. It also supports IRC chat servers and shared whiteboarding solutions, including NetMeeting. The goal is to deliver real-time, or very near real-time, content that is usually multimedia.

*Examples (Vendors and Products)*

**Audio/Video:**   Cisco WebTV, Real Networks Real Server, etc.

**Shared whiteboarding:**   Cisco WebLine, Aspect WebAgent, Microsoft NetMeeting, and WebEx.

| | |
|---|---|
| Layer Number | 2 |
| Component Layer | Presentation |
| Priority | 9 |
| Key Infra Pattern | Stream Publish |
| Key Infra Service | N/A |

## Terminal Server

*Purpose*

Software that services other specialized and/or proprietary terminal devices or protocols.

*Examples (Vendors and Products)*

Citrix Winframe/MetaFrame, Microsoft Terminal Server Edition, IBM 3174 remote controllers, and 3745 front-end processors (FEPs).

| | |
|---|---|
| Layer Number | 2 |
| Component Layer | Presentation |
| Priority | 9 |
| Key Infra Pattern | 2-Tier Transact |
| Key Infra Service | Desktop |

## Voice

*Purpose*

A collaborative POI that allows talking over voice networks to internal people, such as the customer interaction center (CIC) or call center.

*Examples (Vendors and Products)*

Plain old telephone services (POTS) and voice over IP.

| | |
|---|---|
| Layer Number | 2 |
| Component Layer | Presentation |
| Priority | 9 |
| Key Infra Pattern | Real-time Collaborate |
| Key Infra Service | Device |

## WAP Server

*Purpose*

Software that converts internal formats and protocols to those required to run over low bandwidth wireless networks. It also reformats the user interface (UI) to fit small screen sizes.

*Examples (Vendors and Products)*

Nokia, Ericsson, Phone.COM, Alcatel, and Motorola.

| | |
|---|---|
| Layer Number | 2 |
| Component Layer | Presentation |
| Priority | 3 |
| Key Infra Pattern | 3/N-Tier Transact |
| Key Infra Service | Device |

## Web Server

*Purpose*

A combination of two components:

■ An HTTP listener/gateway (such as IIS with HTTP/ISAPI, Apache HTTP/CGI, and Netscape Enterprise Server with HTTP/NSAPI)

■ An HTML-only Web/app server that offers a mix of Web-specific presentation services (such as IIS ASPs and Apache JSPs) with the opportunity to incorporate business logic directly, rather than calling a separate application server

*Examples (Vendors and Products)*

**Technologies:**   HTTP, CGI, Active Server Pages, and Java Server Pages.

**Products:**   Straight Web servers (including Microsoft IIS, Apache, and Netscape Enterprise Server); and Web/app servers (including Allaire ColdFusion, Haht HotSite, and IBM WebSphere Standard Edition).

| | |
|---|---|
| Layer Number | 2 |
| Component Layer | Presentation |
| Priority | 2 |
| Key Infra Pattern | Web Publish |
| Key Infra Service | HTML |

## Application Server

### *Purpose*

Software that executes business logic functions, allowing easy POI differentiation (3/N-Tier focused) or specific nailing to Web front ends (2-Tier). These software suites usually include a Web (or Web/app) server component. Previously, many solutions were built from separate execution, integrity, gateway, interaction, and toolkit services. Since single products now offer all these services as a bundle (even with standard service provider interfaces—for example, J2EE and .NET frameworks), those features are no longer split out as separate components of an application server. However, we still see enough differentiation in the integration server solutions to keep the separate component definitions.

### *Examples (Vendors and Products)*

**Technologies:**   TP Monitors, J2EE Enterprise Java Beans (EJB), Microsoft .NET (Web Services), CORBA, and Proprietary.

**Products:**   BEA WebLogic Enterprise Edition, IBM WebSphere Advanced and Enterprise Editions, Sun iPlanet/ONE, Microsoft COM+/.NET, IBM CICS, and BEA Tuxedo.

| | |
|---|---|
| Layer Number | 3 |
| Component Layer | Application |
| Priority | 1 |
| Key Infra Pattern | 3/N-Tier Transact |
| Key Infra Service | N/A |

## Adapter Toolkit

*Purpose*

Software that enables development of application adaptors, exploiting application or data specific standards or proprietary APIs.

*Examples (Vendors and Products)*

Specific Adapter Toolkits of EAI vendors.

| | |
|---|---|
| Layer Number | 4 |
| Component Layer | Integration |
| Priority | 4 |
| Key Infra Pattern | 3/N-Tier Transact |
| Key Infra Service | Transactional Integration (EAI, IEI) |

## Application Adapter

*Purpose*

Software that connects integration rules engines and their transports to specific applications in a particular instance. This is accomplished by exploiting application or data specific standards or proprietary APIs.

*Examples (Vendors and Products)*

Pre-built adapters from EAI vendors or ERP vendors.

| | |
|---|---|
| Layer Number | 4 |
| Component Layer | Integration |
| Priority | 4 |
| Key Infra Pattern | 3/N-Tier Transact |
| Key Infra Service | Transactional Integration (EAI, IEI) |

## Computer Telephony Integration (CTI) Server

*Purpose*

Software that integrates applications and telephony, and manages and routes (based on skills, wait time, etc.) telephone calls, e-mail, and agent-end user collaboration. CTI routing algorithms can be based on criteria supplied by customer databases (such as CRM), agent skills, wait time for an agent, and so forth.

*Examples (Vendors and Products)*

Genesys, Quintus, Prospect, IBM CallPath, TAPI, TSAPI, CSTA, and CT Connect.

| | |
|---|---|
| Layer Number | 4 |
| Component Layer | Integration |
| Priority | 3 |
| Key Infra Pattern | 3/N-Tier Transact |
| Key Infra Service | Voice |

## Integration Server

*Purpose*

Software that does basic routing (not workflow, and not transactional) and data transformation between applications, often running in a hub-and-spoke configuration. Previously, we have broken these two out into separate functions, but we rarely see them as independent products. Now we have lumped them into a single component. Soon we expect to lump more of the remaining separate components in the integration layer into this overall integration server component.

*Examples (Vendors and Products)*

Viewlocity (was Frontec), NEON/IBM MQSI, SeeBeyond (formerly STC), and Mercator.

| | |
|---|---|
| Layer Number | 4 |
| Component Layer | Integration |
| Priority | 1 |
| Key Infra Pattern | 3/N-Tier Transact |
| Key Infra Service | Transactional Integration (EAI, IEI) |

## EDI Gateway

### *Purpose*

Software that moves data and transforms it from flat format into standard data formats (such as X12 and EDIFACT) for use by business partners. Other services include scheduling, monitoring, acknowledgment, encryption, authentication, and nonrepudiation.

### *Examples (Vendors and Products)*

Sterling Commerce, IBM, Harbinger, St. Paul Software, GEIS, Telecom Finland, Actis, and Sun/Netscape Alliance.

| | |
|---|---|
| Layer Number | 4 |
| Component Layer | Integration |
| Priority | 9 |
| Key Infra Pattern | 3/N-Tier Transact |
| Key Infra Service | Transactional Integration (EAI, IEI) |

## File Exchange Server

### *Purpose*

Software that moves data and schedules the move with some features for recoverability (including checkpoint restart). It may offer encryption, authentication, and other EB-oriented features and may also leverage OS-based FTP and scheduling (such as UNIX cron) capabilities.

### *Examples (Vendors and Products)*

Sterling Software Connect:Direct, Connect:Mailbox, Micro-Tempus, IBM NDM, CA XCOM, and MLINK.

| | |
|---|---|
| Layer Number | 4 |
| Component Layer | Integration |
| Priority | 9 |
| Key Infra Pattern | 3/N-Tier Transact |
| Key Infra Service | Transactional Integration (EAI, IEI) |

## Integration Transport

*Purpose*

Software that enables particular application adaptors to talk to centralized integration server hubs, where asynchronous (store and forward) and event-oriented behavior is critical. Often bundled with Integration (EAI) or IEI server.

*Examples (Vendors and Products)*

IBM MQ Series and Microsoft MSMQ (predominantly for internal EAI uses); SOAP (Simple Object Access Protocol that sends XML via simple RPC mechanism over HTTP and is most applicable to IEI uses).

| | |
|---|---|
| Layer Number | 4 |
| Component Layer | Integration |
| Priority | 3 |
| Key Infra Pattern | 3/N-Tier Transact |
| Key Infra Service | Transactional Integration (EAI, IEI) |

## Middleware Encryption

*Purpose*

Software that secures and protects middleware transports. Several products are specific to MQ Series as a system-to-system transport.

*Examples (Vendors and Products)*

Nanoteq, MQ Armour, Primeur DataSecure, and Candle MQSecure.

| | |
|---|---|
| Layer Number | 4 |
| Component Layer | Integration |
| Priority | 9 |
| Key Infra Pattern | 3/N-Tier Transact |
| Key Infra Service | Security (Isolation) |

## Inter-Enterprise Integration (IEI) Server

*Purpose*

Software that integrates business processes across business boundaries. Currently, IEI servers overlap the functionality provided by integration servers. However, they will evolve into mere inter-business adaptors for those more general-purpose integration servers. Their primary focus is, and should be, community of interest management, XML formatting, and providing firewall-friendly transports.

*Examples (Vendors and Products)*

NetFish, WebMethods, Extricity, Bridges2Islands, and Microsoft's Biz-Talk Server 2000.

| | |
|---|---|
| Layer Number | 4 |
| Component Layer | Integration |
| Priority | 2 |
| Key Infra Pattern | 3/N-Tier Transact |
| Key Infra Service: | Transactional Integration (EAI, IEI) |

## Process Execution Engine

*Purpose*

Workflow software that executes workflow rules designed by a process modeler.

*Examples (Vendors and Products)*

Vitria BusinessWare, IBM MQ Workflow, New Era of Networks eProcess Enabler, Tibco IntegrationManager or InConcert, Mercator Enterprise Broker, webMethods Business Integrator, SeeBeyond (formerly STC) eBusiness Process Manager, Microsoft Biztalk Orchestration.

| | |
|---|---|
| Layer Number | 4 |
| Component Layer | Integration |
| Priority | 3 |
| Key Infra Pattern | 3/N-Tier Transact |
| Key Infra Service | Transactional Integration (EAI, IEI) |

## Process Modeler

*Purpose*

Workflow software that designs workflow processes for execution by the process execution engine.

*Examples (Vendors and Products)*

**UML tools:**   Rational Rose and Visio.

| | |
|---|---|
| Layer Number | 4 |
| Component Layer | Integration |
| Priority | 3 |
| Key Infra Pattern | 3/N-Tier Transact |
| Key Infra Service | Transactional Integration (EAI, IEI) |

## Data Access Middleware

*Purpose*

Software that enables applications (including middle-tier app servers) to access DBMS-based data. Usually, this software provides a protocol to communicate across a network, not only a standard API like ODBC.

*Examples (Vendors and Products)*

Oracle SQL*Net and Net8, and ODBC drivers.

| | |
|---|---|
| Layer Number | 5 |
| Component Layer | Database |
| Priority | 9 |
| Key Infra Pattern | 3/N-Tier Transact |
| Key Infra Service | Database |

## Database Gateway

*Purpose*

Software that enables applications to access a variety of back-end DBMS-based data, transforming calls into native calls for each DBMS supported.

*Examples (Vendors and Products)*

IBI EDA/SQL, Sybase OmniSQL, OLE DB and ODBC drivers.

| | |
|---|---|
| Layer Number | 5 |
| Component Layer | Database |
| Priority | 9 |
| Key Infra Pattern | 3/N-Tier Transact |
| Key Infra Service | Database |

## DBMS

*Purpose*

Software that stores data in formats to allow easy and fast retrieval, along with efficient writing of data, often relational in structure (RDBMS).

*Examples (Vendors and Products)*

Oracle, Sybase, Ingres, IBM DB2, and Microsoft SQL Server.

| | |
|---|---|
| Layer Number | 5 |
| Component Layer | Database |
| Priority | 4 |
| Key Infra Pattern | 3/N-Tier Transact |
| Key Infra Service | Database |

## Voice Messaging Store

*Purpose*

Software that enables voice-mail and messaging.

*Examples (Vendors and Products)*

Octel, Centigram, and Lucent.

| | |
|---|---|
| Layer Number | 5 |
| Component Layer | Database |
| Priority | 9 |
| Key Infra Pattern | 3/N-Tier Transact |
| Key Infra Service | Voice |

## Application Server HA

*Purpose*

High-availability solutions that are specifically for application server implementations. These are often options in the application server software, but may also include hardware solutions. If available, we recommend not using server operating system layer HA solutions for EB situations (except in the case of DBMS servers).

*Examples (Vendors and Products)*

Clustering

| | |
|---|---|
| Layer Number | 6 |
| Component Layer | Server |
| Priority | 2 |
| Key Infra Pattern | 3/N-Tier Transact |
| Key Infra Service | N/A |

## Application Server HW

*Purpose*

Hardware platforms that support application server software.

*Examples (Vendors and Products)*

Sun, Compaq, IBM Intel, RISC, or S/390 servers.

| | |
|---|---|
| Layer Number | 6 |
| Component Layer | Server |
| Priority | 2 |
| Key Infra Pattern | 3/N-Tier Transact |
| Key Infra Service | N/A |

## Application Server OS

*Purpose*

Operating System software for platforms that support application server software.

*Examples (Vendors and Products)*

UNIX (Sun Solaris, HP-UX, IBM AIX), Microsoft NT and Windows 2000 server, and IBM OS/390.

| | |
|---|---|
| Layer Number | 6 |
| Component Layer | Server |
| Priority | 2 |
| Key Infra Pattern | 3/N-Tier Transact |
| Key Infra Service | N/A |

## Database Server HA

*Purpose*

High-availability solutions that are specifically for database server implementations. These are often options in the database server software, but may also include hardware solutions. If available, we recommend not using server operating system layer HA solutions for EB situations (except in the case of DBMS servers).

*Examples (Vendors and Products)*

Oracle replication and clustering.

| | |
|---|---|
| Layer Number | 6 |
| Component Layer | Server |
| Priority | 9 |
| Key Infra Pattern | 3/N-Tier Transact |
| Key Infra Service | Database |

## Database Server HW

*Purpose*

Hardware platforms that support database server software.

*Examples (Vendors and Products)*

Sun, Compaq, IBM Intel or RISC or S/390 servers.

| | |
|---|---|
| Layer Number | 6 |
| Component Layer | Server |
| Priority | 9 |
| Key Infra Pattern | 3/N-Tier Transact |
| Key Infra Service | Database |

## Database Server OS

### *Purpose*

Operating System software for platforms that support database server software.

### *Examples (Vendors and Products)*

UNIX (Sun Solaris, HP-UX, IBM AIX), Microsoft NT and Windows 2000 Server, and IBM OS/390.

| | |
|---|---|
| Layer Number | 6 |
| Component Layer | Server |
| Priority | 9 |
| Key Infra Pattern | 3/N-Tier Transact |
| Key Infra Service | Database |

## Integration Server HA

### *Purpose*

High-availability solutions that are specifically for integration server implementations. These are often options in the integration server software, but may include hardware solutions. They are generally used to avoid single point of failure for this component.

### *Examples (Vendors and Products)*

Clustering and Microsoft Component Load Balancing (Windows 2000).

| | |
|---|---|
| Layer Number | 6 |
| Component Layer | Server |
| Priority | 2 |
| Key Infra Pattern | 3/N-Tier Transact |
| Key Infra Service | Transactional Integration (EAI, IEI) |

## Integration Server HW

*Purpose*

Hardware platforms that support integration server software.

*Examples (Vendors and Products)*

Sun, Compaq, HP, and IBM servers.

| | |
|---|---|
| Layer Number | 6 |
| Component Layer | Server |
| Priority | 2 |
| Key Infra Pattern | 3/N-Tier Transact |
| Key Infra Service | Transactional Integration (EAI, IEI) |

## Integration Server OS

*Purpose*

Operating System software for platforms that support integration server software.

*Examples (Vendors and Products)*

UNIX (Sun Solaris, HP-UX, IBM AIX), Microsoft NT and Windows 2000 Server, and IBM OS/390.

| | |
|---|---|
| Layer Number | 6 |
| Component Layer | Server |
| Priority | 2 |
| Key Infra Pattern | 3/N-Tier Transact |
| Key Infra Service | Transactional Integration (EAI, IEI) |

## File Server and Network-Attached Storage (NAS)

*Purpose*

File systems or storage subsystems that are connected *directly* to the network for direct access, either OS/HW combinations (NT/Windows 2000, NetWare, and UNIX) or in an appliance-style box without any standard OS to configure. Users access the system directly over TCP/IP and native protocols (such as NFS or CIFS) rather than with special storage channel protocols like SCSI. FTP servers are another example of a file-server component.

*Examples (Vendors and Products)*

Network Appliance, Auspex, EMC Celerra, MTI Vivant, or other NFS or Microsoft CIFS appliances and other OS/HW combinations (NT/Windows 2000, NetWare, and NFS).

| | |
|---|---|
| Layer Number | 6 |
| Component Layer | Server |
| Priority | 9 |
| Key Infra Pattern | Store and Forward Collaborate |
| Key Infra Service | File System |

## Web Server HA

*Purpose*

High-availability solutions that are specifically for Web-server implementations. These are often options in the Web-server software, but may include hardware solutions. If available, we recommend not using server operating system layer HA solutions for EB situations (except in the case of DBMS servers).

*Examples (Vendors and Products)*

Clustering and Windows NT/Windows 2000 Load Balancing Service (WLBS). See also network layer load balancers (not part of the Web server).

| | |
|---|---|
| Layer Number | 6 |
| Component Layer | Server |
| Priority | 2 |
| Key Infra Pattern | 3/N-Tier Transact |
| Key Infra Service | HTML |

## Web Server HW

*Purpose*

Hardware platforms that support Web-server software.

*Examples (Vendors and Products)*

Sun, Compaq, HP, and IBM servers.

| | |
|---|---|
| Layer Number | 6 |
| Component Layer | Server |
| Priority | 2 |
| Key Infra Pattern | 3/N-Tier Transact |
| Key Infra Service | HTML |

## Web Server OS

*Purpose*

Operating System software for platforms that support Web-server software.

*Examples (Vendors and Products)*

UNIX (Sun Solaris, HP-UX, IBM AIX), Linux, Microsoft NT and Windows 2000 Server, and IBM OS/390.

| | |
|---|---|
| Layer Number | 6 |
| Component Layer | Server |
| Priority | 2 |
| Key Infra Pattern | 3/N-Tier Transact |
| Key Infra Service | HTML |

## Business Continuance HW

*Purpose*

Hardware devices that include disk storage and tape transports (often with robotics). Such devices support business resumption in the event of a failure, and day-to-day backup and recovery requirements.

*Examples (Vendors and Products)*

**Tape transport vendors:** IBM, Sony, STK, and Quantum.

**Automation vendors:** ATL, IBM, and STK.

| | |
|---|---|
| Layer Number | 7 |
| Component Layer | Storage |
| Priority | 9 |
| Key Infra Pattern | 3/N-Tier Transact |
| Key Infra Service | SAN |

## Business Continuance SW

### *Purpose*

Software that enhances the ability to resume business functions in the event of a system or application failure. Remote mirroring of storage data is one type of software, along with server clustering software, which can reduce the time to recover data.

### *Examples (Vendors and Products)*

Primarily from storage hardware vendors (such as CPQ, EMC, HDS, and MTI), yet often requires server clustering technologies.

| | |
|---|---|
| Layer Number | 7 |
| Component Layer | Storage |
| Priority | 9 |
| Key Infra Pattern | 3/N-Tier Transact |
| Key Infra Service | SAN |

## Host Interconnect

### *Purpose*

Hardware device (such as a PCI card in a server) that connects the operating system servers for an application or database to a storage subsystem over copper or fiber optic cables (typically SCSI, Fibre Channel, or ESCON).

### *Examples (Vendors and Products)*

**Host bus adapter vendors:**   QLogic and Emulex.

**Hardware platform vendors:**   Compaq and Sun.

| | |
|---|---|
| Layer Number | 7 |
| Component Layer | Storage |
| Priority | 9 |
| Key Infra Pattern | 3/N-Tier Transact |
| Key Infra Service | SAN |

## Storage Area Network (SAN)

### Purpose

Physical implementation that separates and offloads storage and B/R traffic from the user/application network using various interconnect technologies. In addition to storage subsystems, traditional storage interconnects (such as Fibre Channel, Ultra SCSI, and ESCON) are typically used, although traditional network protocols like Ethernet can also be used.

### Examples (Vendors and Products)

**Hardware storage vendors:**  EMC, HDS, and MTI.

**System vendors:**  CPQ, Hewlett-Packard, and Sun.

**FC vendors:**  Ancor, Brocade, and McData.

| | |
|---|---|
| Layer Number | 7 |
| Component Layer | Storage |
| Priority | 9 |
| Key Infra Pattern | 3/N-Tier Transact |
| Key Infra Service | SAN |

## Storage Server

*Purpose*

External hardware device that houses storage (such as mechanical disk drives) separate from the application or database server platform. This device is used for information retrieval. Storage servers are typically connected via SCSI, Fibre Channel (potentially a fabric network), or ESCON over dedicated cabling.

*Examples (Vendors and Products)*

**Hardware storage vendors:**  EMC, HDS, and MTI.

**System vendors:**  CPQ, Hewlett-Packard, IBM, and Sun.

| | |
|---|---|
| Layer Number | 7 |
| Component Layer | Storage |
| Priority | 4 |
| Key Infra Pattern | 3/N-Tier Transact |
| Key Infra Service | SAN |

## Automatic Call Distributor (ACD)

### *Purpose*

Facility that manages incoming calls based on the number called, agents available, and a database of handling instructions. Calls are lined up or queued accordingly. The ACD also gathers usage statistics, which include the balance use of phone lines, etc. It can run on PBX or separately for routing and load balancing functions.

### *Examples (Vendors and Products)*

Aspect; Rockwell Galaxy, Spectrum or Transcend; Lucent's CMS; and Nortel Symposium or ACD MAX.

| | |
|---|---|
| Layer Number | 8 |
| Component Layer | Network |
| Priority | 9 |
| Key Infra Pattern | Real-time Collaborate |
| Key Infra Service | Voice |

## Content Delivery Network (CDN)

### *Purpose*

Networks that augment traditional forms of Web delivery by pushing content out to servers close to the user.

### *Examples (Vendors and Products)*

Akamai, Sandpiper/Digital Island, iBeam, Skycache, and Adero.

| | |
|---|---|
| Layer Number | 8 |
| Component Layer | Network |
| Priority | 3 |
| Key Infra Pattern | Web Publish |
| Key Infra Service | HTML |

## Content Security

### *Purpose*

Software that provides content monitoring and filtering to implement security policies against viruses, Java/ActiveX, and inappropriate usage (including porn-site filtering).

### *Examples (Vendors and Products)*

- Firewall plug-ins for virus scanning (CA/Cheyenne, McAfee, Trend Micro)
- Web screening (Microsystems, SpyGlass, Secure Computing)
- Java and ActiveX filtering (Finjan)

| | |
|---|---|
| Layer Number | 8 |
| Component Layer | Network |
| Priority | 3 |
| Key Infra Pattern | Store-and-Forward Collaborate |
| Key Infra Service | Security (Isolation) |

## Directory Server

*Purpose*

Software that stores information about users and applications in a quickly retrievable format (such as a database). This type of storage makes data easily accessible via standard protocols (LDAP). It is often combined with Web SSO solutions and/or public key infrastructure to provide identity infrastructure.

*Examples (Vendors and Products)*

Novell eDirectory, Netscape iPlanet Directory Server, IBM SecureWay Directory Server, and Microsoft Active Directory.

| | |
|---|---|
| Layer Number | 8 |
| Component Layer | Network |
| Priority | 1 |
| Key Infra Pattern | Web Publish |
| Key Infra Service | Security (Identity) |

## Extranet Service Provider (ESP)

*Purpose*

Services that offer a single point of contact for IP transport, firewall and VPN management, hosting, PKI, directory, middleware, professional services, and billing. Unlike pure hosting services, ESPs offer a mix of services specifically targeting B2B Extranets.

*Examples (Vendors and Products)*

No true ESPs currently exist, but emerging players include GE GES, Pilot, Aventail.net, and Telenisus.

| | |
|---|---|
| Layer Number | 8 |
| Component Layer | Network |
| Priority | 2 |
| Key Infra Pattern | Web Publish |
| Key Infra Service | Web Hosting |

## Firewall

*Purpose*

Hardware/software that filters data and applications via a variety of mechanisms (including stateful packet inspection and application proxy) to prevent unauthorized users and applications from entering an organization's enterprise. It may also provide additional functions, such as virus scanning, encryption, network address translation, and virtual private networking capabilities.

*Examples (Vendors and Products)*

Checkpoint FireWall 1 and Cisco Pix.

| | |
|---|---|
| Layer Number | 8 |
| Component Layer | Network |
| Priority | 1 |
| Key Infra Pattern | Web Publish |
| Key Infra Service | Security (Isolation) |

## Hosting Service

*Purpose*

Outsourced hosting offerings that support an organization's Web and application servers and/or provide high bandwidth connections to the "arteries" of the Internet.

*Examples (Vendors and Products)*

Exodus, Digital Island, Internap, Uunet, GTE, and Sprint.

| | |
|---|---|
| Layer Number | 8 |
| Component Layer | Network |
| Priority | 2 |
| Key Infra Pattern | Web Publish |
| Key Infra Service | Web Hosting |

## Internet Access and Transport Service (ISP)

*Purpose*

Internet services (ISPs) that connect an organization's sites and individual users to the Internet via dedicated, dial-up, DSL, and cable modem access technologies.

*Examples (Vendors and Products)*

Uunet, PSInet, Sprint, AT&T, Terra, and Infonet (ISPs).

| | |
|---|---|
| Layer Number | 8 |
| Component Layer | Network |
| Priority | 3 |
| Key Infra Pattern | Web Publish |
| Key Infra Service | WAN |

## Intrusion Detection and Threat Management

*Purpose*

Software and services that monitor an enterprise's firewalls and exposed hosts and report any break-ins or security failures.

*Examples (Vendors and Products)*

**Established products:**   Cisco/NetRanger and ISS/RealSecure)

**Emerging products:**   Abirnet/SessionWall-3, Anzen/Anzen Flight Jacket, Axent/NetProwler, Internet Tools/ID-Trak, and Network Associates/Cyber-Cop Network.

| | |
|---|---|
| Layer Number | 8 |
| Component Layer | Network |
| Priority | 3 |
| Key Infra Pattern | Web Publish |
| Key Infra Service | Security (Isolation) |

## Network Load Balancer

*Purpose*

Switches or appliances that failover and balance traffic load across sets of servers, firewalls, and caches. The scope can cover server load balancing, as well as global or site load balancing.

*Examples (Vendors and Products)*

F5 Networks, Radware, Cisco Local Director, Arrowpoint, Alteon, Foundary, and Resonate.

| | |
|---|---|
| Layer Number | 8 |
| Component Layer | Network |
| Priority | 2 |
| Key Infra Pattern | Web Publish |
| Key Infra Service | HTML |

## Network Pre-Routing (Voice)

*Purpose*

Service that uses the calling number, called number, or other database-influenced factors to determine the appropriate call treatments and routing of a voice call to a particular call center.

*Examples (Vendors and Products)*

GeoTel (now Cisco) and Genesys.

| | |
|---|---|
| Layer Number | 8 |
| Component Layer | Network |
| Priority | 9 |
| Key Infra Pattern | Real-time Collaborate |
| Key Infra Service | Voice |

## Network Protocol and Address Management

*Purpose*

Protocol that is increasingly TCP/IP, though others may apply in non-EB situations (such as SNA and IPX) or specific channels. Wireless and direct voice are not usually over TCP/IP. Beyond this, software is required to enable users to determine and implement effective subnetting strategies, design DHCP and DNS server architectures (for example, clustering vs. distributed redundant servers), and distribute IP addresses to IP devices. Staff must publicly register DNS domain names and obtain public address ranges.

*Examples (Vendors and Products)*

**Protocols:**   Implemented in OS software.

**TCP/IP management solutions:**   Lucent (Quadritek) QIP, Nortel/Bay Networks NetID, Cisco Network Registrar, Check Point MetaIP, and Process Software IP Addressworks.

| | |
|---|---|
| Layer Number | 8 |
| Component Layer | Network |
| Priority | 9 |
| Key Infra Pattern | Store-and-Forward Collaborate |
| Key Infra Service | Network (LAN, WAN) |

## Proxy/Caching Server

*Purpose*

Software/appliances that alleviate traffic across WAN components by storing frequently accessed https, streaming media, and objects that allow repeat requests to be served from inside the LAN. Proxy servers are less scalable than transparently installed caches. Appliance caches are preferable to software-only products.

*Examples (Vendors and Products)*

Cacheflow, Network Appliance, Cisco, Inktomi, Novell ICS (Dell, Compaq), Netscape, Squid, and Microsoft Proxy Server.

| | |
|---|---|
| Layer Number | 8 |
| Component Layer | Network |
| Priority | 2 |
| Key Infra Pattern | Web Publish |
| Key Infra Service | HTML |

## Public Key Infrastructure (PKI)

*Purpose*

Public Key Infrastructure (PKI) that combines the database of keys with the ability to issue keys/certificates, enabling users, devices, and applications to gain authorized access to resources.

*Examples (Vendors and Products)*

Entrust, Verisign, Baltimore/Cybertrust, Netscape, and Microsoft.

| | |
|---|---|
| Layer Number | 8 |
| Component Layer | Network |
| Priority | 2 |
| Key Infra Pattern | Store-and-Forward Collaborate |
| Key Infra Service | Security |

## Service Level Management

*Purpose*

Software platforms that enable users to monitor and track performance of an overall network and network components, also providing insight on service level management.

*Note*

> A separate component per layer for element or layer-specific management solutions may be required for completeness.

*Examples (Vendors and Products)*

HP Openview, Cabletron Spectrum (Platforms), Tivoli, Micromuse, Netcool, BMC, Candle, Inverse, Vitalsigns, and Keynote.

| | |
|---|---|
| Layer Number | 8 |
| Component Layer | Network |
| Priority | 2 |
| Key Infra Pattern | 3/N-Tier Transact |
| Key Infra Service | Management |

## Smart Card

*Purpose*

End-user devices that contain a digital certificate used for authorization and authentication.

*Examples (Vendors and Products)*

Bull, Gemplus, and Keycorp.

| | |
|---|---|
| Layer Number | 8 |
| Component Layer | Network |
| Priority | 9 |
| Key Infra Pattern | Store-and-Forward Collaborate |
| Key Infra Service | Security |

## SSL and Encryption HW

*Purpose*

Hardware products that accelerate encryption processing.

*Examples (Vendors and Products)*

Chrysalis, Rainbow, and Cylink.

| | |
|---|---|
| Layer Number | 8 |
| Component Layer | Network |
| Priority | 2 |
| Key Infra Pattern | Web Publish |
| Key Infra Service | HTML, Security (Isolation) |

## Traffic Shaper

*Purpose*

Hardware devices and software enhancements to products (such as routers) that allow users to prioritize traffic by application, source, and destination via multiple techniques (including weighted-fair queuing and TCP rate control).

*Examples (Vendors and Products)*

**TCP rate control:**  Packeteer

**Queuing:**  Lucent/Xedia and NetReality

| | |
|---|---|
| Layer Number | 8 |
| Component Layer | Network |
| Priority | 9 |
| Key Infra Pattern | 3/N-Tier Transact |
| Key Infra Service | Network (LAN, WAN) |

## Two-Factor Authentication Device

*Purpose*

Physical tokens that generate onetime passwords.

*Examples (Vendors and Products)*

Security Dynamics SecureID cards.

| | |
|---|---|
| Layer Number | 8 |
| Component Layer | Network |
| Priority | 9 |
| Key Infra Pattern | Store-and-Forward Collaborate |
| Key Infra Service | Security |

## VPN Device

*Purpose*

User-supplied products that enable telecommuters and road warriors to connect to internal resources across either the public Internet or VPN services (described above). VPNs may be deployed across dial-up links, cable modems, or DSL.

*Examples (Vendors and Products)*

**VPN product vendors:**   Checkpoint, Nortel, and Cisco.

| | |
|---|---|
| Layer Number | 8 |
| Component Layer | Network |
| Priority | 2 |
| Key Infra Pattern | Store-and-Forward Collaborate |
| Key Infra Service | Security (Isolation) |

## VPN Service

*Purpose*

Carrier-provided network services that link an organization's telecommuters and road warriors to internal resources. Remote access services may be extended to link outside entities (such as business partners, customers, and agents) to the organization.

*Examples (Vendors and Products)*

VPN service providers:
Uunet/Compuserve (MCI Worldcom) and AT&T Global Networking Services.

| | |
|---|---|
| Layer Number | 8 |
| Component Layer | Network |
| Priority | 2 |
| Key Infra Pattern | Store-and-Forward Collaborate |
| Key Infra Service | Security (Isolation) |

## WAN Access Device

*Purpose*

Physical device that connects an organization's site to the outside world (via the Internet) and to other internal sites (via wide area network circuits and services). This typically includes WAN routers; and it may also include frame relay and/or ATM access devices. Routers may include quality of service and VPN functionality, but loading the router down with too many functions is not advised.

*Examples (Vendors and Products)*

**Routers:**   Cisco 7000 (for headquarters) 4500 and 2500 (for branch-office and remote sites); and Nortel products.

| | |
|---|---|
| Layer Number | 8 |
| Component Layer | Network |
| Priority | 9 |
| Key Infra Pattern | All |
| Key Infra Service | Network (WAN) |

## WAN Service

*Purpose*

Physical network that links an organization's branch office, headquarters, and remote office sites together. Circuits and/or services are typically procured from the carrier.

*Examples (Vendors and Products)*

Frame relay, ATM services, or leased lines from AT&T, MCI Worldcom, Sprint, and Qwest.

| | |
|---|---|
| Layer Number | 8 |
| Component Layer | Network |
| Priority | 9 |
| Key Infra Pattern | All |
| Key Infra Service | Network (WAN) |

## Web SSO

*Purpose*

Software that provides users with the ability to sign on to a Web server once and connect to multiple Web applications.

*Examples (Vendors and Products)*

Netegrity and Dascom.

| | |
|---|---|
| Layer Number | 8 |
| Component Layer | Network |
| Priority | 2 |
| Key Infra Pattern | 3/N-Tier Transact |
| Key Infra Service | Security (Identity) |

## Wireless and Mobile Device

*Purpose*

Mobile communication devices that currently include cell phones, PDAs, and laptop computers.

*Examples (Vendors and Products)*

**Handheld products:**   Nokia, Ericsson, Motorola, Palm, and Psion.

**PC vendor products:**   Laptops.

| | |
|---|---|
| Layer Number | 8 |
| Component Layer | Network |
| Priority | 9 |
| Key Infra Pattern | Real-time Collaborate |
| Key Infra Service | Voice |

## Wireless Service

*Purpose*

Satellite services (for example, VSAT or LEOS) and terrestrial services (such as digital cellular) that provide mobile communications.

*Examples (Vendors and Products)*

**Digital cellular:**   Sprint, AT&T, Bell Atlantic, and Vodaphone/Mannes-man.

**VSAT services:**   Hughes.

**LEOS:**   Iridium.

| | |
|---|---|
| Layer Number | 8 |
| Component Layer | Network |
| Priority | 3 |
| Key Infra Pattern | Real-time Collaborate |
| Key Infra Service | Voice |

# Glossary

The following list contains many generic and specialized terms used in this book.

**adaptive infrastructure strategy** A strategy that helps keep businesses agile, by creating reusable infrastructure components, patterns, and services. Adaptive infrastructure processes allow businesses to easily introduce new business initiatives while continuing to improve initiatives already under way.

**application programming interface (API)** Programming hooks that provide a way for external processes to communicate with and control a specific computer program. This book discusses three generic types of APIs used for different purposes: Infra-APIs, Intra-APIs, and Inter-APIs.

**back-end** The part of the application that stores and processes data. In client/server computing, this usually refers to processes that occur on the server side. See also "front-end."

**business process automation (BPA)** Systems that automate business processes.

**business-to-business (B2B)** Any system or process that connects a business with its suppliers, partners, or customers.

**client/server computing** A computing model in which the work is shared by multiple computers communicating over a network. Typically, the server accesses the data store and does most of the heavy processing work. The client receives only the portions of the data or application that it needs to do its work. "Thin clients" carry only a small part of the application load, with most of the work being performed on the server, while "smart PCs" carry a much larger load of application software, with most of the work performed on the client.

**Client/Server Publish pattern** An infrastructure pattern defined by the use of a smart PC, such as a sophisticated business intelligence client, with associated session-oriented protocols such as SQLNet inserted between the client and back-end database. This pattern is best used for implementing sophisticated data analysis capabilities for a small, well-defined user base.

**clustering** The process of grouping together a collection of servers or data in a central location to increase efficiency and effectiveness of security, performance, and administration.

**Collaborate patterns** Infrastructure patterns that use peer-to-peer communications to share documents. This book discusses three types of Collaborate patterns: Real-Time Collaborate, Structured Collaborate, and Store-and-Forward Collaborate.

**Common Gateway Interface (CGI)** A method used in some simple Web applications to move data from the client (Web browser) to the Web server using server-side applications or scripts. Typically, this method is used to process the contents of an online form by transmitting data or query strings embedded in a URL.

**Common Object Request Broker Architecture (CORBA)** An open, cross-platform, and cross-language framework that allows widely disparate programs to communicate with each other in a heterogeneous, distributed environment by using an "interface broker."

**component** Any hardware or software used in a computer system or application.

**computer telephony integration (CTI)** The process of connecting a PC to a telephone switch so that the computer can control the switch as needed.

**content delivery network (CDN)** An application or network service that provides content distribution and management.

**cookies** Small amounts of data stored on a user's computer, typically containing user-specific information such as preferences, automatic logon data, or other configuration information.

**customer relationship management (CRM)** Applications or processes that help businesses manage customer relationships, typically by storing and analyzing extensive sets of customer data.

**data warehousing** A strategy in which data is extracted from large transactional databases and other sources and stored in smaller databases, to make data analysis easier.

**database administrator (DBA)** A person who is specifically responsible for maintaining databases.

**database management system (DBMS)** Any system designed specifically to store and manage data in an organized format.

**demilitarized zone (DMZ)** A portion of a network, located either immediately inside, outside, or between firewalls. Used for security purposes as a buffer zone between the internal network and external networks, such as the Internet.

**Direct access storage device (DASD)** A magnetic disk drive, typically of the type used in mainframe or minicomputer environments, although the term may also encompass hard disk drives on servers and desktop PCs.

**Directory Access Protocol (DAP)** A predecessor of the Lightweight Directory Access Protocol (LDAP), used to locate and transmit information stored in user or customer directories.

**discretionary costs** Enhancements to a product that would be beneficial to complete, but can be pared down or postponed if there are budget or time constraints.

**domain naming system (DNS)** The system used to translate host computer names into IP addresses. DNS can also refer to the Domain Name Server, which implements the Domain Name System.

**Dynamic Host Configuration Protocol (DHCP)** A protocol used in TCP/IP networks to automatically provide static and dynamic allocation and management of IP addresses.

**dynamic link library (DLL)** A set of executable code stored as a separate module for processing purposes.

**e-Business** Any business conducted online over a public or private network using computer applications. e-Business traditionally was conducted using electronic data interchange (EDI) before the late 1990s, then became Web-based, and is now moving to multiple points of interaction (POI).

**e-Commerce** Any sales transactions conducted online. Typically considered a part of e-Business, but not the whole. e-Commerce applications often include online product catalogs, shopping carts, and credit card verification services.

**Electronic Data Interchange (EDI)** An early method of connecting businesses by using a common standardized format to exchange data, typically for transactional purposes (billing or payment).

**e-mail** A client/server application that involves distribution of formatted messages from computer to computer across networks. See also "Simple Mail Transfer Protocol (STMP)."

**enterprise application integration (EAI)** A message broker service that moves much of the responsibility for integrating applications out of the application and into a reusable, unified, systematic service that all applications can share. Also called *transactional integration*.

**Enterprise JavaBeans (EJB)** A server-side component architecture used to develop highly scalable and secure applications for the Java platform.

**enterprise resource planning (ERP)** A business management system that integrates all facets of the business, including planning, manufacturing, sales, marketing, and accounting.

**enterprise systems** Mission-critical systems on which the entire company depends, such as payroll, accounting, and inventory management.

**Extensible Markup Language (XML)** A subset of the Standard Generalized Markup Language (SGML) designed for use over the Internet. With XML, designers can create customized tags to provide functionality that is not available with HTML. Such tags can be codified as standards that business partners or industries can use to communicate and share data over the Internet. As a simple example, a specialized tag for "part number" can be used to identify part numbers in a set of Web-based information, for formatting or data analysis purposes.

**extranet** Any private network used for data exchange typically between businesses, government agencies, or other organizations and their associated customers, suppliers, or business partners.

**fat client** See "client/server computing."

**Federated Database Architecture (FDA)** An architecture that provides autonomous, local processing for individual data stores, as well as a way to integrate the stores globally for applications.

**Fibre Channel (FC)** A set of standards for rapidly transferring data between workstations, mainframes, PCs, storage devices, and other peripherals at speeds up to 10 Gbps. Widely seen as a replacement technology for the Small Computer System Interface (SCSI) for data transfer between computers and storage devices.

**File Transfer Protocol (FTP)** A standard protocol for transferring files across TCP/IP networks, particularly the Internet.

**front-end** The part of the application that displays data and provides user interaction. In client/server computing, the term usually refers to processes that occur on the client side. See also "back-end."

**full-time equivalent (FTE)** A term used when staffing resources to refer to several employees whose workload and work hours, when viewed as a whole, equals that of one full-time employee.

**graphical user interface (GUI)** A display format that enables the user to operate in a visually rich environment, typically by using a mouse to point and click on icons, images, buttons, or lists of menu items on the screen.

**Hypertext Markup Language (HTML)** A set of standard tags used to mark up documents intended for use on the Web. The Web browser interprets the tags embedded in an HTML file and uses them as instructions on how to create the final formatted display.

**Hypertext Transfer Protocol (HTTP)** The protocol used for communication between Web servers and Web clients or "browsers." This protocol, which is transparent to the user, allows the movement of data and documents across the Internet.

**Identity Infrastructure** An adaptive infrastructure service in which the entire authentication process and the components that this process relies upon are separated out into a common infrastructure service shared by all applications. As an example, the Identity Infrastructure might include a Web Single Sign-on (Web SSO) service, which helps avoid the need for users to maintain multiple user names and passwords to access multiple applications.

**information technology (IT)** A term often used in abbreviated form to describe generically the field of computing and all of its related technologies.

**Infra-API** Low-level technology services, such as security, naming, or object invocation, that application developers and infrastructure developers can use to create business logic. Increasingly, Infra-APIs and the services they encapsulate are provided off-the-shelf as a built-in part of application servers, such as EJB or .NET.

**infrastructure** The underlying structure of physical hardware, installed components, or services used to support a wide range of human activity, from transportation to power distribution to computing.

**infrastructure developer** A person responsible for designing or programming the shared portions of the infrastructure, particularly the APIs that are used to connect applications to shared infrastructure.

**Infrastructure Impact Assessment (IIA)** A set of techniques used to plan, build, and execute patterns. IIA involves measuring infrastructure patterns to see if they fit correctly during the project prototyping and operations phases.

**infrastructure packaging** A way of compartmentalizing, marketing, and funding infrastructure so that it provides easily identifiable value to the business.

**infrastructure pattern** A way of organizing infrastructure components to facilitate rapid mapping from business requirements to end-to-end infrastructure designs. Creating standard infrastructure patterns helps to streamline the process of providing infrastructure for application developers and business units. This book identifies three major types of infrastructure patterns: Transact, Publish, and Collaborate.

**Infrastructure Pattern Matching (IPM)** A set of techniques used to match infrastructure patterns to applications by asking who the users are, where they are located, and what work they will perform. Using IPM, infrastructure planners highlight business-critical design tradeoffs and adjust infrastructure investment priorities.

**infrastructure planner** A person responsible for designing, implementing, and managing infrastructure.

**infrastructure product** A set of services packaged in such a way as to provide easily identifiable value to the business. See also "infrastructure packaging."

**integrated development environment (IDE)** Set of integrated tools that work together like a single application to automate many common programming tasks. Tools typically include a code editor, compiler, debugger, and GUI builder. Typical languages using IDE include Java, Visual Basic, and PowerBuilder.

**interactive voice response (IVR)** Computer systems that react to remote, touch-tone telephones, using recordings for messaging. For example, when you call many businesses, you get a voice message asking you to press different numbers on the keypad to access various options.

**Inter-API** APIs that help the business logic communicate *between* applications.

**inter-enterprise integration (IEI)** Integration services that make it possible to communicate information and exchange data between organizations, such as in a business-to-business (B2B) context.

**interface definition language (IDL)** A language designed for describing the data structures passed between parts of an application, to provide a language-independent intermediate representation. Examples include CORBA or DCOM. Typical mainframe applications can be migrated into a component framework by wrapping them inside an IDL.

**Internet** The global public network used for data exchange between consumers, businesses, government institutions, and organizations.

**Intra-API** Intra-APIs help business logic communicate *within* individual applications, and are typically not exposed to other applications. Since they are not reused outside a given application, they are created and managed only by the application's developers.

**intranet** Any private network used for data exchange typically between employees of a particular business, government institution, or organization.

**IP** A generic term used to refer to networks, applications, or systems that use the Internet Protocol. See "Transmission Control Protocol/Internet Protocol (TCP/IP)."

**Java** A programming language most often used for Web applications. It provides a level of presentation and processing sophistication not available through standard Web pages.

**Java Database Connectivity (JDBC)** A standard used to support communication between Java applications and back-end databases.

**Java 2 Enterprise Edition (J2EE)** A version of the Java programming language designed for use in developing enterprise applications.

**layers** User-defined logical subdivisions of information or data.

**legacy systems** The older computing systems in a company, which typically do not represent the latest technology.

**lifecycle** The entire set of processes involved in creating and maintaining a computer system, typically involving several phases expressed as "plan, build, run, change, exit."

**Lightweight Directory Access Protocol (LDAP)** A standard protocol used to communicate customer or other user directory information across a TCP/IP network such as the Internet. Because of the type of data it handles, LDAP is often employed by applications that require user authentication.

**load balancing** A technique used to improve reliability, performance, and manageability of server clusters by intelligently managing traffic into a cluster of servers and distributing the processing load using various strategies, such as "round robin," least connections, and CPU load.

**local area network (LAN)** A computer network that operates over short distances, such as a within a building. See also "wide area network (WAN)."

**middleware** Applications used to communicate or transfer data between front-end and back-end systems.

**Moore's Law** Gordon Moore's observation that a graph of chip performance as a function of time trended toward a doubling of transistor density (and therefore processing power) every 24 months.

**.NET** A Microsoft standard designed to make many common applications interoperable over the Web. When fully realized, this platform will encompass servers, operating systems, software, and reusable services, including Web-based data storage and device software. Promised features will include automatic synchronization of remote data across platforms; increased XML support; increased integration of e-mail, fax, and telephones.

**network load balancing (NLB)** See "load balancing."

**network operating system (NOS)** Any operating system that provides the services required by a network, such as user account management, peer-to-peer communication, file and print queuing, remote access services (RAS), and others.

**network operations center (NOC)** A central location used to manage networks.

**non-discretionary costs** Costs for those things that you must spend money on to keep the business going. For example, Internet service might be a non-discretionary cost if your business conducts a significant part of its business over the Internet.

**object-oriented programming (OOP)** A programming method that involves the creation and reuse of large blocks of code, called "objects." Typically, special programming languages, such as C++ or Java, enable OOP.

**1-Tier Transact pattern** An infrastructure pattern that includes batch processing applications or online transaction processing (OLTP) applications, typically running on a mainframe. Although the application itself is fully centralized, users may be widely distributed over wide area networks (WANs) communicating with the host using data terminals or PCs.

**online analytical processing (OLAP)** Databases and systems that process and arrange large amounts of data into meaningful results used for high-speed analysis with data warehouses. Also called multi-dimensional databases.

**online transaction processing (OLTP)** A generic term referring to any kind of online transaction, ranging from ATM transactions to issuing airline tickets online.

**open database connectivity (ODBC)** A Microsoft standard that provides a way for applications easily to transfer information to and from a wide array of common databases.

**operating system** The underlying set of software that manages computer resources such as the display, keyboard, drives, network connections, and other operating components.

**packaging** See "infrastructure packaging."

**patterns** See "infrastructure patterns."

**periodic process** See "strategic infrastructure planning."

**per-project process** See "tactical infrastructure planning."

**personal digital assistant (PDA)** A handheld computing device used to store personal information such as address books, calendars, to-do lists, notes, media players, and calculators.

**platform** An organizational concept that refers to grouping individual component technologies into technical layers (or domains) to provide a base infrastructure for common technologies. A platform is a common infrastructure on which the hardware, software, and networking all function.

**points of interaction (POI)** Multiple interfaces used to communicate the same basic set of data to a user community, often through handheld devices such as cell phones and personal digital assistants (PDAs), but also through technologies such as interactive voice response (IVR).

**Portable Document Format (PDF)** A specialized file format developed by Adobe Corporation for presenting online documents, typically on CD, downloaded over the Web, or distributed as e-mail attachments.

**portfolio** An infrastructure planning tool that helps organize the process of identifying, cataloging, and managing patterns, platforms, and services on an ongoing basis.

**Predictive Cost Modeling (PCM)** Techniques that help planners quickly determine the cost of infrastructure development projects by taking Infrastructure Pattern Matching (IPM) processes and moving them to a higher level of detail on risks, resources, bills-of-material, and costs.

**Publish pattern** Any application that allows the user to download, view, listen to, or analyze data. Examples include reporting and analysis tools, Web brochure-ware, and streaming audio. This book discusses three types of Publish patterns: Client/Server Publish, Web Publish, and Stream Publish.

**quality of service (QoS)** A measurement of the level of service that a service provider supplies to a subscriber.

**rapid application design (RAD) tools** Automated programming tools that help application developers design, build, compile, and test applications faster than they would be able to do using manual techniques.

**Real-Time Collaborate pattern** An infrastructure pattern that supports two-way transmission of audio and video in real time. Applications in this category use streaming audio, video, graphics, or text to share information between users. The communication can flow either through a server for scalability, or directly from peer to peer. Common examples include Microsoft NetMeeting, Voice Over Internet (VoIP), AOL instant messaging, and videoconferencing.

**relational database management system (RDBMS)** A database management system (DBMS) that provides relational capabilities, typically by storing data in cross-referenced tables.

**remote access services (RAS)** A network operating system feature that allows remote users to connect to the internal network system, typically using dial-up modems.

**return on investment (ROI)** The amount of profit returned as a proportion of the amount of money invested.

**reusability** The ability of infrastructure platforms, patterns, components, and services to be shared and reused by multiple applications. Reusability is a key concept in adaptive infrastructure.

**scalability** The ability of a computer system to handle increases in traffic or processing loads. The increased loads may be random and unpredictable, or planned out over time.

**Secure Socket Layer (SSL)** A standard software interface that provides authentication and data encryption security between a client and a server by sending data over a "socket," which is a secure channel at the connection layer in most TCP/IP applications.

**server load balancing (SLB)** See "load balancing."

**service** A set of reusable applications or processes delivered to an end user by a service provider.

**service level** A user requirement codified as a defined performance goal for service delivery. For example, to work properly, an application might require a TCP/IP network operating at T1 bandwidth (1.5 Mbps). These requirements are then defined as its "service level requirements."

**Simple Mail Transfer Protocol (SMTP)** A standard communications protocol used by e-mail servers to transmit e-mail messages sent by clients.

**Simple Object Access Protocol (SOAP)** A lightweight protocol that allows different programs running in different environments to communicate with each other using HTTP and XML.

**SQLnet** Software used to connect Oracle clients and servers and communicate using various protocols.

**Starter Kit** A set of components, patterns, and/or services presented as an initial group to be considered by readers of this book.

**storage area network (SAN)** A network with its own dedicated set of servers and storage devices used specifically to store data for backup, mirroring, or redundancy purposes.

**Store-and-Forward Collaborate pattern** An infrastructure pattern that involves the basic transfer, replication, and storage of files or documents. Common examples include word processing files and spreadsheets distributed through files systems, e-mail attachments, or print queues. Most organizations also put desktop support and software distribution into this pattern.

**stovepipe** A term used to describe infrastructure components that are dedicated to specific applications, and not easily shared or reused.

**strategic infrastructure planning** A form of infrastructure planning that determines standard infrastructure patterns and services on a regular cycle, such as annually. Also called "periodic planning." See also "tactical infrastructure planning."

**Stream Publish pattern** An infrastructure pattern used for real-time publishing of streaming content, such as audio, video, and text. Content is published to a multimedia player and the file plays in near real-time as it downloads. See also "Real-Time Publish pattern." Common examples include Internet radio stations and film-clip Web sites.

**streaming media** Special audio or video files that play back simultaneously as they are downloaded, as opposed to normal multimedia files that must be played back after downloading. Streaming media typically require special servers and file formats.

**Structured Collaborate pattern** An infrastructure pattern used to identify applications that provide shared access and automated, coordinated change to documents, files, or other data structures. Common examples include Lotus Notes groupware and workflow applications (except simple e-mail), document management applications, Web content management systems, many software development environments, and shared groupware calendars.

**supply chain management (SCM)** Applications or processes that help businesses manage their supply chains, typically by storing and analyzing extensive sets of vendor and inventory data.

**tactical infrastructure planning** A form of infrastructure planning that is completed on a per-project basis for each new application or technology being introduced into the organization. Also called "per-project" planning.

**thin client** See "client/server computing."

**3/N-Tier Transact pattern** An infrastructure pattern consisting of a thin client communicating with a client-neutral, server-based application, which in turn communicates with a back-end database server. Common examples include PeopleSoft v8 and SAP R/3. With a Web server, the presentation is generated on another Web server tier, but still rendered by the Web browser. Since this design is truly N-tier rather than just 3-Tier, this pattern is called 3/N-Tier. This is the most scalable and flexible Transact pattern.

**Total Cost of Ownership (TCO)** The complete cost of a PC to the business, including not just the purchase price, but also any administration, maintenance, support, upgrade, and training costs needed to keep the PC operational.

**Transact patterns** Infrastructure patterns that support applications where user actions make durable changes to the state of the business or business processes. They include any application that writes structured information to a system or a data set. This book discusses three types of Transact patterns: 1-Tier Transact, 2-Tier Transact, and 3/N-Tier Transact.

**Transactional Integration service** See "Enterprise Application Integration (EAI)."

**Transmission Control Protocol/Internet Protocol (TCP/IP)** A set of networking protocols that provide communication across a wide range of different network types and computing platforms. TCP handles data packaging and un-packaging, while IP handles data addressing and delivery.

**2-Tier Transact pattern** An infrastructure pattern that uses a smart PC on the desktop, communicating directly with a back-end database server. This category includes most traditional client/server applications that became popular earlier in the 1990s, but also includes Web applications that intertwine CGI/ASP/JSP presentation and application logic. Common examples include applications programmed using Visual Basic or Powerbuilder, and most Web applications using Microsoft active server pages (ASP) or Java server pages (JSP).

**Universal Description, Discovery, and Integration (UDDI)** A worldwide business registry that promotes e-Commerce by allowing businesses to register online, locate partners, and easily exchange data and online transactions using XML. The original registry was created through the efforts of Microsoft, IBM, and Ariba and now includes many Global 1000 companies.

**User Datagram Protocol (UDP)** An alternative to TCP often used with IP to transmit units of data (known as *datagrams*) between computers on a network. UDP eliminates some of the data handling services provided by TCP, and thus works quicker for specific applications that don't need these services.

**venture funding** Funding by investors for projects that have a typically high risk factor. The theory of venture funding is that high-risk projects may create extremely high returns, effectively covering the cost of other less-profitable investments.

**Very Small Aperture Terminal (VSAT)** A system that uses satellite-based, point-to-multipoint data communications to provide wireless network services.

**virtual private network (VPN)** A private network that operates across the Internet using secure communication. Typically used to connect remote users to an organization's internal networks without using dedicated lines, wide area networks (WANs), or remote access services (RAS).

**Voice Over Internet (VoIP)** A standard way of transmitting voice information over the Internet or other TCP/IP networks.

**Web** An Internet-based service used to transmit formatted documents and multimedia files, typically using HTML and HTTP, but also using PDF, XML, streaming media, and many other technologies.

**Web browser** A software application such as Microsoft Internet Explorer and Netscape Navigator used to view Web-based information over the Internet, intranet, or extranets.

**Web Publish pattern** An infrastructure pattern that uses HTML browsers and HTTP protocol to enable read-only access to structured HTML or XML documents.

**Web Services Description Language (WSDL)** An XML-based language used as part of UDDI to catalog the services that each UDDI subscriber has to offer.

**Web Single Sign-On (Web SSO)** A service that allows users to access multiple secure Web sites, Web applications, or online databases using a single user name and password.

**wide area network (WAN)** A network that connects users over a large geographical area, typically using dedicated lines supplied by local telephone companies.

**Wireless Application Protocol (WAP)** A standard protocol that allows Web applications to present information in a format small enough to fit on the screen of a cell phone, PDA, or other small wireless devices.

**XML** See "Extensible Markup Language (XML)."

# Index